CGP has CCEA GCSE Maths revision sorted!

CCEA GCSE Maths can be quite a handful. But don't worry — this fantastic CGP book contains all the know-how you need for the Foundation Tier course.

It's full of no-nonsense explanations, worked examples and exam practice questions for the M1, M2, M5 & M6 units. There's just no better guide to GCSE Maths.

How to access your free Online Edition

This book includes a free Online Edition to read on your PC, Mac or tablet.
To access it, just go to **cgpbooks.co.uk/extras** and enter this code...

1842 0490 1036 9239

By the way, this code only works for one person. If somebody else has used this book before you, they might have already claimed the Online Edition.

CGP — still the best! ☺

Our sole aim here at CGP is to produce the highest quality books —
carefully written, immaculately presented and dangerously close to being funny.

Then we work our socks off to get them out to you
— at the cheapest possible prices.

Contents

About the Exams

The Exams 1

Section One — Number

Place Value and Ordering Numbers [M1] 2
BODMAS and Wordy Questions [M1] 3
Adding and Subtracting [M1] 4
Multiplying and Dividing by 10, 100, etc. [M1] 5
Multiplying & Dividing Whole Numbers [M1] 6
Multiplying & Dividing with Decimals [M1] 7
Negative Numbers [M1] 8
Multiples and Factors [M1] 9
LCM and HCF [M2] 10
Prime Numbers [M1] 11
Prime Factors [M2] 12
Rounding [M1] 13
Rounding [M1, M2] 14
Estimating [M5] 15
Powers [M1] 16
Powers [M2] 17
Roots [M1] 18
Different Number Systems [M6] 19
Revision Questions for Section One 20

Section Two — Fractions, Ratios and Percentages

Fractions [M1] 21
Fractions [M2] 23
Fractions, Decimals and Percentages [M1] 24
Fractions and Recurring Decimals [M2] 25
Ratios [M5] 26
Direct Proportion Problems [M5] 28
Percentages [M1] 30
Repeated Percentage Change [M2] 33
Revision Questions for Section Two 34

Section Three — Algebra

Algebra — Simplifying [M1] 35
Algebra — Simplifying [M1, M6] 36
Algebra — Multiplying Out Brackets [M1, M2] 37
Algebra — Taking Out Common Factors [M1, M2] ... 38
Solving Equations [M1] 39
Solving Equations [M2] 40
Expressions, Formulas and Functions [M1] 41
Formulas and Equations from Words [M1] 42
Trial and Improvement [M6] 43
Inequalities [M1, M6] 44
Rearranging Formulas [M6] 45
Sequences [M5] 46
Sequences [M6] 47
Revision Questions for Section Three 48

Section Four — Graphs

Coordinates [M1] 49
Line Segments [M2] 50
Straight-Line Graphs [M1] 51
Drawing Straight-Line Graphs [M1] 52
Straight-Line Graphs — Gradients [M2] 53
Real-Life Graphs [M1, M2] 54
Conversion Graphs [M5] 55
Distance-Time Graphs [M5] 56
Solving Equations Using Graphs [M6] 57
Quadratic Graphs [M6] 58
Revision Questions for Section Four 59

Section Five — Measures and Angles

Metric Units [M1]	60
Imperial Units [M5]	61
Area and Volume Conversion [M1]	62
Reading Scales [M5]	63
Time Intervals [M1]	64
Compound Units [M1]	65
Compound Units [M2]	66
Angle Basics [M1]	67
Five Angle Rules [M1, M5]	68
Parallel Lines [M1]	69
Geometry Problems [M1]	70
Angles in Shapes [M6]	71
Bearings [M6]	72
Maps [M5]	73
Maps and Scale Drawings [M5, M6]	74
Pythagoras' Theorem [M2]	75
Revision Questions for Section Five	76

Section Six — Shapes and Area

Properties of 2D Shapes [M1]	77
Perimeter and Area [M1]	79
Perimeter and Area [M2]	80
Circles [M1]	81
3D Shapes [M1]	82
Cubes and Cuboids [M1]	83
Prisms [M2]	84
Plans and Elevations [M1]	85
Construction [M5]	86
Construction [M6]	87
Loci and Construction [M6]	88
Loci and Construction — Examples [M6]	89
Translation [M5, M6]	90
Reflection [M5, M6]	91
Rotation [M5, M6]	92
Enlargement [M5, M6]	93
Revision Questions for Section Six	94

Section Seven — Statistics and Probability

Planning an Investigation [M1]	95
Sampling and Bias [M1]	96
Collecting Data [M1]	97
Mean, Median, Mode and Range [M1]	99
Frequency Tables — Finding Averages [M1]	100
Two-Way Tables [M1]	101
Venn Diagrams [M1, M2]	102
Pictograms and Bar Charts [M1]	103
Pie Charts [M1]	104
Other Charts and Graphs [M1]	105
Scatter Diagrams [M2]	107
Grouped Frequency Tables [M2]	108
Interpreting Data [M1]	109
Comparing Data Sets [M1]	110
Probability Basics [M5]	111
More Probability [M5]	112
Expected Frequency [M5]	113
Probability Experiments [M6]	114
Revision Questions for Section Seven	115

Answers	116
Index	123

Published by CGP

Written by Richard Parsons

Editors: Adam Bartlett, Luke Bennett, Paul Jordin, Luke Molloy, Caroline Purvis, Rosa Roberts, Rachael Rogers, David Ryan, Caley Simpson and George Wright

With thanks to Mona Allen and Glenn Rogers for the proofreading.

ISBN: 978 1 78908 563 1

Clipart from Corel®
Printed by Bell and Bain Ltd, Glasgow

Text, design, layout and original illustrations © Richard Parsons 2020
All rights reserved.

Photocopying more than one section of this book is not permitted, even if you have a CLA licence.
Extra copies are available from CGP with next day delivery • 0800 1712 712 • www.cgpbooks.co.uk

About the Exams

The Exams

This page has all the info about the exams along with a few tips to help you ace them.

There Are Four Different Units

1) CCEA Foundation GCSE maths is split into four different units: M1, M2, M5 and M6. Each unit covers different bits of maths and some units build on what you learn in others.

2) You will only take exams in two units — either M1 or M2 AND either M5 or M6. The two most common combinations are 'M1 and M5' and 'M2 and M6'.

3) The combination you take will depend on the grade you're hoping to get. M1 and M5 are targeted at grades D-G, while M2 and M6 are targeted at grades C*-G.

4) Below is a summary of the Foundation exams.

You could also get your GCSE by sitting a combination of Foundation and Higher unit exams — your teacher should be able to tell you more about this.

- 1 hour 45 mins
- 100 marks
- 45% of the total GCSE.

You'll take one of these unit exams...

- 1 hour 45 mins
- 100 marks
- 45% of the total GCSE.
- Tests content from units M1 and M2.

Stuff from M1 crops up in the other unit exams, so you need to learn M1 whatever combination you're taking.

...and then one of these unit exams.

- You'll sit two papers (Paper 1 and Paper 2).
- Each is 1 hour and has 50 marks.
- Together they make up 55% of the total GCSE.
- Both papers test content from units M1 and M5.

You're not allowed a calculator for Paper 1 of the M5 and M6 exams (but you are allowed one for all of the other exams).

- You'll sit two papers (Paper 1 and Paper 2).
- Each is 1 hour and has 50 marks.
- Together they make up 55% of the total GCSE.
- Both papers test content from units M1, M2, M5 and M6.

So if you're doing M6, you'll need to know everything in this book. Sorry.

5) Every page in this book has been stamped with one of these stamps so you know exactly which bits you need to learn.

6) You'll find most stamps at the top of the page but if a page covers more than one unit, each separate bit will be stamped.

These Top Tips Will Help in the Exams

1) Always make sure you read the question properly.
For example, if the question asks you to give your answer in metres, don't give it in centimetres.

2) Show each step in your working.
You're less likely to make a mistake if you write things out in stages. And even if your final answer's wrong, you'll probably pick up some marks if the examiner can see that your method is right.

3) Check that your answer is sensible.
Worked out an angle of 450° or 0.045° in a triangle? You've probably gone wrong somewhere...

4) If you have any time left at the end of the exam, check all your answers. Look back through your answers and make sure you haven't made any silly mistakes. Don't just stare at the hottie in front.

A 0.01 kg elephant? That's not sensible...

Place Value and Ordering Numbers

Ah, the wondrous and glorious world of GCSE Maths. OK — I'll admit it, maybe one or two bits are more like whiffy socks but we'll deal with them later. For now, let's start off with the basics....

Always Look at Big Numbers in Groups of Three

EXAMPLE: Write the number 2 351 243 in words.

1) The number has spaces which break it up into groups of 3:

    So many MILLION — 2 351 243 — And the rest
    So many THOUSAND

2) So this is: Two million, three hundred and fifty-one thousand, two hundred and forty-three.

Putting Numbers in Order of Size

EXAMPLE: Write these numbers in ascending order:
12   84   623   32   486   4563   75   2143

Ascending order just means smallest to largest.

1) First put them into groups, the ones with fewest digits first:

    2-digit   3-digit   4-digit
    12 84 32 75   623 486   4563 2143

2) Then just put each separate group in order of size:

    12 32 75 84   486 623   2143 4563

To put decimals into ascending order:
1) Do the whole-number bit first, then the bit after the decimal point.
2) Group them by the number of 0s immediately after the decimal point. The group with the most 0s at the start comes first.

If you were asked to put the numbers in descending order, the number with the fewest 0s would come first.

EXAMPLE: Write these numbers in order, from smallest to largest:
0.531   0.098   0.14   0.0026   0.7   0.007   0.03

1) These are all between 0 and 1, so group them by the number of 0s after the decimal point:

    2 initial 0s   1 initial 0   no initial 0s
    0.0026 0.007   0.098 0.03   0.531 0.14 0.7

2) Once they're in groups, just order them by comparing the first non-zero digits. (If the first digits are the same, look at the next digit along instead.)

    0.0026 0.007   0.03 0.098   0.14 0.531 0.7

In decimals, like in whole numbers, the value of the digits decreases from left to right.

0.256
tenths / hundredths / thousandths

Don't call numbers big or small to their face — they're sensitive...

There's nothing too tricky about putting numbers into order of size — just remember the tips above. In fact, you might even find it strangely satisfying. A bit like alphabetising your book collection.

Q1 Write these numbers in words: a) 1 234 531 b) 23 456 c) 3402 d) 203 412   [4 marks]

Q2 Write this down as a number: Fifty-six thousand, four hundred and twenty-one   [1 mark]

Q3 Put these numbers in order of size: 23 493 87 1029 3004 345 9   [1 mark]

Q4 Write these numbers in ascending order: 0.37 0.008 0.307 0.1 0.09 0.2   [1 mark]

BODMAS and Wordy Questions

Nothing too strenuous on this page — make the most of that while it lasts.

BODMAS — Brackets, Other, Division, Multiplication, Addition, Subtraction

BODMAS tells you the ORDER in which these operations should be done:
Work out Brackets first, then Other things like squaring, then Divide / Multiply groups of numbers before Adding or Subtracting them.

EXAMPLES:

1. Work out $7 + 9 \div 3$
   1) Follow BODMAS — do the division first... $\quad 7 + 9 \div 3$
   2) ...then the addition: $\quad = 7 + 3$
   $= 10$

   If you don't follow BODMAS, you get:
   $7 + 9 \div 3$
   $= 16 \div 3$
   $= 5.333...$ ✗

2. Calculate $15 - 7^2$
   1) The square is an 'other' so that's first: $\quad 15 - 7^2$
   2) Then do the subtraction: $\quad = 15 - 49$
   $= -34$

3. Find $(5 + 3) \times (12 - 3)$
   1) Start by working out the brackets: $\quad (5 + 3) \times (12 - 3)$
   2) And now the multiplication: $\quad = 8 \times 9$
   $= 72$

Don't Be Scared of Wordy Questions

Wordy, real-life questions will come up a lot on your exams. For these you don't just have to do the maths, you've got to work out what the question's asking you to do. Relax and work through them step by step.

1) READ the question carefully. Work out what bit of maths you need to answer it.
2) Underline the INFORMATION YOU NEED to answer the question — you might not have to use all the numbers they give you.
3) Write out the question IN MATHS and answer it, showing all your working clearly.

EXAMPLE: Cahya buys dog food in boxes of 20 packets. Each box costs £12.50. She has 3 dogs which each eat 2 packets per day. How much will it cost Cahya to buy enough boxes of food for all of her dogs for 4 weeks?

Number of packets for 3 dogs for 1 day = $3 \times 2 = 6$
Number of packets for 3 dogs for 4 weeks = $6 \times 7 \times 4 = 168$
Number of boxes needed = $168 \div 20 = 8.4$ Cahya can't buy part of a box, so she needs to buy 9 boxes.
$9 \times £12.50 = £112.50$

What's your BODMAS? About 50 kg, dude...

It's really important to check your working on BODMAS questions. You might be sure you did the calculation right, but it's surprisingly easy to make a slip. Try this exam-style question:

Q1 Find the value of: a) $15 - 12 \div 3$ b) $5 \times 2 + 3 \times 9$ c) $(3 + 5) \div 2 - 1$ [3 marks]

Section One — Number

Adding and Subtracting

Remember that time when you were stranded at sea and needed to split the bill with that kindly seagull but you didn't have a calculator so you just couldn't do it? Well this page is here to make sure THAT situation doesn't happen again (and it may also help in exams) — get your pen and paper at the ready...

Adding

1) Line up the units columns of each number.
2) Add up the columns from right to left.
3) Carry over any spare tens to the next column.

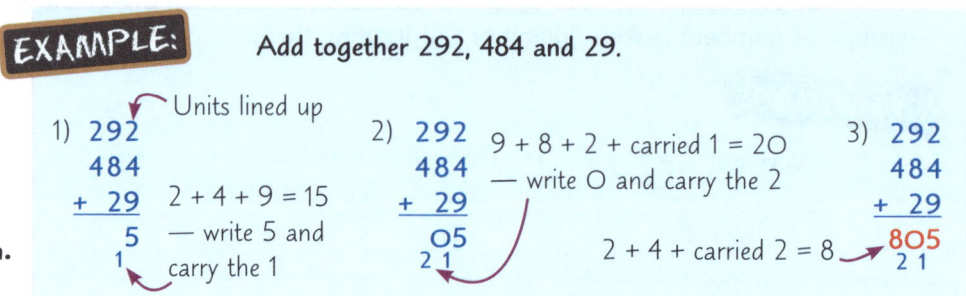

Subtracting

1) Line up the units columns of each number.
2) Working right to left, subtract the bottom number from the top number.
3) If the top number is smaller than the bottom number, borrow 10 from the left.

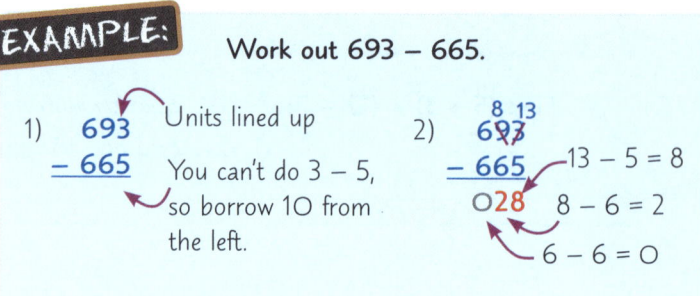

And with Decimals...

The method's just the same, but start instead by lining up the decimal points.

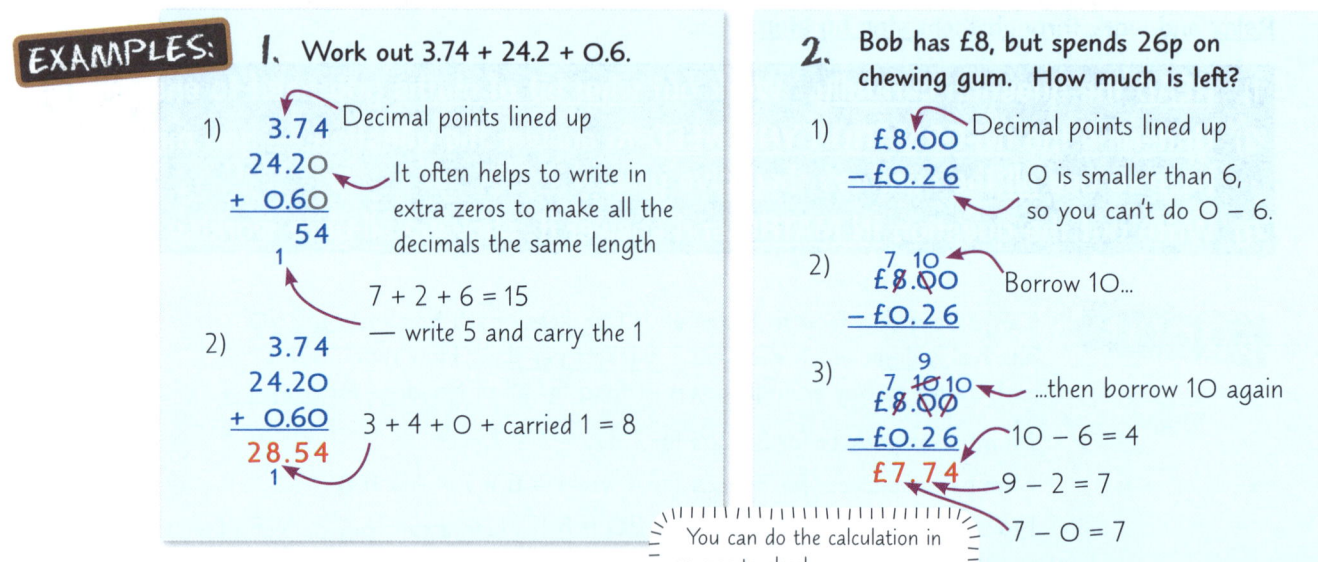

Ones never pull their weight — they always have to be carried...

Test your skills of pen-and-paper maths with these teasers:

Don't forget to include the units in your answers.

Q1 When Oisin was 10 he was 142 cm tall. Since then he has grown 29 cm.
   a) How tall is he now?   b) How much more must he grow to be 190 cm tall?   [2 marks]

Q2 I have 3 litres of water and drink 1.28 litres. How much is left?   [2 marks]

Multiplying and Dividing by 10, 100, etc.

You need to know the stuff on this page — it's nice 'n' simple, and they're likely to test you on it in the exam.

1) Multiplying and Dividing Any Number by 10

Multiply: Move the decimal point ONE place BIGGER and if it's needed, ADD A ZERO on the end.

E.g. 23.6 × 10 = 2 3 6

Divide: Move the decimal point ONE place SMALLER and if it's needed, REMOVE ZEROS after the decimal point.

E.g. 23.6 ÷ 10 = 2 . 3 6

2) Multiplying and Dividing Any Number by 100

Multiply: Move the decimal point TWO places BIGGER and ADD ZEROS if necessary.

E.g. 34 × 100 = 3 4 0 0

Divide: Move the decimal point TWO places SMALLER and REMOVE ZEROS after the decimal point.

E.g. 340 ÷ 100 = 3 . 4

3) Multiplying and Dividing by 1000 or 10 000

Multiply: Move the decimal point so many places BIGGER and ADD ZEROS if necessary.

Divide: Move the decimal point so many places SMALLER and REMOVE ZEROS after the decimal point.

You always move the DECIMAL POINT this much:
1 place for 10,   2 places for 100,
3 places for 1000,   4 places for 10 000,   etc.

4) Multiply and Divide by Numbers like 20, 300, etc.

MULTIPLY by 2 or 3 or 8 etc. FIRST, then move the decimal point so many places BIGGER (↗) according to how many zeros there are.

DIVIDE by 4 or 3 or 7 etc. FIRST, then move the decimal point so many places SMALLER (i.e. to the left ↙).

1. Calculate 234 × 200.
   234 × 2 = 468
   468 × 100 = 46800

2. Calculate 960 ÷ 300.
   960 ÷ 3 = 320
   320 ÷ 100 = 3.2

Adding 0s when they're not needed? Tut, tut, noughty, noughty...

Learn the methods on this page — nothing too taxing. For a bit of a workout, try these:

Q1   Work out   a) 12.3 × 100   b) 3.08 ÷ 1000   c) 360 ÷ 30   [3 marks]

 Multiplying & Dividing Whole Numbers

You need to be really happy doing multiplications and divisions <u>with</u> and <u>without</u> a calculator so you're ready for anything an exam may throw at you. This page covers the <u>brain-only methods</u>...

Multiplying Whole Numbers

The Traditional Method:
1) Split it into <u>separate multiplications</u>.
2) Add up the results in <u>columns</u> (right to left).

There are lots of other multiplication methods — make sure you're comfortable using whichever method you prefer.

EXAMPLES:

1. Work out 46 × 27

```
        4 6
    ×   2 7
    ─────────
    3 2₄2      —— This is 7 × 46
    9 2 0      —— This is 20 × 46
    ─────────
    1 2 4 2    —— This is 322 + 920
```

2. Work out 243 × 18

```
        2 4 3
    ×     1 8
    ─────────
    1 9₃4₂4    —— This is 8 × 243
    2 4 3 0    —— This is 10 × 243
    ─────────
    4₁3 7 4    —— This is 1944 + 2430
```

Dividing Whole Numbers

EXAMPLE: What is 748 ÷ 22?

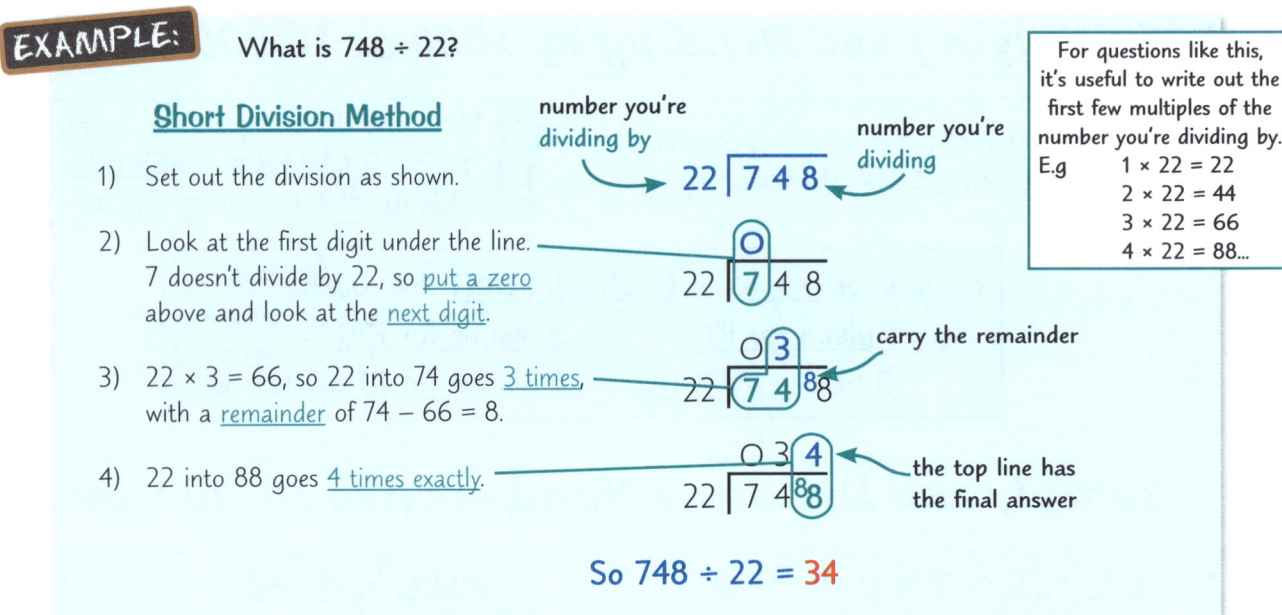

Short Division Method

1) Set out the division as shown.

2) Look at the first digit under the line. 7 doesn't divide by 22, so <u>put a zero</u> above and look at the <u>next digit</u>.

3) 22 × 3 = 66, so 22 into 74 goes <u>3 times</u>, with a <u>remainder</u> of 74 − 66 = 8.

4) 22 into 88 goes <u>4 times exactly</u>.

So 748 ÷ 22 = 34

For questions like this, it's useful to write out the first few multiples of the number you're dividing by.
E.g 1 × 22 = 22
     2 × 22 = 44
     3 × 22 = 66
     4 × 22 = 88...

The other common method for dividing is <u>long division</u> — if you prefer this method, make sure you know it <u>really</u> well, so you'll have no problems with any division in your exam.

If only you could multiply this page and learn it all over again...

There are lots of methods you can use for multiplication — and they all work just as well as each other. It comes down to which method you find easiest to use. Have a go at these practice questions without using a calculator — if you really know your methods, they'll be an absolute doddle. Seriously.

Q1 Work out a) 28 × 12   b) 56 × 11   c) 104 × 16   [3 marks]

Q2 Work out a) 96 ÷ 8   b) 91 ÷ 7   c) 252 ÷ 12   [3 marks]

Q3 James has a plank of wood which is 220 cm long.
    He cuts it into 14 cm pieces. What length of wood will he have left over?   [2 marks]

Multiplying & Dividing with Decimals

You might get a scary question on multiplying or dividing using decimals, but really these aren't any harder than the whole-number versions. You just need to know what to do in each case.

Multiplying Decimals

1) Start by ignoring the decimal points. Do the multiplication using whole numbers.
2) Count the total number of digits after the decimal points in the original numbers.
3) Make the answer have the same number of decimal places.

EXAMPLE: Work out 4.6 × 2.7

46 × 27 = 1242 — We know this 'cos we worked it out on page 6.

4.6 × 2.7 has 2 digits after the decimal points.

4.6 × 2.7 = 12.42

Dividing a Decimal by a Whole Number

For these, you just set the question out like a whole-number division but put the decimal point in the answer right above the one in the question.

EXAMPLE: What is 0.528 ÷ 3?

So 0.528 ÷ 3 = 0.176

Put the decimal point in the answer above the one in the question.

0.   0.1   0.17   0.176
3)0.528   3)0.5²28   3)0.5²2¹8   3)0.5²2¹8

3 into 0 won't go | 3 into 5 goes once, carry the remainder of 2 | 3 into 22 goes 7 times, carry the remainder of 1 | 3 into 18 goes 6 times exactly

Dividing a Number by a Decimal

Two-for-one here — this works if you're dividing a whole number by a decimal, or a decimal by a decimal.

EXAMPLE: What is 36.6 ÷ 0.12?

1) The trick here is to write it as a fraction:
2) Get rid of the decimals by multiplying top and bottom by 100 (see p5):
3) It's now a decimal-free division that you know how to solve:

$36.6 ÷ 0.12 = \frac{36.6}{0.12} = \frac{3660}{12}$

0   03   030   0305
12)3660   12)3³660   12)3³66⁶0   12)3³66⁶0

12 into 3 won't go so carry the 3 | 12 into 36 goes 3 times exactly | 12 into 6 won't go so carry the 6 | 12 into 60 goes 5 times exactly

So 36.6 ÷ 0.12 = 305

Compared to this stuff, whole numbers seem pretty pointless...

Just like you did with whole numbers on p6, use the method you prefer for multiplying or dividing. Have a go at these practice questions without using your calculator.

Q1 Work out   a) 3.2 × 56   b) 0.6 × 10.2   c) 5.5 × 2.154   [6 marks]

Q2 Naomi buys 14 packets of biscuits for a party. Each packet of biscuits costs £1.27. How much does Naomi spend on biscuits in total?   [2 marks]

Q3 Claire has £22.38. She wants to share it equally between her three nephews. How much does each nephew receive?   [2 marks]

Q4 Find   a) 33.6 ÷ 0.6   b) 84.6 ÷ 0.12   c) 4.625 ÷ 5   [6 marks]

Negative Numbers

Numbers less than zero are <u>negative</u>. You should be able to <u>add</u>, <u>subtract</u>, <u>multiply</u> and <u>divide</u> with them.

Adding and Subtracting with Negative Numbers

Use the <u>number line</u> for <u>addition</u> and <u>subtraction</u> involving negative numbers:

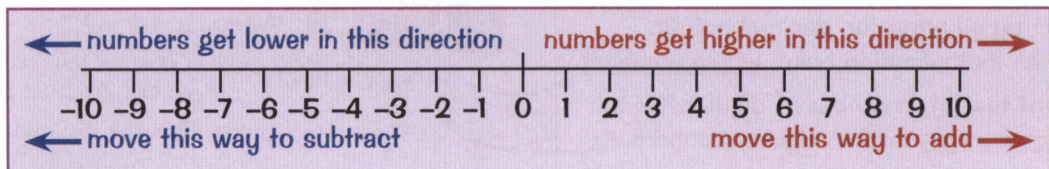

EXAMPLES:

What is −4 + 7?   Start at −4 and move 7 places in the positive direction:

So −4 + 7 = **3**

Work out 5 − 8   Start at 5 and move 8 places in the negative direction:

So 5 − 8 = **−3**

Find −2 − 4   Start at −2 and move 4 places in the negative direction:

So −2 − 4 = **−6**

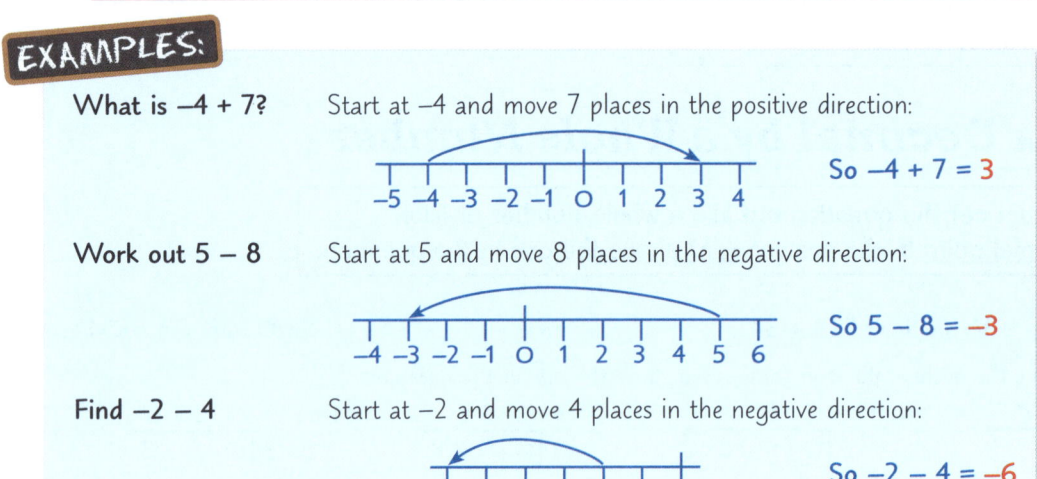

Good evening caller, you're through to the Number Line. What's your problem?

Use These Rules for Combining Signs

+	+	makes	+
+	−	makes	−
−	+	makes	−
−	−	makes	+

These rules are <u>ONLY TO BE USED WHEN</u>:

1) Multiplying or dividing

EXAMPLES:
Find: a) −2 × 3   (invisible + sign)   − + makes − so −2 × 3 = **−6**
         b) −8 ÷ −2   − − makes + so −8 ÷ −2 = **4**

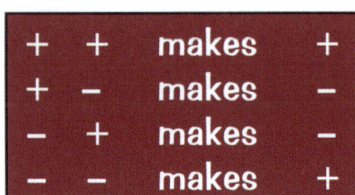

Be careful when squaring or cubing. <u>Squaring</u> a negative number gives a <u>positive</u> number (e.g. −2 × −2 = 4) but <u>cubing</u> a negative number gives a <u>negative</u> number (e.g. −3 × −3 × −3 = −27).

2) Two signs appear next to each other

EXAMPLES:
Work out: a) 5 − −4   − − makes + so 5 − −4 = 5 + 4 = **9**
           b) 4 + −6 − −7 + − makes − and − − makes +
                            so 4 + −6 − −7 = 4 − 6 + 7 = **5**

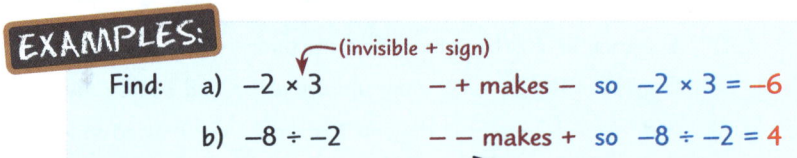
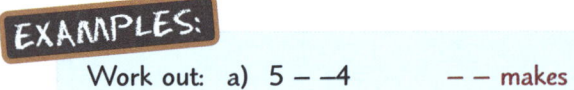

I need cheering up after all that negativity...

Don't just learn the rules in that red box — make sure you know when you can use them too.

Q1   The temperature in Mathstown at 9 am on Monday was 4 °C.
      At 9 am on Tuesday the temperature was −2 °C.
   a) What was the change in temperature from Monday to Tuesday? [1 mark]
   b) The temperature at 9 am on Wednesday was 3 °C lower than on Tuesday.
      What was the temperature on Wednesday? [1 mark]

Section One — Number

Multiples and Factors

If you think 'factor' is short for 'fat actor', you should give this page a read. Stop thinking about fat actors.

Multiples and Factors

The MULTIPLES of a number are just its <u>times table</u>.

 Find the first 8 multiples of 13.

You just need to find the first 8 numbers in the 13 times table:
13   26   39   52   65   78   91   104

The FACTORS of a number are all the numbers that <u>divide into it</u>.

There's a method that guarantees you'll find them all:

1) Start off with 1 × the number itself, then try 2 ×, then 3 × and so on, listing the pairs in rows.
2) Try each one in turn. Cross out the row if it doesn't divide exactly.
3) Eventually, when you get a number <u>repeated</u>, <u>stop</u>.
4) The numbers in the rows you haven't crossed out make up the list of factors.

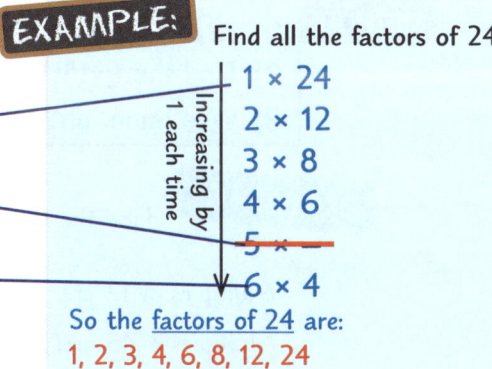

Find all the factors of 24.

1 × 24
2 × 12
3 × 8
4 × 6
5 ×
6 × 4

Increasing by 1 each time

So the <u>factors of 24</u> are:
1, 2, 3, 4, 6, 8, 12, 24

Common Multiples

The COMMON MULTIPLES of two numbers are the multiples found in the <u>times tables</u> of <u>both</u> numbers.

EXAMPLE:

Find the first 3 common multiples of 4 and 5.

Write out the times tables for 4 and 5 until you find 3 numbers that are in both lists:

Multiples of 4:   4   8   12   16   (20)   24   28   32   36   (40)   44   48   52   56   (60)
Multiples of 5:   5   10   15   (20)   25   30   35   (40)   45   50   55   (60)

So the first 3 <u>common multiples</u> of 4 and 5 are 20, 40 and 60.

If you can spot a pattern, it could help you. Here, the common multiples for 4 and 5 are all multiples of 20 (4 × 5).

Common Factors

The COMMON FACTORS of a pair of numbers are the numbers that can be <u>divided into</u> both numbers.

EXAMPLE: Find the common factors of 24 and 36.

1) Write out the factors of both 24 and 36:
2) Find all the numbers that are in both lists.

Factors of 24:
1 × 24
2 × (12)
3 × 8
4 × (6)

Factors of 36:
1 × 36
2 × 18
3 × (12)
4 × 9
(6 × 6)

So the <u>common factors</u> of 24 and 36 are 1, 2, 3, 4, 6 and 12.

The common factor — a thing politicians should learn more about...

This stuff can be very useful for all sorts of topics in maths, so learn the page then try these:

Q1   Find the first 3 common multiples of: a) 3 and 5,   b) 2 and 10.   [4 marks]

Q2   Find the common factors of: a) 20 and 30,   b) 18 and 24.   [4 marks]

LCM and HCF

Two big fancy names but don't be put off — they're both <u>real easy</u>. There are two methods for finding each — this page starts you off with the <u>nice</u>, <u>straightforward</u> methods.

LCM — 'Lowest Common Multiple'

'Lowest Common Multiple' — sure, it sounds kind of complicated, but all it means is this:

The SMALLEST number that will DIVIDE BY ALL the numbers in question.

METHOD:
1) LIST the MULTIPLES of ALL the numbers (see the previous page).
2) Find the SMALLEST one that's in ALL the lists.
3) Wee buns, eh?

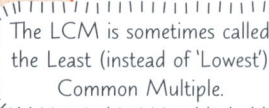

The LCM is sometimes called the Least (instead of 'Lowest') Common Multiple.

EXAMPLE: Find the lowest common multiple (LCM) of 12 and 15.

Multiples of 12 are: 12, 24, 36, 48, (60), 72, 84, 96, ...
Multiples of 15 are: 15, 30, 45, (60), 75, 90, 105, ...

So the lowest common multiple (LCM) of 12 and 15 is 60.
Told you it was easy.

HCF — 'Highest Common Factor'

'Highest Common Factor' — all it means is <u>this</u>:

The BIGGEST number that will DIVIDE INTO ALL the numbers in question.

METHOD:
1) LIST the FACTORS of ALL the numbers (see the previous page).
2) Find the BIGGEST one that's in ALL the lists.

EXAMPLE: Find the highest common factor (HCF) of 36, 54, and 72.

Factors of 36 are: 1, 2, 3, 4, 6, 9, 12, (18), 36
Factors of 54 are: 1, 2, 3, 6, 9, (18), 27, 54
Factors of 72 are: 1, 2, 3, 4, 6, 8, 9, 12, (18), 24, 36, 72

So the highest common factor (HCF) of 36, 54 and 72 is 18.

Just <u>take care</u> listing the factors — make sure you use the <u>proper method</u> (as shown on the previous page) or you might miss one and blow the whole thing out of the water.

BRB, just off to learn my LCMs from my HCFs...

You need to learn what LCM and HCF are, and how to find them. Turn over and write it all down. And after that, I have some lovely Exam Practice Questions for you — bonus.

Q1 Find the lowest common multiple (LCM) of 12, 14 and 21. [2 marks]

Q2 Find the highest common factor (HCF) of 36 and 84. [2 marks]

Prime Numbers

'Prime numbers?' I hear you ask. 'What are these magical things you speak of?'
Read on, my friend, and you shall see...

PRIME Numbers Don't Divide by Anything

Prime numbers are all the numbers that DON'T come up in times tables:

| 2 | 3 | 5 | 7 | 11 | 13 | 17 | 19 | 23 | 29 | 31 | 37 | ... |

The only way to get ANY PRIME NUMBER is: 1 × ITSELF

E.g. The only numbers that multiply to give 7 are 1 × 7
      The only numbers that multiply to give 31 are 1 × 31

EXAMPLE: Show that 24 is not a prime number.

Just find another way to make 24 other than 1 × 24:   2 × 12 = 24

24 divides by other numbers apart from 1 and 24, so it isn't a prime number.

Five Important Facts

1) 1 is NOT a prime number.
2) 2 is the ONLY even prime number.
3) The first four prime numbers are 2, 3, 5 and 7.
4) Prime numbers end in 1, 3, 7 or 9 (2 and 5 are the only exceptions to this rule).
5) But NOT ALL numbers ending in 1, 3, 7 or 9 are primes, as shown here:
   (Only the circled ones are primes.)

② ③ ⑤ ⑦
⑪ ⑬ ⑰ ⑲
21 ㉓ 27 ㉙
㉛ 33 ㊲ 39
㊶ ㊸ ㊼ 49
51 ㊳ 57 ㊾
㉛ 63 ㊌ 69
㋋ ㋍ 77 ㋏
81 ㊣ 87 ㊥
91 93 ㊧ 99

How to FIND Prime Numbers — a very simple method

1) All primes (above 5) end in 1, 3, 7 or 9. So ignore any numbers that don't end in one of those.
2) Now, to find which of them ACTUALLY ARE primes you only need to divide each one by 3 and by 7.
   If it doesn't divide exactly by 3 or by 7 then it's a prime.

This simple rule using just 3 and 7 is true for checking primes up to 120.

EXAMPLE: Find all the prime numbers in this list: 71, 72, 73, 74, 75, 76, 77, 78

① First, get rid of anything that doesn't end in 1, 3, 7 or 9: 71, ~~72~~, 73, ~~74~~, ~~75~~, ~~76~~, 77, ~~78~~

② Now try dividing 71, 73 and 77 by 3 and 7:

71 ÷ 3 = 23.667   71 ÷ 7 = 10.143   so 71 is a prime number
73 ÷ 3 = 24.333   73 ÷ 7 = 10.429   so 73 is a prime number
77 ÷ 3 = 25.667   BUT: 77 ÷ 7 = 11 — 11 is a whole number,
                          so 77 is NOT a prime, because it divides by 7.

So the prime numbers in the list are 71 and 73.

Two is the oddest prime of all — it's the only one that's even...

Learn the sections above, then cover the page and try this Exam Practice Question without peeking:

Q1   Below is a list of numbers. Write down all the prime numbers from the list.
     39, 51, 46, 35, 61, 53, 42, 47
     [1 mark]

Section One — Number

Prime Factors

This page is all about breaking a number down until all that's left of it are its prime factors...
But it's not as cruel as it sounds. Really.

Finding Prime Factors — The Factor Tree

Any number can be broken down into a string of prime numbers all multiplied together — this is called 'expressing it as a product of prime factors', or its 'prime factorisation'.

EXAMPLES:

1. Express 420 as a product of prime factors.

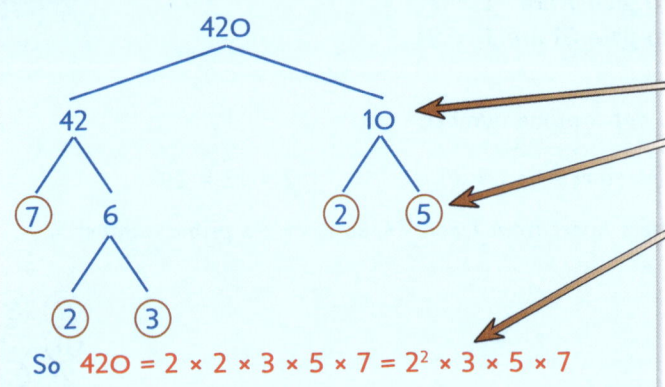

So $420 = 2 \times 2 \times 3 \times 5 \times 7 = 2^2 \times 3 \times 5 \times 7$

To write a number as a product of its prime factors, use the Factor Tree method:
1) Start with the number at the top, and split it into factors as shown.
2) Every time you get a prime, ring it.
3) Keep going until you can't go further (i.e. you're just left with primes), then write the primes out in order. If there's more than one of the same factor, you can write them as powers.

A few things to look out for:
1) If a number ends in 5, it's a multiple of 5, so you can divide by 5 for the first prime factor.
2) If the number is even, you can divide by 2 to find the first prime factor.
3) If you can, dividing by 10 is a good idea. 10 will split into 2 and 5, giving you two prime factors straight off the bat.

2. Express 585 as a product of prime factors.

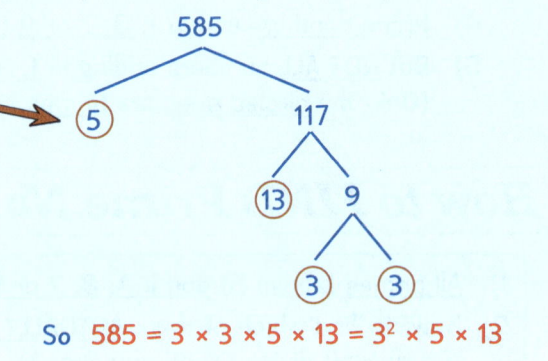

So $585 = 3 \times 3 \times 5 \times 13 = 3^2 \times 5 \times 13$

A Number's Prime Factors are Unique

1) No matter which numbers you choose at each step, you'll find that the prime factorisation is exactly the same.
2) This is because each number has a unique set of prime factors.
3) For example, if you split 420 from the first example like this...
   ... you end up with the same prime factorisation: $2^2 \times 3 \times 5 \times 7$.

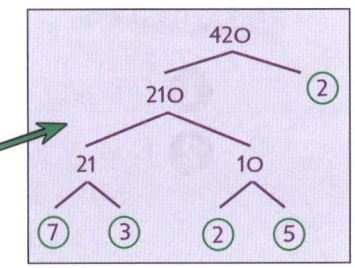

Where are primes manufactured? In a factor-tree...

All this talk about prime factors just makes me want to get stuck into some Exam Style Questions.
'Me too!' I hear you cry? Grand — I've got some here just for you.

Q1 Express the following as products of prime factors: a) 275   b) 100   c) 364   [6 marks]

Q2 Niall writes 450 as $2 \times 5^2 \times 9$ as its product of prime factors.
Where has he gone wrong? What should the prime factors be?   [2 marks]

Q3 Express 10 780 as a product of prime factors.   [2 marks]

Section One — Number

Rounding

You need to be able to use 3 different rounding methods.
This page covers decimal places and rounding to the nearest whole numbers, tens, etc.

Decimal Places (d.p.)

To round to a given number of decimal places:

① Identify the position of the 'last digit' from the number of decimal places.
② Then look at the next digit to the right — called the decider.
③ If the decider is 5 or more, then round up the last digit.
   If the decider is 4 or less, then leave the last digit as it is.
④ There must be no more digits after the last digit (not even zeros).

If you're rounding to 2 d.p. the last digit is the second digit after the decimal point.

EXAMPLE: What is 7.45839 to 2 decimal places?

7.45839 = 7.46

LAST DIGIT to be written (2nd decimal place because we're rounding to 2 d.p.)
DECIDER
The LAST DIGIT rounds UP because the DECIDER is 5 or more.

If you have to round up a 9 (to 10), replace the 9 with 0, and add 1 to the digit on the left.
E.g. Round 45.698 to 2 d.p:

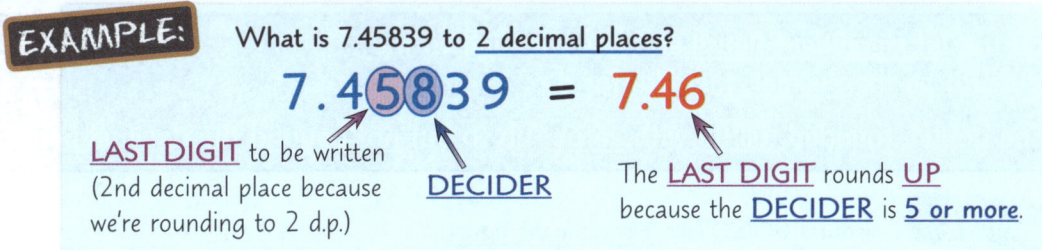

45.698 → 45.69 → 45.70 to 2 d.p.
last digit — round up
The question asks for 2 d.p. so you must put 45.70 not 45.7.

To the Nearest Whole Number, Ten, Hundred etc.

You might be asked to round to the nearest whole number, ten, hundred, thousand, or million:

① Identify the last digit, e.g. for the nearest whole number it's the units position, and for the 'nearest ten' it's the tens position, etc.
② Round the last digit and fill up to the decimal point with zeros.

EXAMPLE: Round 6751 to the nearest hundred.

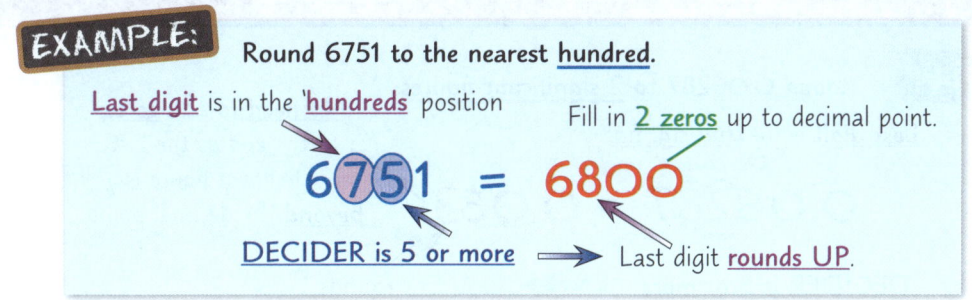

Last digit is in the 'hundreds' position   Fill in 2 zeros up to decimal point.

6751 = 6800

DECIDER is 5 or more → Last digit rounds UP.

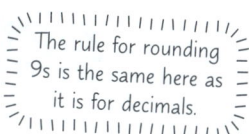

The rule for rounding 9s is the same here as it is for decimals.

Well, I think that's put those decimals in their place...

This is important stuff, so learn the steps of the basic method and then have a crack at these:

Q1   Give 21.435 correct to: a) 1 d.p.   b) 2 d.p.   c) the nearest whole number   [3 marks]
Q2   Round 4968 to the nearest: a) ten   b) hundred   c) thousand   [3 marks]
Q3   Round the following to 2 d.p.:   a) 0.845   b) 5.907   c) 88.396   [3 marks]

Rounding

... And here's the third method for rounding numbers — rounding to a given number of significant figures.

Significant Figures (s.f.)

The 1st significant figure of any number is the first digit which isn't a zero.

The 2nd, 3rd, 4th, etc. significant figures follow immediately after the 1st — they're allowed to be zeros.

Rounding to 1 Significant Figure (s.f.)

To round to 1 significant figure:

1. Find the 1st significant figure and use the digit to the right of it as the decider, just like for d.p.
2. Once you've rounded, fill up with zeros, up to but not beyond the decimal point.

EXAMPLE: Round 506.07 to 1 significant figure.

The 1st sig. fig. is 5.   Need two zeros to fill up to decimal point.

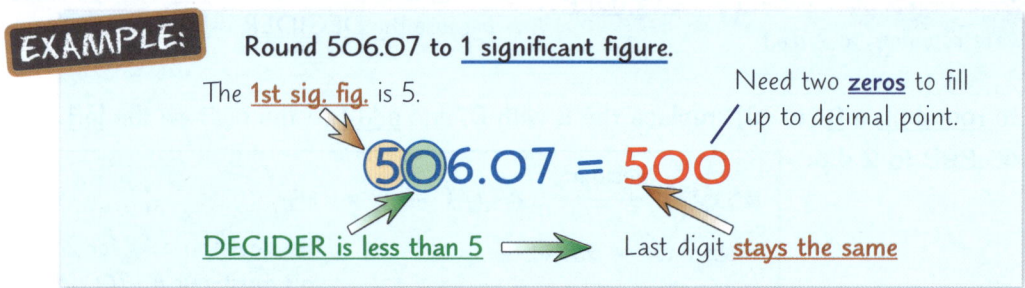

DECIDER is less than 5 ⟹ Last digit stays the same

Rounding to Any Number of Significant Figures (s.f.)

To round to any given number of significant figures:

1. Find the last digit — if you're rounding to, say, 3 s.f., then the 3rd significant figure is the last digit.
2. Use the digit to the right of it as the decider, just like for d.p.
3. Once you've rounded, fill up with zeros, up to but not beyond the decimal point.

EXAMPLE: Round 0.06287 to 2 significant figures.

Last digit is the 2nd sig. fig.   No need to add zeros to the end as the last significant figure is beyond the decimal point.

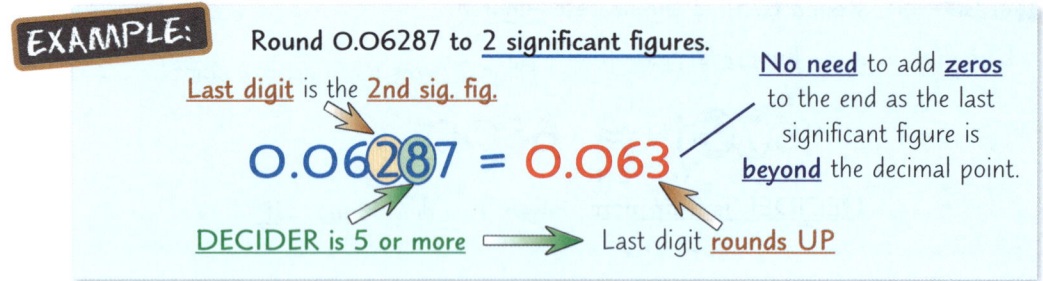

DECIDER is 5 or more ⟹ Last digit rounds UP

Julius Caesar, Elizabeth I, Einstein — all significant figures...

Remember, you can fill in spaces with zeros, but only up to the decimal point. Now have a go at these:

Q1   Round each of these to 1 s.f.:   a) 14.5   b) 198   c) 0.349   d) 0.08732   [4 marks]

Q2   Round 76.841 to: a) 2 s.f.   b) 3 s.f.   c) 4 s.f.   [3 marks]

Estimating

'Estimate' doesn't mean 'take a wild guess', it means 'look at the numbers, make them a bit easier, then do the calculation'. Your answer won't be as accurate as the real thing but hey, it's easier on your brain.

Estimating Calculations

1. Round everything off to 1 significant figure.
2. Then work out the answer using these nice easy numbers.
3. Show all your working or you won't get the marks.

Have a look at the previous page to remind yourself how to round to 1 s.f.

EXAMPLES:

1. Estimate the value of 42.6 × 12.1.

   1) Round each number to 1 s.f.   42.6 × 12.1 ≈ 40 × 10
   2) Do the calculation with the rounded numbers.   = 400

   ≈ means 'approximately equal to'.

   You might have to say if it's an underestimate or an overestimate. Here, you rounded both numbers down, so it's an underestimate.

2. Jo has a cake-making business. She spent £984.69 on flour last year. A bag of flour costs £1.89, and she makes an average of 5 cakes from each bag of flour. Work out an estimate of how many cakes she made last year.

   1) Estimate number of bags of flour — round numbers to 1 s.f.

   Number of bags of flour = $\frac{984.69}{1.89}$ ≈ $\frac{1000}{2}$ = 500

   2) Multiply to find the number of cakes.

   Number of cakes ≈ 500 × 5 = 2500

Don't panic if you get a 'real-life' estimating question — just round everything to 1 s.f. as before.

Estimating Square Roots

Estimating square roots can be a bit tricky, but there are only 2 steps:
1) Find two square numbers, one either side of the number you're given.
2) Decide which number it's closer to, and make a sensible estimate of the digit after the decimal point.

See p18 for more on square roots.

EXAMPLE: Estimate the value of $\sqrt{87}$ to 1 d.p.

87 is between 81 (= 9^2) and 100 (= 10^2).
It's closer to 81, so its square root will be closer to 9 than 10: $\sqrt{87}$ ≈ 9.3
(the actual value of $\sqrt{87}$ is 9.32737..., so this is a reasonable estimate).

And he definitely said Tim ate the calculation? How odd...

If you're asked to estimate something in the exam, make sure you show all your steps (including what each number is rounded to) to prove that you didn't just use a calculator. That would be naughty.

Q1 Estimate the value of: a) $\frac{586.7}{9.8 \times 3.1}$ [2 marks]   b) $\frac{22.3 \times 11.4}{0.532}$ [2 marks]

Q2 Kate buys 17 kg of turnips at a cost of £1.93 per kg. Estimate the total cost.   [2 marks]

Q3 Estimate the value of: a) $\sqrt{60}$ [2 marks]   b) $\sqrt{39}$ [2 marks]

Section One — Number

Powers

Now we're getting on to the good stuff. Although powers in maths aren't exactly the same as the ones superheroes have, they can be just as thrilling. Or more so if you ask me...

Square Numbers

1) When you multiply a whole number by itself, you get a square number.
2) They're called square numbers because they're like the areas of this pattern of squares (there's more about area on p79):
3) Square numbers are written to the power 2 because you multiply 2 lots of the number together, e.g. $2^2 = 2 \times 2 = 4$. It would be a good idea to learn the squares below:

1^2	2^2	3^2	4^2	5^2	6^2	7^2	8^2	9^2	10^2	11^2	12^2	13^2	14^2	15^2
1	4	9	16	25	36	49	64	81	100	121	144	169	196	225
(1×1)	(2×2)	(3×3)	(4×4)	(5×5)	(6×6)	(7×7)	(8×8)	(9×9)	(10×10)	(11×11)	(12×12)	(13×13)	(14×14)	(15×15)

Cube Numbers

1) When you multiply a whole number by itself, then by itself again, you get a cube number.
2) They're called cube numbers because they're like the volumes of this pattern of cubes (there's more about volume on p83):
3) Cube numbers are written to the power 3 because you multiply 3 lots of the number together, e.g. $2^3 = 2 \times 2 \times 2 = 8$. These ones would be useful to learn by heart:

1^3	2^3	3^3	4^3	5^3	10^3
1	8	27	64	125	1000
(1×1×1)	(2×2×2)	(3×3×3)	(4×4×4)	(5×5×5)	(10×10×10)

Powers of Ten

1) Powers of ten are 10 to any power. Unlike square and cube numbers, the power changes and the number stays the same (10).
2) The powers of ten are really easy — the power tells you how many lots of 10 you multiply together. In other words, it tells you how many zeros there are after the 1:

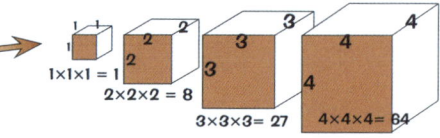

$10^1 = 10$ $10^2 = 100$ $10^3 = 1000$ $10^4 = 10\,000$

EXAMPLE: Write 1 000 000 as a power of 10.
1) Count up how many zeros the number has.   1 000 000 has 6 zeros
2) Write this as a power of 10. $= 10^6$

Numbers may sometimes be square, but they're never boring...

A lot to take in here — when you've got it, cover the page and try these Exam Practice Questions:

Q1 Work out the following: a) 3^2 b) 7^2 c) 2^3 d) 5^3 [4 marks]

Q2 a) Write 10^9 as a proper number. b) Write one hundred thousand as a power of ten. [2 marks]

Q3 List all the numbers under 1000 that are both square numbers and cube numbers. [1 mark]

Section One — Number

Powers

You've seen 'squared' and 'cubed' numbers — these are just 'to the power 2' and 'to the power 3'. But as the 'powers of ten' hint at, any number can be a power if it puts its mind to it...

Powers are a very Useful Shorthand

1) Powers are 'numbers multiplied by themselves so many times':

$$2\times2\times2\times2\times2\times2\times2 = 2^7 \text{ ('two to the power 7')}$$
$$6\times6\times6\times6\times6 = 6^5 \text{ ('six to the power 5')}$$
$$4\times4\times4 = 4^3 \text{ ('four cubed')}$$

2) Use the $x^\blacksquare$ button on your calculator to find powers, e.g. press 3.7 $x^\blacksquare$ 3 $=$ to get $3.7^3 = 50.653$.

3) Anything to the power 1 is just itself, e.g. $4^1 = 4$.

4) 1 to any power is still 1, e.g. $1^{457} = 1$.

5) Anything to the power 0 is just 1, e.g. $5^0 = 1$, $67^0 = 1$, $x^0 = 1$.

The Three Power Rules

1) When MULTIPLYING, you ADD the powers.

e.g. $3^4 \times 3^6 = 3^{4+6} = 3^{10}$ $8^3 \times 8 = 8^3 \times 8^1 = 8^{3+1} = 8^4$

Warning: Rules 1 and 2 don't work for things like $2^3 \times 3^7$, only for powers of the same number.

2) When DIVIDING, you SUBTRACT the powers.

e.g. $5^4 \div 5^2 = 5^{4-2} = 5^2$ $p^8 \div p^7 = p^{8-7} = p^1 = p$

Don't be put off by letters — they obey the same rules.

3) When RAISING one power to another, you MULTIPLY the powers.

e.g. $(4^2)^4 = 4^{2\times 4} = 4^8$, $(x^4)^6 = x^{4\times 6} = x^{24}$

EXAMPLE: $a = 5^9$ and $b = 5^4 \times 5^2$. What is the value of $\frac{a}{b}$?

1) Work out b — add the powers: $b = 5^4 \times 5^2 = 5^{4+2} = 5^6$

2) Divide a by b — subtract the powers: $\frac{a}{b} = 5^9 \div 5^6 = 5^{9-6}$
$= 5^3 = 125$

So (super) powers really DO exist...

Learn this page off by heart, then cover it up and have a go at these...

Q1 Use your calculator to find: a) 6.2^3 b) 11^4 c) 2.3^5 [3 marks]

Q2 Simplify: a) $4^2 \times 4^3$ b) $7^6 \div 7^3$ c) $(q^2)^4$ [3 marks]

Q3 Work out: a) $(5^3)^2$ b) $3^6 \times 3^4$ c) $8^3 \div 8^3$ [3 marks]

Q4 Find $\frac{6^3 \times 6^5}{6^6}$ without using a calculator.   [2 marks]

Section One — Number

Roots

Take a deep breath, and get ready to tackle this page. Good luck with it, I'll be rootin' for ya...

Square Roots

'Squared' means 'multiplied by itself': $8^2 = 8 \times 8 = 64$
SQUARE ROOT $\sqrt{}$ is the reverse process: $\sqrt{64} = 8$

'Square Root' means 'What Number Multiplied by Itself gives...'

EXAMPLES:

1. What is $\sqrt{49}$?

   49 is a square number — make sure you know all the square numbers on p16 so you can answer questions like this without a calculator.

   7 times by itself gives 49: $49 = 7 \times 7$
   So $\sqrt{49} = 7$

2. What is $\sqrt{29.16}$?

   Use your calculator. Press: $\sqrt{}$ 29.16 = 5.4

3. Find both square roots of 36.

   $6 \times 6 = 36$, so positive square root = 6
   $-6 \times -6 = 36$, so negative square root = -6

   All numbers also have a NEGATIVE SQUARE ROOT — it's just the '−' version of the normal positive one.

This little rule for multiplying roots might come in handy in your exam:

$\sqrt{a} \times \sqrt{a} = a$

Be careful — this is only true if you're multiplying together two roots which are the same.

Cube Roots

'Cubed' means 'multiplied by itself and then by itself again': $2^3 = 2 \times 2 \times 2 = 8$
CUBE ROOT $\sqrt[3]{}$ is the reverse process: $\sqrt[3]{8} = 2$

'Cube Root' means 'What Number Multiplied by Itself and then by Itself Again gives...'

You need to be able to write down the cube roots of the cube numbers given on p16 without a calculator. To find the cube root of any other number you can use your calculator — press $\sqrt[3]{}$.

EXAMPLES:

1. What is $\sqrt[3]{27}$?

   27 is a cube number.

   3 times by itself and then by itself again gives 27: $27 = 3 \times 3 \times 3$
   So $\sqrt[3]{27} = 3$

2. What is $\sqrt[3]{4913}$?

   Press: $\sqrt[3]{}$ 4913 = 17

   Make sure you know how to use your calculator to find higher order roots — the buttons might be slightly different to these ones.

You can use your calculator to find any root of a number, using the $\sqrt[x]{}$ or $\sqrt[\square]{}$ buttons.

"Cue brute", that's what I call Charley when I play him at snooker...

Once you've got the meanings of square root and cube root well and truly sorted, have a go at these.

Q1 Find: a) $\sqrt{196}$ without using a calculator. b) $\sqrt[3]{9261}$ c) $\sqrt[7]{2187}$ [3 marks]

Q2 The volume of a cube is 1.728 cm³. Find the length of one of its sides, in cm. [2 marks]

Q3 Work out $\sqrt[3]{19.34} + (1.3 + 2.5)^2$. Write down the full calculator display. [1 mark]

Different Number Systems

There are lots of different number systems, such as decimal (the system you usually use) and Roman numerals. This page covers another you need to know for your exam — binary.

The Binary Number System Uses Two Digits

1) Our standard number system uses ten different digits (0-9) and is called decimal or base-10. The place value in decimal numbers increases from right to left in powers of 10 (1, 10, 100, 1000 etc). So 101 = (1 × 100) + (0 × 10) + (1 × 1)

2) Binary (or base-2) is a different number system which uses only two different digits (0 and 1). The place value in binary numbers increase each time in powers of 2 (1, 2, 4, 8 etc).

3) For example, the binary number 101 ("one zero one" — DEFINITELY NOT "one hundred and one") has a 1 in the place value 1 (on the right), a 0 in the place value 2 and a 1 in the place value 4 (on the left). So as a decimal number, 101 = (1 × 4) + (0 × 2) + (1 × 1) = 5.

4) This table shows the binary equivalents of the decimal numbers 0-15:

0 = 0	4 = 100	8 = 1000	12 = 1100
1 = 1	5 = 101	9 = 1001	13 = 1101
2 = 10	6 = 110	10 = 1010	14 = 1110
3 = 11	7 = 111	11 = 1011	15 = 1111

Binary Numbers are easier to Convert using Tables

Drawing a table with binary place values in the first row makes binary to decimal conversion easier.

EXAMPLE: Convert the binary number 1010 to a decimal number.

1) Draw up a table with binary place values in the top row. Start with 1 at the right, then move left, doubling each time.

8	4	2	1
1	0	1	0

Each column is just a power of 2. i.e. $2^3, 2^2, 2^1, 2^0$.

2) Write the binary number 1010 in the row below.

3) Add up all the top row numbers that have a 1 in their column:
8 + 2 = 10
So 1010 is 10 as a decimal number.

This works with all binary numbers — just draw as many columns as you need, doubling each time.

Convert Decimal to Binary by Subtracting

When converting from decimal to binary, it's easier to draw a table of binary place values, then subtract them from largest to smallest. Have a look at this example:

EXAMPLE: Convert the decimal number 79 into a binary number.

1) Draw a table with binary place values up until the next number bigger than 79.

128	64	32	16	8	4	2	1
0	1	0	0	1	1	1	1

2) Move along the table, only subtracting the number in each column from your running total if it gives a positive answer or zero.

79 − 128 = −49
79 − 64 = 15
15 − 32 = −17
15 − 16 = −1
15 − 8 = 7
7 − 4 = 3
3 − 2 = 1
1 − 1 = 0

3) Put a 1 in every column that gives a positive answer or zero, and a 0 in the rest.

So 79 converted to a binary number is **1001111**.

There are other methods to convert decimal to binary, so just choose the one you are most comfortable with.

There are 10 types of people in this world...

... those who understand binary, and those who don't. Go over the page again, then try these:

Q1 Convert these binary numbers to decimal: a) 111 b) 100010 c) 110 1100 [3 marks]

Q2 Convert these to binary numbers: a) 22 b) 40 c) 63 [3 marks]

Revision Questions for Section One

Well, that wraps up Section One — time to put yourself to the test and find out how much you really know.
- Try these questions and tick off each one when you get it right.
- When you've done all the questions for a topic and are completely happy with it, tick off the topic.

Ordering Numbers and Arithmetic (p2-8)

Calculators are only allowed in questions 3, 11, 12, 13, and 24. Sorry.

1) Write this number out in words: 21 306 515
2) Put these numbers in order of size: 2.2, 4.7, 3.8, 3.91, 2.09, 3.51
3) Using the numbers 2, 4 and 5, and +, −, × and ÷, find the smallest possible positive number you can make. You can use each number/operation ONCE only. You may also use brackets but can NOT use powers or combine the digits to make other numbers (e.g. 245).
4) Tickets for a show cost £12 each. A senior's ticket is half price. A child's ticket is a third of the full price. How much does it cost for a family of 2 adults, 2 children and 1 senior to watch the show?
5) Work out: a) 235 + 678   b) 1090 − 461   c) 54.3 + 75.6
6) Find: a) £1.20 × 100   b) 2.3 × 1000   c) 44 × 200
7) Work out: a) 51 × 27   b) 338 ÷ 13   c) 3.3 × 19   d) 4.2 ÷ 12
8) Find: a) −10 − 6   b) −35 ÷ −5   c) −4 + −5 + 22 − −7

Primes, Factors and Multiples (p9-12)

9) What are multiples? Find the first six multiples of: a) 10   b) 4
10) Find all the common factors of 12 and 60.
11) Find: a) the HCF of 42 and 28   b) the LCM of 8 and 10
12) Find all the prime numbers between 40 and 60 (there are 5 of them).
13) Express each of these as a product of prime factors: a) 210   b) 1260

Rounding and Estimating (p13-15)

14) Round: a) 17.65 to 1 d.p.   b) 6743 to 2 s.f.   c) 0.0561 to 1 s.f.
15) Find: a) 891 302 to the nearest thousand   b) 3 643 510 to the nearest million.
16) Estimate the value of: a) $\dfrac{17.8 \times 32.3}{6.4}$ b) $\dfrac{96.2 \times 7.3}{0.463}$
17) Estimate the value of: a) $\sqrt{20}$ b) $\sqrt{90}$ c) $\sqrt{172}$

Powers and Roots (p16-18)

18) Find: a) 7^2 b) 1^3 c) 3^3 d) 13^2 e) 6^3
19) Write these numbers as squares or cubes: a) 9   b) 125   c) 144
20) Work out: a) 10^3 b) 10^7 c) 100 000 as a power of ten.
21) Simplify: a) $4^6 \div 4^2$ b) $3^3 \times 3^7$ c) $9^4 \div 9^1$
22) If $f = 7^6 \times 7^4$ and $g = 7^5$, what is $f \div g$?
23) Find without using a calculator: a) $\sqrt{121}$ b) $\sqrt[3]{64}$ c) $8^2 - 2^3$
24) Use a calculator to find: a) $\sqrt{23.04}$ b) $\sqrt[3]{512}$ c) $\sqrt[5]{161051}$

Number Systems (p19)

25) What is our standard number system called?
26) Write in binary: a) 12   b) 25   c) 93
27) Write in decimal: a) 1111   b) 10101   c) 1011011

Section One — Number

Section Two — Fractions, Ratios and Percentages

Fractions

These pages show you how to cope with fraction calculations without your beloved calculator.

Cancelling Down Fractions

To cancel down or simplify a fraction, divide top and bottom by the same number, till they won't go further:

EXAMPLE: Simplify $\frac{18}{24}$. These fractions are equivalent fractions — they are equal in value even though they look different.

Cancel down in a series of easy steps — keep going till the top and bottom don't have any common factors.

$$\frac{18}{24} \xrightarrow{\div 3} \frac{6}{8} \xrightarrow{\div 2} \frac{3}{4}$$

The number on the top of the fraction is the numerator, and the number on the bottom is the denominator.

Mixed Numbers and Improper Fractions

Mixed numbers are things like $3\frac{1}{3}$, with an integer part and a fraction part. Improper fractions are ones where the top number is larger than the bottom number. You need to be able to convert between the two.

EXAMPLES:

1. Write $4\frac{2}{3}$ as an improper fraction.
   1) Think of the mixed number as an addition:
      $4\frac{2}{3} = 4 + \frac{2}{3}$
   2) Turn the integer part into a fraction:
      $4 + \frac{2}{3} = \frac{12}{3} + \frac{2}{3} = \frac{12+2}{3} = \frac{14}{3}$

2. Write $\frac{31}{4}$ as a mixed number.
   Divide the top number by the bottom.
   1) The answer gives the whole number part.
   2) The remainder goes on top of the fraction.
   $31 \div 4 = 7$ remainder 3 so $\frac{31}{4} = 7\frac{3}{4}$

Use Common Denominators to Order Fractions

This comes in handy for ordering fractions by size, and for adding or subtracting fractions (see next page). You need to find a number that all the denominators divide into — this will be your common denominator. The simplest way is to find the lowest common multiple (see p10) of the denominators:

EXAMPLE: Put these fractions in ascending order of size: $\frac{8}{3}, \frac{5}{4}, \frac{12}{5}$

The LCM of 3, 4 and 5 is 60, so make 60 the common denominator:

$\frac{8}{3} \xrightarrow{\times 20} \frac{160}{60}$ $\frac{5}{4} \xrightarrow{\times 15} \frac{75}{60}$ $\frac{12}{5} \xrightarrow{\times 12} \frac{144}{60}$

So the correct order is $\frac{75}{60}, \frac{144}{60}, \frac{160}{60}$ — i.e. $\frac{5}{4}, \frac{12}{5}, \frac{8}{3}$

Don't forget to use the original fractions in the final answer.

I prefer my numbers shaken, not stirred...

Have a go at these Exam Practice Questions to check you've got your head around the fraction basics.

Q1 Write each of the following in its simplest form:
   a) $\frac{30}{75}$ [1 mark]   b) $\frac{96}{108}$ [1 mark]   c) $\frac{42}{98}$ [1 mark]

Q2 Write: a) $2\frac{3}{5}$ as an improper fraction [1 mark]   b) $\frac{16}{7}$ as a mixed number [1 mark]

Q3 Put these fractions in order of size, from largest to smallest: $\frac{7}{8}, \frac{7}{9}, \frac{5}{6}$. [2 marks]

Fractions

Yep, still going — there's a lot you need to know about fractions.

Adding, Subtracting — Sort the Denominators First

1) Make sure the denominators are the same (see previous page).
2) Add (or subtract) the top lines only.

If you're adding or subtracting mixed numbers, it usually helps to convert them to improper fractions first.

EXAMPLE: Calculate $\frac{1}{3} + \frac{2}{9}$.

1) Find a common denominator: $\frac{1}{3} + \frac{2}{9} = \frac{3}{9} + \frac{2}{9}$

2) Combine the top lines: $= \frac{3+2}{9} = \frac{5}{9}$

EXAMPLE: Calculate $3\frac{1}{8} - \frac{1}{4}$.

1) Rewrite the mixed number as an improper fraction: $3\frac{1}{8} - \frac{1}{4} = \frac{25}{8} - \frac{1}{4}$

2) Find a common denominator: $= \frac{25}{8} - \frac{2}{8}$

3) Combine the top lines: $= \frac{25-2}{8} = \frac{23}{8}$

Fractions of Something

EXAMPLE: What is $\frac{9}{20}$ of £360?

The order that you multiply and divide in doesn't matter — just start with whatever's easiest. It's often easier to divide first as it keeps the numbers smaller.

'$\frac{9}{20}$ of £360' means '$\frac{9}{20}$ × £360'.

Multiply by the top of the fraction and divide by the bottom:

$\frac{9}{20}$ × £360 = (£360 ÷ 20) × 9
= £18 × 9 = £162

Expressing as a Fraction

EXAMPLE: Write 180 as a fraction of 80.

Write the first number over the second and cancel down: $\frac{180}{80} = \frac{9}{4}$

I tried expressing my feelings as fractions — it didn't go so well...

Little bit tougher, this page. Have a go at these to check you've grasped everything.

Q1 Calculate: a) $\frac{8}{9} + \frac{19}{27}$ [2 marks] b) $1\frac{1}{4} - \frac{7}{20}$ [2 marks]

Q2 Dean has made 30 sandwiches. $\frac{7}{15}$ of the sandwiches he has made are vegetarian, and $\frac{3}{7}$ of the vegetarian sandwiches are cheese sandwiches. How many cheese sandwiches has he made? [2 marks]

Section Two — Fractions, Ratios and Percentages

Fractions

A couple more methods to deal with on this page — things are getting fractionally tougher...

Adding, Subtracting when Both Denominators Change

If one denominator isn't a multiple of the other, you'll need to change both fractions before you can add or subtract.

EXAMPLE: Calculate $\frac{2}{3} - \frac{1}{5}$.

Find a common denominator: $\frac{2}{3} - \frac{1}{5} = \frac{10}{15} - \frac{3}{15}$

Combine the top lines: $= \frac{10-3}{15} = \frac{7}{15}$

EXAMPLE: Calculate $2\frac{1}{4} + 1\frac{1}{6}$.

1) Rewrite the mixed numbers as improper fractions: $2\frac{1}{4} + 1\frac{1}{6} = \frac{9}{4} + \frac{7}{6}$

2) Find a common denominator: $= \frac{27}{12} + \frac{14}{12}$

If you use the LCM in step 2 you won't have to cancel down later.

3) Combine the top lines: $= \frac{27+14}{12} = \frac{41}{12} = 3\frac{5}{12}$

Multiplying Fractions

Multiply top and bottom separately. Then simplify your fraction as far as possible.

EXAMPLE: Find $\frac{8}{5} \times \frac{7}{12}$.

Multiply the top and bottom separately: $\frac{8}{5} \times \frac{7}{12} = \frac{8 \times 7}{5 \times 12}$

Then simplify — top and bottom both divide by 4: $= \frac{56}{60} = \frac{14}{15}$

Dividing Fractions

Turn the second fraction UPSIDE DOWN and then multiply:

When you're multiplying or dividing with mixed numbers, always turn them into improper fractions first.

EXAMPLE 1: Calculate $\frac{5}{9} \div \frac{3}{4}$.

Turn $\frac{3}{4}$ upside down and multiply:
$\frac{5}{9} \div \frac{3}{4} = \frac{5}{9} \times \frac{4}{3} = \frac{5 \times 4}{9 \times 3} = \frac{20}{27}$

EXAMPLE 2: Find $2\frac{1}{3} \div 3\frac{1}{2}$.

Rewrite the mixed numbers as improper fractions: $2\frac{1}{3} \div 3\frac{1}{2} = \frac{7}{3} \div \frac{7}{2}$

Turn $\frac{7}{2}$ upside down and multiply: $= \frac{7}{3} \times \frac{2}{7} = \frac{7 \times 2}{3 \times 7}$

$= \frac{14}{21} = \frac{2}{3}$

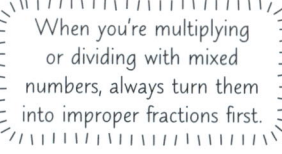

No fractions were harmed in the making of these pages...

...although one was slightly frightened for a while, and several were tickled.
When you think you've learnt all this, try this Exam Practice Question.

Q1   Calculate: a) $\frac{4}{9} + \frac{1}{2}$ [2 marks]   b) $5\frac{2}{3} - 9\frac{1}{4}$ [2 marks]

c) $\frac{5}{8} \times 1\frac{5}{6}$ [2 marks]   d) $\frac{10}{7} \div \frac{8}{3}$ [2 marks]

Section Two — Fractions, Ratios and Percentages

Fractions, Decimals and Percentages

Fractions, decimals and percentages are three different ways of describing when you've got part of a whole thing. They're closely related and you can convert between them. These tables show some really common conversions which you should know straight off without having to work them out:

Fraction	Decimal	Percentage
$\frac{1}{2}$	0.5	50%
$\frac{1}{4}$	0.25	25%
$\frac{3}{4}$	0.75	75%
$\frac{1}{3}$	0.333333...	$33\frac{1}{3}$%
$\frac{2}{3}$	0.666666...	$66\frac{2}{3}$%
$\frac{5}{2}$	2.5	250%

Fraction	Decimal	Percentage
$\frac{1}{10}$	0.1	10%
$\frac{2}{10}$	0.2	20%
$\frac{1}{5}$	0.2	20%
$\frac{2}{5}$	0.4	40%
$\frac{1}{8}$	0.125	12.5%
$\frac{3}{8}$	0.375	37.5%

The more of those conversions you learn, the better — but for those that you don't know, you must also learn how to convert between the three types. These are the methods:

Fraction — Divide → Decimal — × by 100 → Percentage

E.g. $\frac{7}{20}$ is 7÷20   = 0.35   e.g. 0.35 × 100   = 35%

Fraction ← The awkward one — Decimal ← ÷ by 100 — Percentage

Converting decimals to fractions is awkward. To convert terminating decimals to fractions:
The digits after the decimal point go on the top, and a 10, 100, 1000, etc. on the bottom — so you have the same number of zeros as there were decimal places.

Terminating decimals are ones where the digits don't go on forever — see the next page.

$0.6 = \frac{6}{10}$ $0.78 = \frac{78}{100}$ $0.024 = \frac{24}{1000}$ etc.   These can often be cancelled down — see p21.

EXAMPLE:  In a survey of 300 supermarket shoppers, 126 said that Nutty Shreds was their favourite type of cereal. What percentage said that Nutty Shreds was their favourite type of cereal?

Write down the fraction of shoppers that said Nutty Shreds was their favourite. $\frac{126}{300}$

Divide to convert the fraction to a decimal. $\frac{126}{300}$ is 126 ÷ 300 = 0.42

Multiply by 100 to find the percentage.   0.42 × 100 = 42%

The proportion of the shoppers that said that Wheatybits was their favourite type of cereal was 0.15. What fraction of shoppers in the survey said that Wheatybits was their favourite type of cereal?

0.15 has 2 decimal places, so 15 goes on the top and 100 goes on the bottom of the fraction. $\frac{15}{100}$

Cancel down to give the fraction in its simplest form. $\frac{15}{100} = \frac{3}{20}$

Eight out of ten cats prefer the perfume Eighty Purr Scent...

Learn the top tables and the conversion processes. Then it's time to break into a mild sweat...

Q1   Which is greater: a) 57% or $\frac{5}{9}$,   b) 0.2 or $\frac{6}{25}$,   c) $\frac{7}{8}$ or 90%?   [3 marks]

Q2   Write 0.555 as a fraction in its simplest form.   [2 marks]

Section Two — Fractions, Ratios and Percentages

Fractions and Recurring Decimals

You might think that a decimal is just a decimal. But oh no — things get a lot more juicy than that...

Recurring or Terminating...

1) Recurring decimals have a pattern of numbers which repeats forever.

   For example, $\frac{1}{3}$ is the decimal 0.333333...

2) It doesn't have to be a single digit that repeats.

   E.g. You could have 0.143143143...

3) The repeating part is usually marked with dots on top of the number.

4) If there's one dot, only one digit is repeated. If there are two dots, then everything from the first dot to the second dot is the repeating bit.

   E.g. $0.2\dot{5} = 0.2555555...$
   $0.\dot{2}\dot{5} = 0.25252525...$
   $0.\dot{2}6\dot{5} = 0.265265265...$

5) Terminating decimals don't go on forever.

   E.g. $\frac{1}{20}$ is the terminating decimal 0.05

6) All terminating and recurring decimals can be written as fractions.

Fraction	Recurring decimal or terminating decimal?	Decimal
$\frac{1}{2}$	Terminating	0.5
$\frac{1}{3}$	Recurring	$0.\dot{3}$
$\frac{1}{4}$	Terminating	0.25
$\frac{1}{5}$	Terminating	0.2
$\frac{1}{6}$	Recurring	$0.1\dot{6}$
$\frac{1}{7}$	Recurring	$0.\dot{1}4285\dot{7}$
$\frac{1}{8}$	Terminating	0.125
$\frac{1}{9}$	Recurring	$0.\dot{1}$
$\frac{1}{10}$	Terminating	0.1

Turning Fractions into Recurring Decimals

This isn't so different from turning a fraction into a terminating decimal, but you need to make sure you've found the whole repeating pattern before you write your final answer.

EXAMPLE: Without using a calculator, write $\frac{5}{11}$ as a recurring decimal.

1) Remember, $\frac{5}{11}$ means $5 \div 11$, so you can just do the division. The trick is to treat the 5 as a decimal — write it as 5.000...

   For more about division with decimals, see p7.

   11 into 50 goes 4 times...

   0.4
   $11 \overline{| 5.{}^5 0 {}^6 0\ 0\ 0\ 0}$
   ...and carry the 6

   11 into 60 goes 5 times...

   $0.4\ 5$
   $11 \overline{| 5.{}^5 0 {}^6 0 {}^5 0\ 0\ 0}$
   ...and carry the 5

   $0.4\ 5\ 4\ 5$
   $11 \overline{| 5.{}^5 0 {}^6 0 {}^5 0 {}^6 0 {}^5 0}$

2) Keep going until you can see the repeating pattern. Write the recurring decimal using dots above the repeating part.

   $5 \div 11 = 0.454545...$
   so $\frac{5}{11} = 0.\dot{4}\dot{5}$

Oh, what's recurrin'?...

This seems pretty tricky, I admit, but you'll be on the right track if you know what those dots on top of a decimal mean, and how to turn a fraction into a decimal by dividing — even without a calculator.

Q1 Without a calculator, use division to show that $\frac{1}{6} = 0.1\dot{6}$ [3 marks]

Ratios

Ratios are a pretty important topic — they can crop up in all sorts of questions, so you need to be prepared. Make sure you understand the examples on the next two pages, then get practising.

Reducing Ratios to their Simplest Form

1) To reduce a ratio to a simpler form, divide all the numbers in the ratio by the same thing (a bit like simplifying a fraction — see p21).
   It's in its simplest form when there's nothing left you can divide by.

   EXAMPLE: Write the ratio 15:18 in its simplest form.

   For the ratio 15:18, both numbers have a factor of 3, so divide them by 3.   ÷3 (15:18) ÷3 = 5:6

   We can't reduce this any further. So the simplest form of 15:18 is 5:6.

   ### A handy trick for the calculator papers — use the fraction button
   If you enter a fraction with the ▭ or $a^b/_c$ button, the calculator automatically cancels it down when you press =.
   So for the ratio 8:12, just enter $\frac{8}{12}$ as a fraction, and you'll get the reduced fraction $\frac{2}{3}$.
   Now you just change it back to ratio form, i.e. 2:3. Ace.

2) If the ratio has mixed units — convert to the smaller unit then simplify.

   EXAMPLE: Reduce the ratio 24 mm : 7.2 cm to its simplest form.

   1) Convert 7.2 cm to millimetres.
   2) Simplify the resulting ratio. Once the units on both sides are the same, get rid of them for the final answer.

   24 mm : 7.2 cm
   = 24 mm : 72 mm
   = ÷24 ↘ 1:3 ↙ ÷24

Writing Ratios as Fractions

1) To write one part as a fraction of another part — put one number over the other.

   E.g. if apples and oranges are in the ratio 2:9 then we say there are $\frac{2}{9}$ as many apples as oranges or $\frac{9}{2}$ times as many oranges as apples.

2) To write one part as a fraction of the total — add up the parts to find the total, then put the part you want over the total.

   E.g. a pie dough is made by mixing flour, butter and water in the ratio 3:2:1.
   The total number of parts is 3 + 2 + 1 = 6.
   So $\frac{3}{6} = \frac{1}{2}$ of the dough is flour, $\frac{2}{6} = \frac{1}{3}$ is butter and $\frac{1}{6}$ is water.

The simpler the ratio the better as far as I'm concerned...

Whole number ratios are easy to simplify, but you need to make sure you can do the awkward cases too.

Q1 Simplify: a) 25:35   b) 2.5 kg : 750 g   c) 40 s : 4 min   [5 marks]

Q2 Niamh mixes red paint, blue paint and white paint in the ratio 2:3:5 to make some lilac paint.
   a) Write the amount of blue paint Niamh uses as a fraction of the amount of red paint she uses.   [1 mark]
   b) What fraction of the lilac paint is made up of white paint?   [2 marks]

Section Two — Fractions, Ratios and Percentages

Ratios

I'm afraid you're not done with ratios just yet. There are some more examples to get your head around here...

Scaling Up Ratios

If you know the ratio between parts and the actual size of one part,
you can scale the ratio up to find the other parts.

 Mortar is made from mixing sand and cement in the ratio 7:2. How many buckets of mortar will be made if 21 buckets of sand are used in the mixture?

You need to multiply by 3 to go from 7 to 21 on the left-hand side (LHS) — so do that to both sides:

So 21 buckets of sand and 6 buckets of cement are used.

sand : cement

×3 (7 : 2) ×3
= 21 : 6

Amount of mortar made = 21 + 6 = 27 buckets

The two parts of a ratio are always in direct proportion (see p28-29). So in the example above, sand and cement are in direct proportion, e.g. if the amount of sand doubles, the amount of cement doubles.

Proportional Division

In a proportional division question a TOTAL AMOUNT is split into parts in a certain ratio.
The key word here is PARTS — concentrate on 'parts' and it all becomes quite painless:

EXAMPLE: Jess, Mo and Greg share £9100 in the ratio 2:4:7. How much does Mo get?

1) **ADD UP THE PARTS**:
   The ratio 2:4:7 means there will be a total of 13 parts: 2 + 4 + 7 = 13 parts

2) **DIVIDE TO FIND ONE "PART"**:
   Just divide the total amount by the number of parts: £9100 ÷ 13 = £700 (= 1 part)

3) **MULTIPLY TO FIND THE AMOUNTS**:
   We want to know Mo's share, which is 4 parts: 4 parts = 4 × £700 = £2800

 In an office, the ratio of people who drink tea to people who drink coffee is 8:5. 18 more people drink tea than coffee. How many people drink coffee?

You know how many more people drink tea than coffee, so work out how many more parts drink tea than coffee.   8 − 5 = 3 parts

Then divide to find how many people there are in one part.   1 part = 18 ÷ 3 = 6 people

The ratio tells you that 5 parts of the people drink coffee, so multiply by 5 to calculate the number that drink coffee.   Coffee = 5 parts = 5 × 6 = 30 people

---

I always divide sweets in the ratio me:you = 3:1...

There's loads of stuff to learn about ratios, so have another look over it and then try these questions:

Q1   Orange squash is made of water and concentrate in the ratio 11:2.
     a) What fraction of the squash is made up from concentrate?   [1 mark]
     b) How many litres of water are needed if 6 litres of concentrate are used?   [1 mark]

Q2   The ages of Ben, Tanvi and Pam are in the ratio 5:3:1.
     Their combined age is 108. How old is Tanvi?   [2 marks]

Direct Proportion Problems

Direct proportion problems all involve amounts that <u>increase</u> or <u>decrease</u> together. Awww.

Learn the *Golden Rule* for *Proportion* Questions

There are lots of questions which at first sight seem completely different but in fact they can all be done using the GOLDEN RULE...

DIVIDE FOR ONE, THEN TIMES FOR ALL

 5 pints of milk cost £2.60. How much will 3 pints cost?

The GOLDEN RULE tells you to:
<u>Divide the price by 5</u> to find how much FOR ONE PINT,
then <u>multiply by 3</u> to find how much FOR 3 PINTS.

1 pint: £2.60 ÷ 5 = 0.52 = 52p
3 pints: 52p × 3 = 156p = **£1.56**

My favourite cereal is muesli.

 Emma is handing out some leaflets. She gets paid per leaflet she hands out. If she hands out 300 leaflets she gets £12.00.
How many leaflets will she have to hand out to earn £28.50?

<u>Divide by 12.00</u> to find how many leaflets she has to hand out to earn <u>£1</u>.

<u>Multiply by 28.50</u> to find how many leaflets she has to hand out to earn <u>£28.50</u>.

To earn £1: 300 ÷ 12.00 = 25 leaflets

To earn £28.50: 25 × 28.50 = 712.5
So she'll need to hand out **713** leaflets.

You need to round your answer up because 712 wouldn't be enough.

Scaling *Recipes* Up or Down

 Judy is making orange and pineapple punch using the recipe shown on the right.
She wants to make enough to serve 20 people.
How much of each ingredient will Judy need?

Fruit Punch (serves 8)
800 ml orange juice
140 g fresh pineapple

The GOLDEN RULE tells you to <u>divide each amount by 8</u> to find how much FOR ONE PERSON, then <u>multiply by 20</u> to find how much FOR 20 PEOPLE.

So for 1 person you need:
800 ml ÷ 8 = 100 ml orange juice
140 g ÷ 8 = 17.5 g pineapple

And for 20 people you need:
⇒ 20 × 100 ml = **2000 ml orange juice**
⇒ 20 × 17.5 g = **350 g pineapple**

The Three Mathsketeers say "divide for one, then times for all"...

The trick here is knowing when to use the golden rule. Only use it when two things are in direct proportion, e.g. when doubling one quantity doubles the other. Learning the examples above will help.

Q1   Seven pencils cost £1.40.   a) How much will four pencils cost?   [2 marks]
     b) What is the maximum number of pencils you could buy for £6.50?   [2 marks]

Q2   It costs £43.20 for 8 people to go on a rollercoaster 6 times.
     How much will it cost for 15 people to go on the rollercoaster 5 times?   [4 marks]

Section Two — Fractions, Ratios and Percentages

Direct Proportion Problems

These types of questions might not work in quite the same way, but I promise it's all still direct proportion...

Best Buy Questions

A slightly different type of direct proportion question is comparing the 'value for money' of 2 or 3 similar items. For these, follow the second GOLDEN RULE...

Divide by the PRICE in pence (to get the amount per penny)

EXAMPLE: The local 'Supplies 'n' Vittals' stocks two sizes of Jamaican Gooseberry Jam, as shown on the right. Which of these represents better value for money?

Follow the GOLDEN RULE —
divide by the price in pence to get the amount per penny.

In the 350 g jar you get   350 g ÷ 80p = 4.38 g per penny
In the 100 g jar you get   100 g ÷ 42p = 2.38 g per penny

The 350 g jar is better value for money, because you get more jam per penny.

350 g at 80p   100 g at 42p

In some cases it might be easier to divide by the weight to get the cost per gram.
If you're feeling confident then you can do it this way — if not, the golden rule always works.

Exchange Rates

1) An exchange rate tells you what one unit of one currency is worth in another currency. For example, £1 = $1.25 means that for every £1, you'd get 1.25 US dollars.

2) If the exchange rate is in the form £1 = ..., then to go from pounds to the other currency you'll need to multiply by the exchange rate. To go from the other currency to pounds, you'll need to divide by the exchange rate.

Because the exchange rate already tells you how much you'll get for one unit, you won't usually need to do the 'divide for one' step when answering questions.

EXAMPLE: Josh changes £200 into euro for his holiday to Italy. The exchange rate is £1 = €1.11. How much, in euro, does Josh receive?

£1 is €1.11, so to find out what £200 is in euro, multiply by 1.11.   200 × 1.11 = 222

So Josh receives €222.

The hotel room Josh stays in costs €75 a night. How much does the room cost in pounds?

Divide by 1.11 to work out how many pounds there are in 75 euro.   75 ÷ 1.11 = 67.5675...

Then round to 2 d.p. to give an answer in pounds and pence.   = £67.57

Calm down, you're blowing this page all out of proportion...

A mixed bag on this page — soak it all in and then have a crack at these questions.

Q1 Tomato ketchup comes in bottles of three sizes: 250 g for 50p, 770 g for £1.40 and 1600 g for £3.20. Which bottle represents the best value for money? [3 marks]

Q2 Ayida changes £600 into dollars for a trip to America. The exchange rate is £1 = $1.25. How many dollars will she receive? [1 mark]

Percentages

You're going to see 5 different types of percentage question on the next three pages. The first few shouldn't give you too much trouble. Especially if you remember:

> 1) 'Per cent' means 'out of 100', so 20% means '20 out of 100' = $\frac{20}{100}$.
>
> 2) To work out the percentage OF something replace the word OF with a multiplication (×).

Five Different Question Types

Type 1 — "Find x% of y"

If you have a calculator, turn the percentage into a decimal, then multiply.

EXAMPLE: Find 18% of £4.

18% of £4 — Replace 'of' with '×'.
= 18% × £4
Change 18% to a decimal and multiply.
= 0.18 × £4 = £0.72

Find the other 50% of my sandwich

If you don't have a calculator, you can use this clever method instead:

EXAMPLE: Find 35% of 600 kg.

100% = 600 kg

1) Find 10% by dividing by 10:   10% = 600 ÷ 10 = 60 kg
2) Find 5% by dividing 10% by 2:   5% = 60 ÷ 2 = 30 kg
3) Use these values to make 35%:   35% = (3 × 10%) + 5%
                                               = (3 × 60) + 30 = 210 kg

You can also find 1% by dividing by 100.

Type 2 — "Express x as a percentage of y"

Divide x by y, then multiply by 100.

EXAMPLES:

1. Give 36p as a percentage of 80p.

Divide 36p by 80p, then multiply by 100: $\frac{36}{80}$ × 100 = 45%

If you don't have a calculator you'll have to simplify the fraction (see p21).

2. The depth of a pond was measured at the start and end of a particularly dry month. At the start of the month it was 1.32 m deep and at the end of the month it was 84 cm deep. Give the depth at the end of the month as a percentage of the depth at the start.

1) Make sure both amounts are in the same units.   1.32 m = 132 cm
2) Divide 84 cm by 132 cm, then multiply by 100: $\frac{84}{132}$ × 100 = 64% (to the nearest percent)

Fact: 70% of people understand percentages, the other 40% don't...

It's all fairly straightforward here — just make sure you can do percentages with and without a calculator.

Q1   a) Without using a calculator, find 36% of 300.   [3 marks]
       b) Use a calculator to find 39% of 505.   [2 marks]

Q2   A full bottle of pearade holds 1.2 litres. After pouring a glass there is 744 ml left in the bottle. What percentage of the original amount is left in the bottle?   [2 marks]

Section Two — Fractions, Ratios and Percentages

Percentages

By my calculations, you're already 40% of the way through those 5 types of question...

Type 3 — New Amount After a % Increase or Decrease

There are <u>two different ways</u> of finding the new amount after a percentage increase or decrease:

1) Find the % then Add or Subtract.

Find the % of the <u>original amount</u>. <u>Add</u> this on to (or <u>subtract</u> from) the <u>original value</u>.

 A dress has increased in price by 30%.
It originally cost £40. What is the new price of the dress?

1) Find 30% of £40:   30% of £40 = 30% × £40
2) It's an <u>increase</u>, so   = 0.3 × 40 = £12
   <u>add on</u> to the original: £40 + £12 = £52

2) The Multiplier Method

This time, you first need to find the <u>multiplier</u> — the decimal that represents the <u>percentage change</u>.

E.g. 5% increase is 1.05 (= 1 + 0.05)   26% decrease is 0.74 (= 1 − 0.26)

Then you just <u>multiply</u> the <u>original value</u> by the <u>multiplier</u> and voilà — you have the answer.

A % <u>decrease</u> has a multiplier <u>less than 1</u>,
a % <u>increase</u> has a multiplier <u>greater than 1</u>.

 A hat is reduced in price by 20% in the sales.
It originally cost £12. What is the new price of the hat?

1) Find the <u>multiplier</u>:   20% decrease = 1 − 0.20 = 0.8
2) Multiply the <u>original value</u> by the <u>multiplier</u>:   £12 × 0.8 = £9.60   ← Voilà

Type 4 — Simple Interest

Compound interest is covered on page 33.

Simple interest means a certain percentage of the <u>original amount only</u> is paid at regular intervals (usually once a year). So the amount of interest is <u>the same every time</u> it's paid.

 Regina invests £380 in an account which pays 3% simple interest each year.
How much interest will she earn in 4 years?

1) Work out the amount of interest earned <u>in one year</u>:   3% = 3 ÷ 100 = 0.03
                                                               3% of £380 = 0.03 × £380 = £11.40
2) Multiply by 4 to get the <u>total interest</u> for <u>4 years</u>:   4 × £11.40 = £45.60

Simple Interest — it's simple, but it's not that interesting...

Another two types of percentages for you here — try the methods out on these practice questions.

Q1   A unicorn costing £4000 is reduced by 15% in a sale. What is its new price?   [2 marks]

Q2   Al puts £110 into a bank account that pays 6% simple interest each year. What will his bank balance be after 3 years if he doesn't pay in or take out any money?   [3 marks]

Percentages

Watch out for these trickier types of percentage question — they'll often include lots of real-life context.

Type 5 — Finding the Percentage Change

1) This is the formula for giving a change in value as a percentage — **LEARN IT, AND USE IT**:

$$\text{PERCENTAGE 'CHANGE'} = \frac{\text{'CHANGE'}}{\text{ORIGINAL}} \times 100$$

2) Typical questions will ask 'Find the percentage increase/profit/error' or 'Calculate the percentage decrease/loss/discount', etc.

Tariq buys a plain plate for £2. He paints it, then sells it at a craft fair for £3.75. Find his profit as a percentage.

1) Here the 'change' is profit, so the formula looks like this: percentage profit = $\frac{\text{profit}}{\text{original}} \times 100$

2) Work out the profit (amount made − original cost).   profit = £3.75 − £2 = £1.75

3) Calculate the percentage profit.   percentage profit = $\frac{£1.75}{£2} \times 100 = 87.5\%$

AER is Used for Savings and APR is Used for Borrowing

1) **AER** (Annual Equivalent Rate) is a rate used to work out how much interest a savings account pays over a full year.

2) It's used to compare savings accounts which pay interest at different intervals (e.g. annually, monthly).

Erin's savings account has an AER of 6.5%. She deposits £3000 in the account. How much interest will she earn in a year?

Calculate 6.5% of £3000.   0.065 × £3000 = £195

3) **APR** (Annual Percentage Rate) is a rate used to work out how much it costs you to borrow money — e.g. when you take out a loan, get a mortgage to buy a house or pay for something on a credit card.

4) It takes into account both the interest charged on what you borrowed, and any extra charges that you might have to pay (e.g. the fee you pay the bank for arranging a mortgage).

5) It allows you to make meaningful comparisons between lenders.

Ivor wants to take out a £200 loan. He goes to two lenders with different rates:
- Mako Money offers him a loan with 14% APR.
- Great White Loans offers an annual interest rate of 10% with a £5 initial fee.

If Ivor pays the loan back in full after one year, which is the better offer?

Work out how much he'll have to pay at the end of the year with each lender:

Mako Money: £200 plus 14% = £200 × 1.14 = £228
Great White Loans: £200 plus 10%, plus £5 fees
= (£200 × 1.1) + £5 = £225

So Great White Loans is offering the better deal.

The % change in my understanding of this topic is 100%...

Read over the page again and make sure it's all straight in your head, then give this question a go.

Q1 Naresh is 172 cm tall. One year ago, he was 164 cm tall.
    Find the percentage increase in his height over the year.   [3 marks]

Repeated Percentage Change

One more sneaky % type for you... In a repeated percentage change, the amount added on/taken away changes each time — it's a percentage of the new amount, rather than the original amount.

Compound Interest is a Repeated Percentage Increase

Compound interest is a good example of repeated percentage change — it means the interest is added on each time, and the next lot of interest is calculated using the new total rather than the original amount.

EXAMPLE: Daniel invests £10 000 in a savings account which pays 4% compound interest per annum. How much money will there be in his account after 3 years?

1) Work out the multiplier: Multiplier = 4% increase = 1.04
2) Find the amount in the savings account each year until you get to 3 years.
   After 1 year: £10 000 × 1.04 = £10 400
   After 2 years: £10 400 × 1.04 = £10 816
   After 3 years: £10 816 × 1.04 = **£11 248.64**

'Per annum' just means 'each year'.

You Can Also Have a Repeated Percentage Decrease

Some questions are about things that decrease in value or number over time.

EXAMPLE: Susan has just bought a car for £6500. The car depreciates by 16% each year. How many years will it be before the car is worth less than £5000?

1) Work out the multiplier: 16% decrease = 1 − 0.16 = 0.84
2) Calculate the value of the car each year — stop when the value drops below £5000.
   After 1 year: £6500 × 0.84 = £5460
   After 2 years: £5980 × 0.84 = £4586.40

So it will be **2 years** before the car is worth less than £5000.

'Depreciates' means 'decreases in value'.

Sometimes the Multiplier Changes

Some quantities don't change by the same amount each time — for example, they might increase one year and then decrease the next. So you'll need to work out more than one multiplier.

EXAMPLE: In 2016 Baako's Bakery made a profit of £25 000. In 2017, the profit was 12% lower than in 2016. In 2018, the profit was 15% higher than in 2017. How much profit did Baako's Bakery make in 2018?

1) First, work out the profit in 2017.
   100% − 12% = 88%
   88% of £25 000 = 0.88 × 25 000 = £22 000
2) Then work out the profit in 2018. Make sure you use the value you've just found.
   100% + 15% = 115%
   115% of £22 000 = 1.15 × 22 000 = **£25 300**

I thought you'd depreciate all the work I've put into this page...

Write down the value after each increase/decrease — it'll help you keep track of where you're up to.

Q1 Priya's bank account pays 2.5% compound interest per annum and her bank balance is £3200. If she doesn't pay in or withdraw money, what will Priya's bank balance be after 3 years? [3 marks]

Section Two — Fractions, Ratios and Percentages

Revision Questions for Section Two

Lots of things to remember in Section Two — there's only one way to find out what you've taken in...
- Try these questions and tick off each one when you get it right.
- When you've done all the questions for a topic and are completely happy with it, tick off the topic.

Fractions and Decimals (p21-25)

1) Write the following as mixed numbers in their simplest form:
   a) $\frac{30}{16}$ b) $\frac{24}{10}$ c) $\frac{70}{25}$

2) Amy has completed $\frac{5}{8}$ of a video game, Brad has completed $\frac{7}{11}$ of the game and Cameron has completed $\frac{15}{22}$ of the game. Who has the largest fraction of the game left to complete?

3) Calculate: a) $\frac{4}{7}$ of 560   b) $\frac{2}{5}$ of £150

4) Work out without a calculator: a) $\frac{25}{6} \div \frac{8}{3}$ b) $\frac{2}{3} \times 4\frac{2}{5}$ c) $\frac{5}{8} + \frac{9}{4}$ d) $\frac{2}{3} - \frac{1}{7}$

5) Write: a) 0.04 as: (i) a fraction   (ii) a percentage   b) 65% as: (i) a fraction   (ii) a decimal

6) a) What is a recurring decimal?   b) Write $\frac{2}{9}$ as a recurring decimal.

Ratios (p26-27)

7) Reduce: a) 18:22 to its simplest form   b) 4.9 kg : 1400 g to its simplest form

8) A pencil case contains pencils and rubbers. The ratio of pencils to rubbers is 7:2. What fraction of the items in the pencil case are pencils?

9) Sarah is in charge of ordering stock for a clothes shop. The shop usually sells red scarves and blue scarves in the ratio 5:8. Sarah orders 50 red scarves. How many blue scarves should she order?

10) Ryan, Joel and Sam are sharing 800 lollipops. They split the lollipops in the ratio 5:8:12.
    a) What fraction of the lollipops does Ryan get?   b) How many lollipops does Sam get?

Direct Proportion Problems (p28-29)

11) 3 gardeners can plant 360 flowers in a day. How many flowers could 8 gardeners plant in a day?

12) CGP's secret pasta sauce recipe is shown on the right. The recipe serves 6 people. How much of each ingredient is needed to make enough for 17 servings?

- 18 ml olive oil
- 360 g tomatoes
- 9 g garlic powder
- 72 g onions

13) A DIY shop sells varnish in two different sized tins. A 500 ml tin costs £8 and a 1800 ml tin costs £30. Which tin represents the better value for money?

14) Maria is changing $130 of leftover holiday money back into pounds. The bank offers her an exchange rate of £1 = $1.45. How many pounds will she get?

Percentages (p30-33)

15) Find: a) 70% of 600   b) 90% of 1200   c) 45% of 250

16) A tree's height has increased by 15% in the last year. A year ago it was 17.6 m tall. What is its height now?

17) If x = 20 and y = 95:   a) Find x% of y.   b) Find the new value after y is increased by x%.
                            c) Express x as a percentage of y.

18) A bakery sold 700 items in one day. 25% of the items sold were pies. 8% of the pies sold were chicken pies. How many chicken pies were sold by the bakery?

19) An antique wardrobe decreased in value from £800 to £520. What was the percentage decrease?

20) Collectable baseball cards increase in value by 10% each year. A particular card is worth £80. How much will it be worth in 3 years?

Section Two — Fractions, Ratios and Percentages

Section Three — Algebra

Algebra — Simplifying

Algebra really terrifies so many people. But honestly, it's not that bad. You just have to make sure you understand and learn these basic rules for dealing with algebraic expressions.

Terms

There's more on multiplying letters together on the next page.

Before you can do anything else with algebra, you must understand what a term is:

A TERM IS A COLLECTION OF NUMBERS, LETTERS AND BRACKETS, ALL MULTIPLIED/DIVIDED TOGETHER

Terms are separated by + and − signs. Every term has a + or − attached to the front of it.

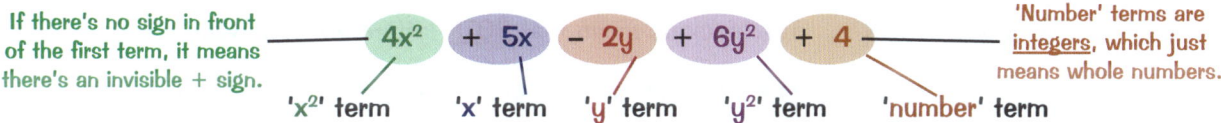

If there's no sign in front of the first term, it means there's an invisible + sign.

'Number' terms are integers, which just means whole numbers.

Simplifying or 'Collecting Like Terms'

To simplify an algebraic expression made up of all the same terms (e.g. all x's), just add or subtract them.

EXAMPLES:

1. Simplify $q + q + q + q + q + q$
   Just add up all the q's:
   $q + q + q + q + q + q = 6q$

   'q' just means '1q'.

2. Simplify $4t + 5t − 2t$
   Again, just combine the terms — but don't forget the '−' before the 2t:
   $4t + 5t − 2t = 7t$

If you have a mixture of different letters, or letters and numbers, it's a bit more tricky. To simplify an algebraic expression like this, you combine 'like terms' (e.g. all the x terms, all the y terms, all the number terms etc.).

EXAMPLE: Simplify $2x − 4 + 5x + 6$

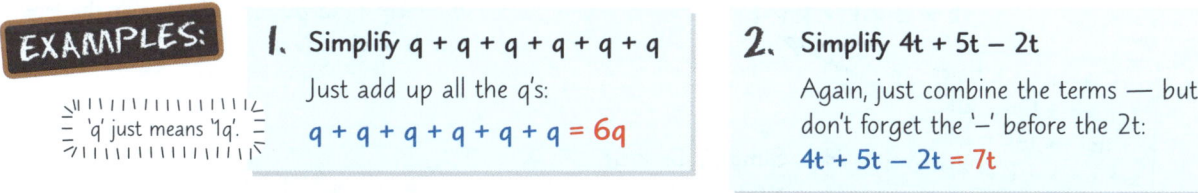

1) Put bubbles round each term — be sure you capture the +/− sign in front of each.
2) Then you can move the bubbles into the best order so that like terms are together.
3) Combine like terms.

EXAMPLE: Simplify $6m + 3n + 2m + 8n$

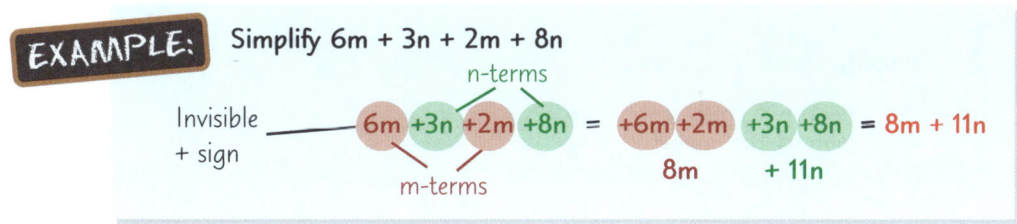

Collecting like terms — less exciting than collecting stamps...

There are lots of pretty colours on this page (sorry about that). Anyway, here are some questions to try:

Q1 Simplify a) $a + a + a + a + a + a$ [1 mark] b) $3b + 5b − b$ [1 mark]

Q2 Simplify $5x + y − 2x + 7y$ [2 marks]

Algebra — Simplifying

On this page we'll look at some rules that will help you simplify expressions that have letters and numbers multiplied together.

Letters Multiplied Together

Watch out for these combinations of letters in algebra that regularly catch people out:

1) abc means $a \times b \times c$ and 3a means $3 \times a$. The ×'s are often left out to make it clearer.
2) gn^2 means $g \times n \times n$. Note that only the n is squared, not the g as well.
3) $(gn)^2$ means $g \times g \times n \times n$. The brackets mean that BOTH letters are squared.
4) Powers tell you how many letters are multiplied together — so $r^6 = r \times r \times r \times r \times r \times r$.
5) -3^2 isn't very clear. It should either be written $(-3)^2 = 9$, or $-(3^2) = -9$ (you'd usually take -3^2 to be -9).

There's more on powers on p16-17.

 **EXAMPLES:**

1. Simplify $k \times k \times k \times k$
   You have 4 k's multiplied together:
   $k \times k \times k \times k = k^4$

   Careful — k times itself 4 times is k^4, not 4k (4k means $k + k + k + k$ or $4 \times k$).

2. Simplify $a \times b \times 6$
   This one's dead easy — just combine into one term (and put the number at the front):
   $a \times b \times 6 = 6ab$

3. Simplify $5s \times 3t$
   Multiply the numbers together, then the letters together:
   $5s \times 3t = 5 \times 3 \times s \times t = 15st$

Power Rules and Algebra

You can use the power rules from p17 on algebraic expressions too:
1) When multiplying, you add the powers.
2) When dividing, you subtract the powers.

 **EXAMPLES:**

1. Simplify $v^2 \times v^3$
   You're multiplying, so add the powers:
   $v^2 \times v^3 = v^{2+3} = v^5$

2. Simplify $\dfrac{w^{11}}{w^8}$
   This time, you're dividing — so subtract the powers:
   $\dfrac{w^{11}}{w^8} = w^{11-8} = w^3$

Ahhh algebra, it's as easy as abc, or (ab)² or something like that…

If you're struggling to use the power rules on algebra, try writing the expressions out in full to see how they work — so $v^2 \times v^3 = v \times v \times v \times v \times v = v^5$. Then have a go at these Exam Practice Questions.

Q1 Simplify a) $e \times e \times e \times e \times e$ [1 mark]   b) $3f \times 6g$ [1 mark]

Q2 Simplify a) $h^4 \times h^5$ [1 mark]   b) $\dfrac{s^9}{s^6}$ [1 mark]

Section Three — Algebra

Algebra — Multiplying Out Brackets

If you have an algebraic expression with brackets in, you might be asked to get rid of them by multiplying out the brackets. Your multiplying skills from the previous page will come in handy here.

Multiplying Brackets by a Number

There are a few key things to remember before you start multiplying out brackets:

1) The thing outside the brackets multiplies each separate term inside the brackets.
2) Be very careful with MINUS SIGNS — remember the rules for multiplying them from p8.

EXAMPLES:

1. Expand $3(2x + 5)$
Multiply the $2x$ and 5 inside by the 3 outside:
$3(2x + 5) = (3 \times 2x) + (3 \times 5)$
$= 6x + 15$

2. Expand $-4(3p^2 - 7q^3)$
Be very careful with the minus signs here:
$-4(3p^2 - 7q^3) = (-4 \times 3p^2) + (-4 \times -7q^3)$
$= -12p^2 + 28q^3$

Note that the minus sign outside the brackets reverses all the signs when you multiply.

If you're given more than one set of brackets to expand like $2(x + 2) + 3(x - 4)$, you'll have to simplify at the end by collecting like terms (see p35).

EXAMPLE: Expand and simplify $3(x + 2) + 4(4 - x)$.

First, expand each of the brackets separately (as you did above):
$3(x + 2) + 4(4 - x) = (3 \times x) + (3 \times 2) + (4 \times 4) + (4 \times -x)$
$= 3x + 6 + 16 - 4x$

Careful with the negatives here — the 4 and $-x$ multiply to give $-4x$.

Then collect like terms to simplify the expression:
$= 3x - 4x + 6 + 16 = -x + 22$ OR $22 - x$

Multiplying Brackets by a Term

Multiplying by a term is pretty much the same as multiplying by a number, but with some key differences:

- When letters are multiplied together, they are just written next to each other, e.g. pq.
- Remember from the previous page that $r \times r = r^2$, and when you multiply terms with numbers and letters in, you multiply the numbers together then the letters.

EXAMPLES:

1. Expand $4a(3b - 2)$
Multiply the $3b$ and -2 inside by the $4a$ outside:
$4a(3b - 2) = (4a \times 3b) + (4a \times -2)$
$= 12ab - 8a$
$4 \times -2 = -8$

2. Expand $2e(e - 3)$
This time, be careful when you multiply $2e$ by e — you'll end up with a $2e^2$:
$2e(e - 3) = (2e \times e) + (2e \times -3)$
$= 2e^2 - 6e$

Go forth and multiply out brackets...

Don't rush when multiplying out brackets — you'll make mistakes and throw away marks. Try these Exam Practice Questions to see how it's done (expanding brackets that is, not throwing away marks).

Q1 Expand $-6(3x - 2)$ [1 mark]
Q2 Expand $3x(x - 5)$ [1 mark]
Q3 Expand and simplify $5(y + 2) + 3(3 - y)$ [2 marks]

Algebra — Taking Out Common Factors

Right, now you know how to expand brackets, it's time to put them back in. This is known as factorising.

Taking Out a Number

If all the terms of the expression you're trying to factorise have a number part, you can look for the highest common factor (see p10) of all the numbers and take it outside the brackets. Here's the method to follow:

1) Take out the highest common factor of all the numbers. This is the biggest number that the numbers in all the terms divide by.
2) Open the brackets and fill in all the bits needed to reproduce each term.
3) Check your answer by multiplying out the brackets again.

EXAMPLES:

1. Factorise $3x - 9$

   3 and 9 both divide by 3. Decide what you need to multiply 3 by to get to $3x$ and 9.

   $3(x - 3)$

   Check: $3(x - 3) = 3x - 9$ ✓

2. Factorise $16x + 20y$

   The biggest number that 16 and 20 both divide by is 4.

   $4(4x + 5y)$

   Check: $4(4x + 5y) = 16x + 20y$ ✓

REMEMBER: The bits taken out and put at the front of the brackets are the common factors. The bits inside are what get you back to the original terms when you multiply out again.

Taking Out a Letter

If the same letter appears in all the terms (but to different powers), you can take out some power of the letter as a common factor.

1) For each letter in turn, take out the highest power (e.g. x, x^2 etc.) that will go into EVERY term.
2) If both terms of the expression have a number part, you might be able to take out a number as well.

EXAMPLES:

1. Factorise $y^3 - y$

   Highest power of y in both terms. Decide what you need to multiply y by to get y^3 and $-y$.

   $y(y^2 - 1)$

   Check: $y(y^2 - 1) = y^3 - y$ ✓

2. Factorise $3x^2 + 6x$

   Biggest number that'll divide into 3 and 6. Highest power of x that will go into both terms.

   $3x(x + 2)$

   Check: $3x(x + 2) = 3x^2 + 6x$ ✓

Have you got the Common Factor...

Make sure you find all the common factors — if you don't, the expression won't be fully factorised.

Q1 Factorise: a) $21x - 14y$ [1 mark] b) $24x + 56y$ [1 mark]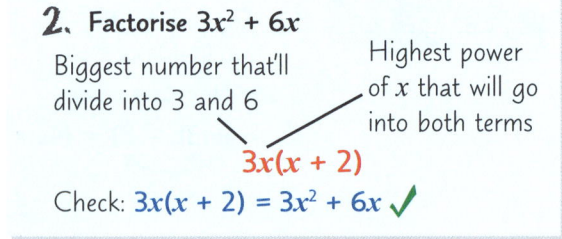

Q2 Factorise fully: a) $2a + a^2$ [1 mark] b) $4r^2 - 22rs$ [2 marks]

Solving Equations

'Solving equations' basically means 'find the value of x (or whatever letter is used) that makes the equation true'. To do this, you usually have to rearrange the equation to get x on its own.

The 'Common Sense' Approach

The trick here is to realise that the unknown quantity 'x' is just a number and the 'equation' is a cryptic clue to help you find it.

EXAMPLE: Solve the equation $3x + 4 = 46$. ← This just means 'find the value of x'.

This is what you should say to yourself:
'Something + 4 = 46', hmmm, so that 'something' must be 42.
So that means $3x = 42$, which means '3 × something = 42'.
So it must be $42 \div 3 = 14$, so $x = 14$.

If you were writing this down in an exam question, just write down the bits in blue.

In other words, don't think of it as algebra, but as 'find the mystery number'.

The 'Proper' Way

The 'proper' way to solve equations is to keep rearranging them until you end up with '$x = $' on one side. There are a few important points to remember when rearranging.

Golden Rules
1) Always do the SAME thing to both sides of the equation.
2) To get rid of something, do the opposite.
   The opposite of + is – and the opposite of – is +.
   The opposite of × is ÷ and the opposite of ÷ is ×.
3) Keep going until you have a letter on its own.

EXAMPLES:

1. Solve $x + 7 = 11$. — The opposite of +7 is –7
   $x + 7 = 11$
   (–7) $x + 7 - 7 = 11 - 7$
   $x = 4$

   This means 'take away 7 from both sides'.

2. Solve $x - 3 = 7$. — The opposite of –3 is +3
   $x - 3 = 7$
   (+3) $x - 3 + 3 = 7 + 3$
   $x = 10$

3. Solve $5x = 15$. — 5x means 5 × x, so do the opposite — divide both sides by 5
   $5x = 15$
   (÷5) $5x \div 5 = 15 \div 5$
   $x = 3$

4. Solve $\frac{x}{3} = 2$. — $\frac{x}{3}$ means x ÷ 3, so do the opposite — multiply both sides by 3
   $\frac{x}{3} = 2$
   (×3) $\frac{x}{3} \times 3 = 2 \times 3$
   $x = 6$

Handy hint — x often hides behind the sofa...

It's a good idea to write down what you're doing at every stage — put it in brackets next to the equation (like in the examples above). Try it out on this Exam Practice Question.

Q1 Solve these equations: a) $x + 2 = 8$ [1 mark]   b) $x - 6 = 8$ [1 mark]
c) $4x = 12$ [1 mark]   d) $\frac{x}{5} = 3$ [1 mark]

Section Three — Algebra

Solving Equations

You're not done with solving equations yet — not by a long shot. This is where it gets really fun*.

Two-Step Equations

If you come across an equation like $4x + 3 = 19$ (where there's an x-term and a number on the same side), use the methods from the previous page to solve it — just do it in two steps:

1) **Add or subtract** the number first. 2) **Multiply or divide** to get 'x = '.

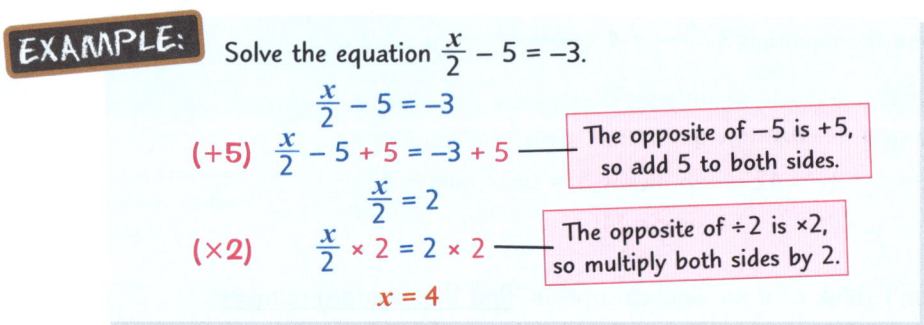

EXAMPLE: Solve the equation $\frac{x}{2} - 5 = -3$.

$\frac{x}{2} - 5 = -3$

(+5) $\frac{x}{2} - 5 + 5 = -3 + 5$ — The opposite of -5 is $+5$, so add 5 to both sides.

$\frac{x}{2} = 2$

(×2) $\frac{x}{2} \times 2 = 2 \times 2$ — The opposite of $\div 2$ is $\times 2$, so multiply both sides by 2.

$x = 4$

Equations with an 'x' on Both Sides

For equations like $2x + 3 = x + 7$ (where there's an x-term on each side), you have to:

1) Get all the x's on one side and all the numbers on the other.
2) Multiply or divide to get 'x = '.

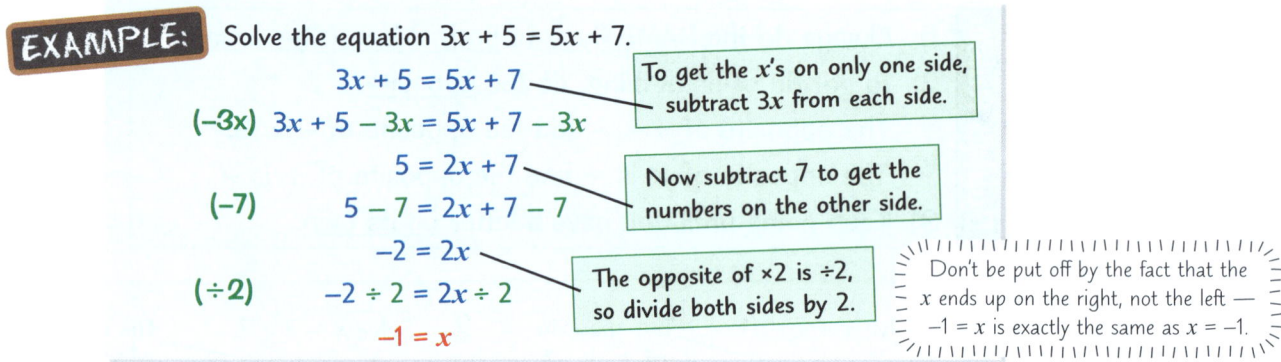

EXAMPLE: Solve the equation $3x + 5 = 5x + 7$.

$3x + 5 = 5x + 7$ — To get the x's on only one side, subtract $3x$ from each side.

(−3x) $3x + 5 - 3x = 5x + 7 - 3x$

$5 = 2x + 7$ — Now subtract 7 to get the numbers on the other side.

(−7) $5 - 7 = 2x + 7 - 7$

$-2 = 2x$ — The opposite of ×2 is ÷2, so divide both sides by 2.

(÷2) $-2 \div 2 = 2x \div 2$

$-1 = x$

Don't be put off by the fact that the x ends up on the right, not the left — $-1 = x$ is exactly the same as $x = -1$.

Equations with Brackets

If the equation has brackets in, you have to multiply out the brackets (see p37) before solving it.

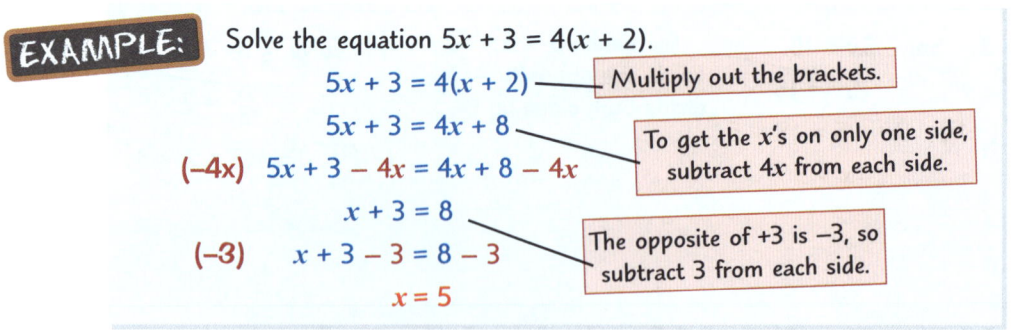

EXAMPLE: Solve the equation $5x + 3 = 4(x + 2)$.

$5x + 3 = 4(x + 2)$ — Multiply out the brackets.

$5x + 3 = 4x + 8$ — To get the x's on only one side, subtract $4x$ from each side.

(−4x) $5x + 3 - 4x = 4x + 8 - 4x$

$x + 3 = 8$ — The opposite of +3 is −3, so subtract 3 from each side.

(−3) $x + 3 - 3 = 8 - 3$

$x = 5$

Solving mysteries would be more exciting...

A good thing about solving equations is that you can always check your answer — just put the value of x you've found back into the original equation, and check that it works. Give it a go on these questions.

Q1   Solve $6x - 5 = 3x + 10$ [2 marks]   Q2   Solve $4(y - 2) = 2y + 6$ [3 marks]

*Fun not guaranteed. Terms and conditions apply.

Expressions, Formulas and Functions

Before we get started, there are a few definitions you need to know:

1) **EXPRESSION** — a collection of terms (see p35). Expressions DON'T have an = sign in them.
2) **EQUATION** — an expression with an = sign in it (so you can solve it).
3) **FORMULA** — a rule that helps you work something out (it will also have an = sign in it).
4) **FUNCTION** — an expression that takes an input value, processes it and produces an output value.

Putting Numbers into Formulas

You might be given a formula and asked to work out its value when you put in certain numbers. All you have to do here is follow this method.

1) Write out the formula.
2) Write it again, directly underneath, but substituting numbers for letters on the RHS (right-hand side).
3) Work it out in stages. Use BODMAS (see p3) to work things out in the right order. Write down values for each bit as you go along.
4) DO NOT attempt to do it all in one go on your calculator — you're more likely to make mistakes.

EXAMPLE: The formula for converting from Celsius (C) to Fahrenheit (F) is $F = \frac{9}{5}C + 32$. Use this formula to convert −10 °C into Fahrenheit.

$F = \frac{9}{5}C + 32$ — 1) Write out the formula.
$F = \frac{9}{5} \times -10 + 32$ — 2) Write it again, substituting numbers for letters on the RHS.
$F = -18 + 32$ — 3) Use BODMAS to work things out in the right order — do the multiplication first, then do the addition.
$F = 14$ so −10 °C = 14 °F

Be careful when substituting negative numbers into a formula — just do it step-by-step.

Functions Produce Outputs from Inputs

1) A function takes an input, processes it (e.g. multiplies it by 5 and adds 2) and outputs a value.
2) If you have to use a function machine, just put in the number, follow the steps and see what comes out.
3) If you're given the output and have to find the input, use the function machine in reverse.

EXAMPLE: The function machine below represents the function 'multiply by 5 and add 2'.

$x \longrightarrow \boxed{\times 5} \longrightarrow \boxed{+2} \longrightarrow y$

If this was an equation, it'd be written as $y = 5x + 2$.

a) Find the value of y when $x = 5$.
Just put 5 into the machine: $5 \xrightarrow{\times 5} 25 \xrightarrow{+2} 27$. So $y = 27$.

b) Find the value of x when $y = 42$.
This time, put $y = 42$ into the machine and work backwards:
$42 \xrightarrow{-2} 40 \xrightarrow{\div 5} 8$. So $x = 8$.

Don't forget to reverse each step as well — so +2 becomes −2 and ×5 becomes ÷5.

Grumpiness = number of annoying people ÷ hours of sleep...

If you have more than one number to put into a formula, make sure you put them in the right places.

Q1 $v = u + at$. Find the value of v when $u = 5$, $a = 4$ and $t = 6$. [2 marks]

Q2 Using the function machine above, find the value of x when $y = 57$. [2 marks]

Formulas and Equations from Words

Making expressions or formulas from words can be a bit confusing as you're given a lot of information in one go. You just have to go through it slowly and carefully and extract the maths from it.

Make Expressions or Formulas from Given Information

Here are some of examples of how to use the information to write expressions and formulas.

EXAMPLE: Aoife is x years old. Leah is 5 years younger than Aoife. Martin is 4 times as old as Aoife. Find a simplified expression for the sum of their ages in terms of x.

Aoife's age is x
Leah's age is $x - 5$ — Leah is 5 years younger, so subtract 5
Martin's age is $4 \times x = 4x$ — 4 times older

The sum of their ages is:
$x + (x - 5) + 4x = 6x - 5$

If you'd been told the sum of their ages, you'd have to set your expression equal to the sum and solve it to find x.

EXAMPLE: In rugby union, tries score 5 points and conversions score 2 points. A team scores a total of P points, made up of t tries and c conversions. Write a formula for P in terms of t and c.

Tries score 5 points —— t tries will score $5 \times t = 5t$ points
Conversions score 2 points —— c conversions will score $2 \times c = 2c$ points
So total points scored are $P = 5t + 2c$

Because you're asked for a formula, you must include the 'P = ' bit to get full marks (i.e. don't just put 5t + 2c).

Use Your Expression to Solve Equations

Sometimes, you might be asked to use an expression to solve an equation.

EXAMPLE: A zoo has x zebras and four times as many lemurs. The difference between the number of zebras and the number of lemurs is 45. How many zebras does the zoo have?

The zoo has x zebras and $4 \times x = 4x$ lemurs.
The difference is $4x - x = 3x$, so $3x = 45$, which means $x = 15$.
So the zoo has 15 zebras.

Once you've formed the equation, you need to solve it to find the value of x.

EXAMPLE: Liên, Naveed and Camille give some books to charity. Naveed gives 6 more books than Liên, and Camille gives 7 more books than Naveed. Between them, they give away 46 books. How many books did they give each?

Let the number of books Liên gives be x.
Then Naveed gives $x + 6$ books
and Camille gives $(x + 6) + 7 = x + 13$ books
So in total they give:
$x + (x + 6) + (x + 13) = 3x + 19$ books

So $3x + 19 = 46$ — You're told this in the question.
$3x = 27$
$x = 9$
So Liên gives 9 books,
Naveed gives $9 + 6 = 15$ books and
Camille gives $15 + 7 = 22$ books.

I have the formula for the perfect cup of tea...

Exam questions might not tell you to write an equation or formula — but sometimes you'll have to come up with one to be able to answer a question. Try writing some for these Exam Practice Questions.

Q1 Noah, Hellä and Joe sell 73 raffle tickets between them. Hellä sells twice as many tickets as Noah, and Joe sells 8 more tickets than Hellä. How many tickets does each person sell? [4 marks]

Q2 Three positive whole numbers have a sum of 48. The second number is five times the first, and the third number is double the second number. What are the three numbers? [3 marks]

Section Three — Algebra

Trial and Improvement

Trial and improvement is a way of finding an approximate solution to an equation that's too hard to be solved using normal methods. You'll be told WHEN to use trial and improvement — don't go using it willy-nilly.

Keep Trying Different Values in the Equation

The basic idea of trial and improvement is to keep trying different values of x that are getting closer and closer to the solution. Here's the method to follow:

1) **SUBSTITUTE TWO INITIAL VALUES** into the equation that give **OPPOSITE CASES**.
   These could be suggested in the question. 'Opposite cases' means one answer too big, one too small.

2) Now **CHOOSE YOUR NEXT VALUE IN BETWEEN THE PREVIOUS TWO**, and **SUBSTITUTE** it into the equation.
   Continue this process, always choosing a new value between the two closest opposite cases (and preferably nearer to the one that was closer to the answer).

3) **AFTER ONLY 3 OR 4 STEPS** you should have 2 numbers which are to the right degree of accuracy but **DIFFER BY 1 IN THE LAST DIGIT**.
   For example, if you had to get your answer to 1 d.p. then you'd eventually end up with say 5.4 and 5.5, with these giving OPPOSITE results of course.

   You'll be asked for a certain level of accuracy (often 1 d.p.) in the question.

4) At this point you ALWAYS take the exact middle value to decide which is the answer you want.
   E.g. for 5.4 and 5.5 you'd try 5.45 to see if the real answer was between 5.4 and 5.45 (so 5.4 to 1 d.p.) or between 5.45 and 5.5 (so 5.5 to 1 d.p.).

It's a good idea to keep track of your working in a table — see example below.

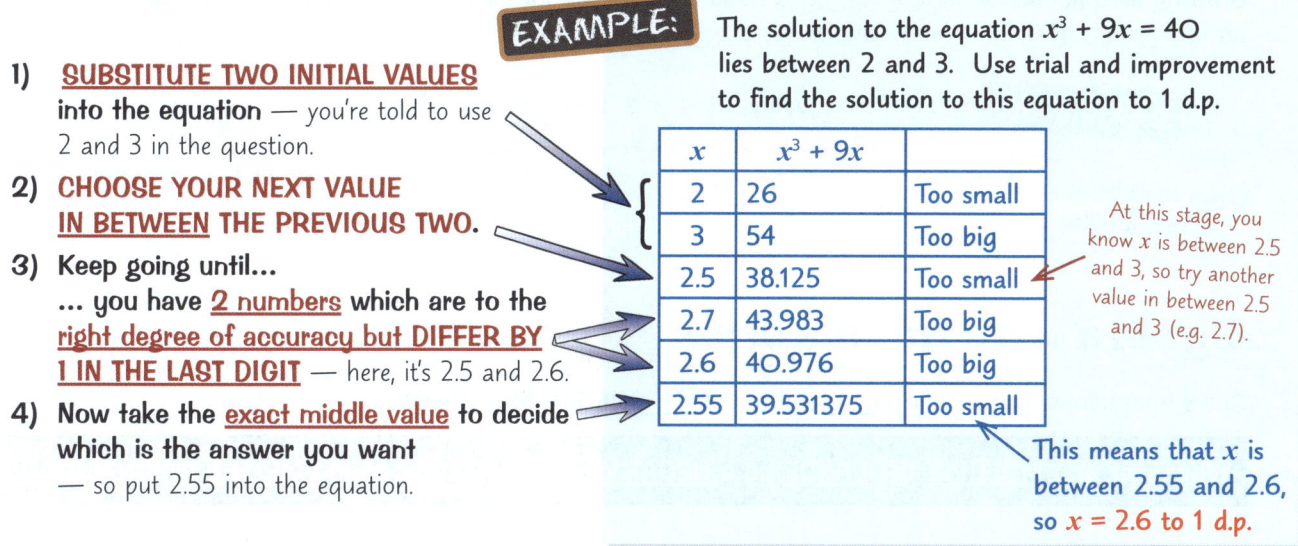

EXAMPLE: The solution to the equation $x^3 + 9x = 40$ lies between 2 and 3. Use trial and improvement to find the solution to this equation to 1 d.p.

1) **SUBSTITUTE TWO INITIAL VALUES** into the equation — you're told to use 2 and 3 in the question.

2) **CHOOSE YOUR NEXT VALUE IN BETWEEN THE PREVIOUS TWO.**

3) Keep going until...
   ... you have 2 numbers which are to the right degree of accuracy but **DIFFER BY 1 IN THE LAST DIGIT** — here, it's 2.5 and 2.6.

4) Now take the exact middle value to decide which is the answer you want — so put 2.55 into the equation.

x	$x^3 + 9x$	
2	26	Too small
3	54	Too big
2.5	38.125	Too small
2.7	43.983	Too big
2.6	40.976	Too big
2.55	39.531375	Too small

At this stage, you know x is between 2.5 and 3, so try another value in between 2.5 and 3 (e.g. 2.7).

This means that x is between 2.55 and 2.6, so $x = 2.6$ to 1 d.p.

Make sure you show all your working — you could lose marks if it's not clear which method you've used.

Trial and improvement — not a good strategy for lion-taming...

Sorry, it's not the most exciting page in the world — but it is a good way of picking up easy marks in the exam just by putting some numbers into equations. Try it out on these Exam Practice Questions:

Q1 $x^3 + 6x = 69$ has a solution between 3 and 4.
Use trial and improvement to find this solution to 1 d.p. [4 marks]

Q2 $x^3 - 12x = 100$ has a solution between 5 and 6.
Use trial and improvement to find this solution to 1 d.p. [4 marks]

Section Three — Algebra

Inequalities

Inequalities are a bit tricky, but once you've learned the tricks involved, most of the algebra for them is identical to ordinary equations (have a look back at pages 39-40 if you need a reminder).

The Inequality Symbols

> means 'Greater than' ≥ means 'Greater than or equal to'
< means 'Less than' ≤ means 'Less than or equal to'

REMEMBER — the one at the BIG end is BIGGEST so x > 4 and 4 < x both say: 'x is greater than 4'.
You might also see the ≠ symbol — this means 'is not equal to'. e.g. 4 + 5 ≠ 7

"I > All of you."

Showing Inequalities

You can work out all the possible values that match an inequality.
You can write them out or draw them on a number line.

EXAMPLE: x is an integer such that $-4 < x \leq 3$. Write down all possible values of x.

Work out what each bit of the inequality is telling you:

$-4 < x$ means 'x is greater than -4',
and $x \leq 3$ means 'x is less than or equal to 3'.

Now just write down all the values that x can take:

$-3, -2, -1, 0, 1, 2, 3$

Remember, integers are just whole numbers (positive and negative, including 0).

-4 isn't included because of the <, but 3 is included because of the ≤.

Drawing inequalities on a number line is dead easy — all you have to remember is that you use an open circle (○) for > or < and a coloured-in circle (●) for ≥ or ≤.

EXAMPLE: Show the inequality $-4 < x \leq 3$ on a number line.

Open circle because -4 isn't included.

Closed circle because 3 is included.

Algebra with Inequalities

Solve inequalities like regular equations but WITH ONE BIG EXCEPTION:

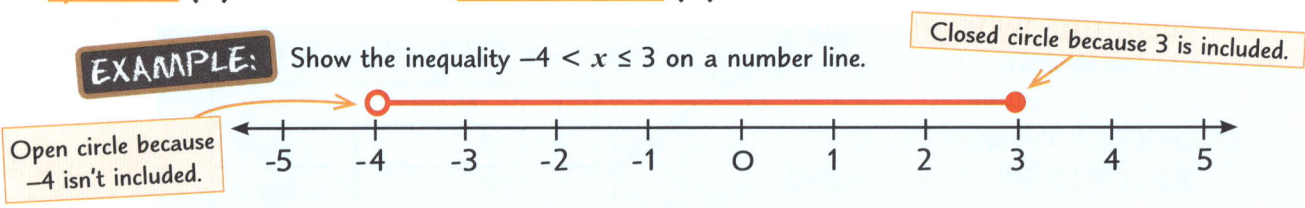

Whenever you MULTIPLY OR DIVIDE by a NEGATIVE NUMBER, you must FLIP THE INEQUALITY SIGN.

EXAMPLES:

1. Solve $3x - 2 \leq 13$.

Just solve it like an equation — but leave the inequality sign in your answer:
(+2) $3x - 2 + 2 \leq 13 + 2$
$3x \leq 15$
(÷3) $3x \div 3 \leq 15 \div 3$
$x \leq 5$

2. Solve $2x + 7 > x + 11$.

Again, solve it like an equation:
(−7) $2x + 7 − 7 > x + 11 − 7$
$2x > x + 4$
(−x) $2x − x > x + 4 − x$
$x > 4$

3. Solve $9 − 2x > 15$.

Watch out for the sign change:
(−9) $9 − 2x − 9 > 15 − 9$
$−2x > 6$
(÷−2) $−2x \div −2 < 6 \div −2$
$x < −3$

The > has turned into a <, because we divided by a negative number.

I saw you flip the inequality sign — how rude...

To check you've got the inequality sign right, pop in a value for x and check the inequality's true.

Q1 n is an integer such that $-1 \leq n < 5$. Write down all the possible values of n. [1 mark]

Q2 Solve the following inequalities: a) $4x + 3 < 27$ [2 marks]   b) $4x \geq 18 - 2x$ [2 marks]

Rearranging Formulas

The subject of a formula is the letter on its own before the = (so x is the subject of x = 2y + 3z).

Changing the Subject of a Formula

Rearranging formulas means making a different letter the subject, e.g. getting 'y = ' from 'x = 3y + 2'. Fortunately, you can use the same methods that you used for solving equations (see p39-40) — here's a quick reminder:

Golden Rules
1) Always do the SAME thing to both sides of the formula.
2) To get rid of something, do the opposite.
   The opposite of + is − and the opposite of − is +.
   The opposite of × is ÷ and the opposite of ÷ is ×.
3) Keep going until you have the letter you want on its own.

EXAMPLE: Rearrange $a = 3b + 4$ to make b the subject of the formula.

$$a = 3b + 4$$
(-4) $\quad a - 4 = 3b + 4 - 4$ — The opposite of +4 is −4, so take away 4 from both sides.
$$a - 4 = 3b$$ — The opposite of ×3 is ÷3, so divide both sides by 3.
$(\div 3)$ $\quad (a - 4) \div 3 = 3b \div 3$
$$\frac{a-4}{3} = b \quad \text{OR} \quad b = \frac{a-4}{3}$$

Careful here — you divide the whole side by 3, not just one term.

EXAMPLE: Rearrange $p = 5(q + 2)$ to make q the subject of the formula.

$$p = 5q + 10$$ — Multiply out the brackets.
(-10) $\quad p - 10 = 5q + 10 - 10$ — The opposite of +10 is −10, so take away 10 from both sides.
$$p - 10 = 5q$$
$(\div 5)$ $\quad (p - 10) \div 5 = 5q \div 5$ — The opposite of ×5 is ÷5, so divide both sides by 5.
$$\frac{p-10}{5} = q \quad \text{OR} \quad q = \frac{p-10}{5}$$

EXAMPLE: Rearrange $m = \frac{n}{4} - 7$ to make n the subject of the formula.

$$m = \frac{n}{4} - 7$$ — The opposite of −7 is +7, so add 7 to both sides.
$(+7)$ $\quad m + 7 = \frac{n}{4} - 7 + 7$
$$m + 7 = \frac{n}{4}$$ — The opposite of ÷4 is ×4, so multiply both sides by 4.
$(\times 4)$ $\quad (m + 7) \times 4 = \frac{n}{4} \times 4$
$$4(m + 7) = n \quad \text{OR} \quad n = 4m + 28$$

If I could rearrange my subjects I'd have Maths all day every day...

This page is really just like solving equations — so if you learn the method for one, you know the method for the other. What a bonus. It's like buy-one-get-one-free but more mathsy.

Q1 Rearrange $u = \frac{v}{3} - 2$ to make v the subject of the formula. [2 marks]

Q2 Rearrange $c = 6d - 12$ to make d the subject of the formula. [2 marks]

Section Three — Algebra

Sequences

Sequences are lists of numbers (or shapes) that follow a rule. You need to be able to spot what the rule is.

Finding the Rule for Number Sequences

The trick to finding the rule for number sequences is to write down what you have to do to get from one number to the next in the gaps between the numbers. There are 2 main types to look out for:

1) Add or subtract the same number — These are known as arithmetic sequences.

E.g. 2, 5, 8, 11, 14, ... (+3 each time) 30, 24, 18, 12, ... (−6 each time)

The RULE: 'Add 3 to the previous term' 'Subtract 6 from the previous term'

2) Multiply or divide by the same number each time — These are known as geometric sequences.

E.g. 2, 6, 18, 54, ... (×3 each time) 40 000, 4000, 400, 40, ... (÷10 each time)

The RULE: 'Multiply the previous term by 3' 'Divide the previous term by 10'

Sometimes you might get sequences that follow a different rule — e.g. you might have to add or subtract a changing number each time, or add together the two previous terms (see the examples below).

EXAMPLE: Find the next two terms in each of the following sequences.

a) 1, 3, 6, 10, 15, ...

'The number you add on increases by one each time' (i.e. +2, +3, +4, ...) so the next two terms are:

15 + 6 = 21
21 + 7 = 28

This is the sequence of triangular numbers.

b) 1, 1, 2, 3, 5, ...

The rule is 'add together the two previous terms', so the next two terms are:

3 + 5 = 8
5 + 8 = 13

This is known as the Fibonacci sequence.

Find Any Term with the nth Term Formula

The nth term formula can be used to find any term in the sequence. It contains an n, which is the position of the term you want — e.g. to find the third term, use $n = 3$.

EXAMPLE: The nth term of a sequence is given by $4n - 5$. Find:

a) the first term,

Substitute $n = 1$ into the formula:
$(4 \times 1) - 5 = 4 - 5 = -1$

b) the eighth term,

Substitute $n = 8$ into the formula:
$(4 \times 8) - 5 = 32 - 5 = 27$

c) the ninety-ninth term.

Substitute $n = 99$ into the formula:
$(4 \times 99) - 5 = 396 - 5 = 391$

The nth term in the example above is linear. If you come across a non-linear nth term, you can still use the same method as above. E.g. the 6th term of $n^2 - 2$ is given by $6^2 - 2 = 34$.

Knitting patterns follow the rule knit one, purl one...

Try out this Exam Practice Question to see how you're getting on with sequences.

Q1 A sequence starts 3, 6, 12, ... There are two possible rules for this sequence. Write down both possible rules and find the next two terms of the sequence in each case. [2 marks]

Section Three — Algebra

Sequences

On the previous page you were introduced to the nth term. Now you'll get to know each other a little better — this page is all about finding an *expression* for the *nth term* when you've been given a sequence.

Finding the nth Term of a Linear Sequence

This method works for sequences with a *common difference* — where you *add* or *subtract* the *same number* each time.

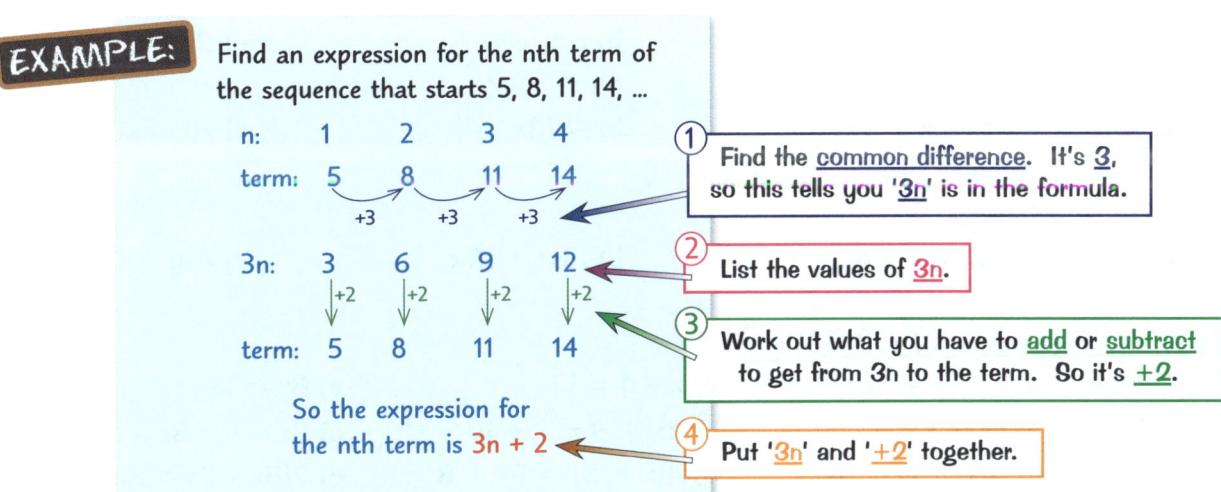

Check your formula by putting the first few values of n back in:
n = 1 gives 3n + 2 = 3 + 2 = 5 ✓
n = 2 gives 3n + 2 = 6 + 2 = 8 ✓

Finding the nth Term for Shape Sequences

If you have a sequence of *shape* patterns, you might need to find the *rule* for the sequence and then use it to work out *how many* shapes there'll be in a later pattern.

EXAMPLE: On the right, there are some patterns made of circles.
a) Draw the next pattern in the sequence.
b) Work out how many circles there will be in the 10th pattern.

a) Just continue the sequence — the circles make a rectangular pattern.

b) Find the rule for the number of circles: there's **2 × 1 = 2 circles** in the first pattern, **2 × 2 = 4 circles** in the second pattern, **2 × 3 = 6 circles** in the third pattern etc. The rule is '**two times the number of the pattern**'. So in the nth pattern, there'll be **2n circles**. In the 10th pattern, there'll be **2 × 10 = 20 circles**.

Shape sequences are sticklers for the rules...

Here are a couple of Exam Practice Questions to make sure you're a sequences whizz...

Q1 Find an expression for the *n*th term of the linear sequence 2, 9, 16, 23, ...   [2 marks]

Q2 A shape sequence starts with these four patterns:
 a) How many dots are in the next pattern in the sequence?   [2 marks]
 b) Find an expression for the number of dots in the *n*th term.   [2 marks]

Section Three — Algebra

Revision Questions for Section Three

There was a lot of nasty algebra in that section — let's see how much you remember.
- Try these questions and tick off each one when you get it right.
- When you've done all the questions for a topic and are completely happy with it, tick off the topic.

Algebra (p35-38)

1) Simplify: a) $e + e + e$ b) $6f + 7f - f$
2) Simplify: a) $2x + 3y + 5x - 4y$ b) $11a + 2 - 8a + 7$
3) Simplify: a) $m \times m \times m$ b) $p \times q \times 7$ c) $2x \times 9y$
4) Simplify: a) $g^5 \times g^6$ b) $c^{15} \div c^{12}$
5) Expand: a) $6(x + 3)$ b) $-3(3x - 4)$ c) $x(5 - x)$
6) Expand and simplify $4(3 + 5x) - 2(7x + 6)$
7) What is factorising?
8) Factorise: a) $8x + 24$ b) $18x^2 + 27x$ c) $4xy - 10x$

Solving Equations (p39-40)

9) Solve: a) $x + 9 = 16$ b) $x - 4 = 12$ c) $6x = 18$
10) Solve: a) $\frac{x}{3} + 1 = 4$ b) $3x + 6 = x + 10$ c) $2x - 7 = 3x - 10$
11) Solve: a) $3(x + 2) = 5x$ b) $4(x + 3) = 5x + 8$ c) $2(5x - 2) = 3(x + 1)$

Expressions, Functions and Formulas (p41-42)

12) $Q = 5r + 6s$. Work out the value of Q when $r = -2$ and $s = 3$.
13) A function starts with a number, doubles it and then subtracts 8. What is the result when 11 is put in the function?
14) Fionn and Robbie have the same number of marbles. Nadia has 26 marbles. Between them, they have 100 marbles. How many marbles does Fionn have?
15) A rectangle measures $2x$ cm by $7x$ cm. An equilateral triangle has the same perimeter as the rectangle. Find the length of one side of the triangle in terms of x.

Trial and Improvement (p43)

16) What is trial and improvement?
17) Given that $x^3 + 8x = 103$ has a solution between 4 and 5, use trial and improvement to find this solution to 1 d.p.

Inequalities and Rearranging Formulas (p44-45)

18) Write the following inequalities out in words: a) $x > -7$ b) $x \leq 6$
19) $0 < k \leq 7$. Find all the possible integer values of k.
20) Solve the following inequalities: a) $x + 4 < 14$ b) $3x + 5 \leq 26$.
21) Rearrange the formula $W = 4v + 5$ to make v the subject.
22) Rearrange the formula $y = \frac{x}{3} + 4$ to make x the subject.

Sequences (p46-47)

23) For each of the following sequences, find the next term and write down the rule you used.
    a) 3, 10, 17, 24, ...   b) 1, 4, 16, 64, ...   c) 2, 5, 7, 12, ...
24) For a sequence with the nth term $5n - 2$, find: a) the first four terms,   b) the 101st term.
25) Find an expression for the nth term of the sequence that starts 6, 13, 20, 27, ...

Coordinates

What could be more fun than points in one quadrant? Points in four quadrants, that's what...

The Four Quadrants

A graph can be plotted on a coordinate plane. This is just a space (or plane) containing an x- and y- axis.

The coordinate plane can be split into four different quadrants (regions).

The top-right region is the easiest because ALL THE COORDINATES IN IT ARE POSITIVE.

You have to be careful in the other regions though, because the x- and y- coordinates could be negative, and that makes life much more difficult.

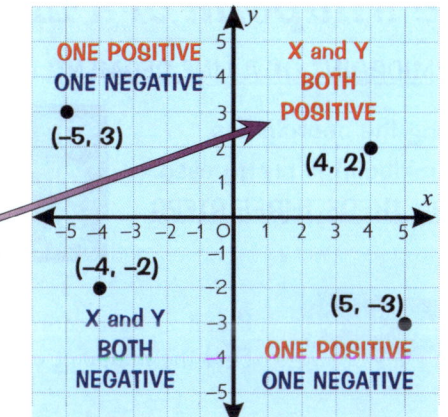

THREE IMPORTANT POINTS ABOUT COORDINATES:

1) The coordinates are always in ALPHABETICAL ORDER, x then y.

2) x is always the flat axis going ACROSS the page.
In other words 'x is a...cross' Get it — x is a '×'. (Hilarious isn't it)

3) Remember it's always IN THE HOUSE (→) and then UP THE STAIRS (↑) so it's ALONG first and then UP, i.e. x-coordinate first, and then y-coordinate.

(x , y)

Finding Coordinates of 2D Shapes

A 2D shape can be drawn on a coordinate plane by plotting the coordinates of its vertices (corners).

There's more about the properties of 2D shapes on p77-78.

EXAMPLE: A rectangle has vertices at (−2, 3), (1, 3) and (1, −2).

Plot these points on a grid and find the coordinates of the missing vertex.

Plot the given points and join them with straight lines.

Work out where the 4th vertex would be on the grid and write down the coordinates.

The 4th vertex would be here at (−2, −2).

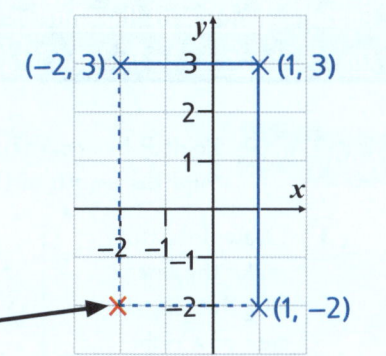

But what if you live in a bungalow...

Learn the 3 points for getting *x* and *y* the right way round and then try these questions.

Q1 Plot point A(−3, 2) and point B(3, 5) on a grid. [2 marks]

Q2 Two adjacent vertices of a square are plotted on the grid on the right. Plot the square's third and fourth vertices and give their coordinates. [3 marks]

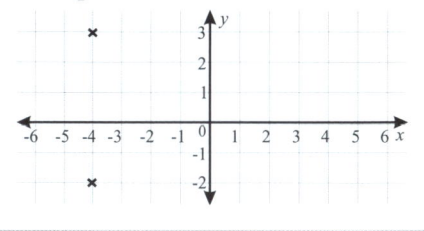

Section Four — Graphs

Line Segments

Put down your pen. Take a deep breath. It's time for the most exciting topic in this book — line segments...

The Midpoint of a Line

The 'MIDPOINT OF A LINE SEGMENT' is the POINT THAT'S BANG IN THE MIDDLE of it.

Finding the coordinates of a midpoint is pretty easy. LEARN THESE THREE STEPS...

1) Find the average of the x-coordinates.
2) Find the average of the y-coordinates.
3) Plonk them in brackets.

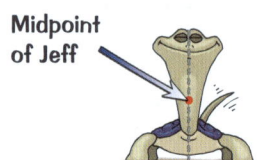
Midpoint of Jeff

EXAMPLE: P and Q have coordinates (1, 2) and (6, 6). Find the midpoint of the line PQ.

Average of x-coordinates = $\frac{1+6}{2}$ = 3.5

Average of y-coordinates = $\frac{2+6}{2}$ = 4

Coordinates of midpoint = **(3.5, 4)**

Use Pythagoras to find the Distance Between Points

You need to know how to find the straight-line distance between two points on a graph. You can do this by turning the straight line into a right-angled triangle and then using Pythagoras' theorem.

Pythagoras' Theorem

Pythagoras' theorem is $a^2 + b^2 = c^2$. This allows you to find the longest length of a right-angled triangle (c), as long as you know the lengths of the two smaller sides (a and b). Learn more about it on p75.

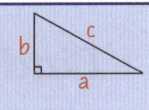

This is how you use the theorem to find the distance between any two points...

1) Sketch a straight line to join up the two points. Then turn the sketch into a right-angled triangle.
2) Find the lengths of the shorter sides of the triangle by subtracting the coordinates.
3) Use Pythagoras to find the length of the longest side. (That's your answer.)

EXAMPLE: Point P has coordinates (10, 3) and point Q has coordinates (2, 9). Find the length of the line PQ.

① Draw lines to make the line PQ the longest side of a right-angled triangle.

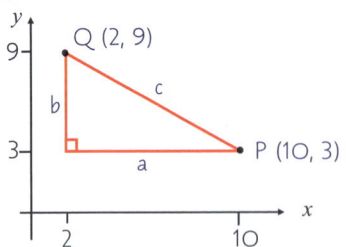

② Find the lengths of the shorter sides:
Length of side a = 10 − 2 = 8
Length of side b = 9 − 3 = 6

③ Use Pythagoras to find side c:
$c^2 = a^2 + b^2 = 8^2 + 6^2 = 64 + 36 = 100$
So: $c = \sqrt{100}$ = **10**

If you only do half the work, you'll only reach your midpoint-ential...

If you wanna make tricky line segment questions a bit less tricky then draw a diagram. It'll help loads.

Q1 Point A has coordinates (5, 2) and point B has coordinates (9, 8). Find:

a) The coordinates of the midpoint of AB. [2 marks]

b) The length from point A to point B. [5 marks]

Straight-Line Graphs

If you thought I-spy was a fun game, wait 'til you play 'recognise the straight-line graph from the equation'.

Vertical and Horizontal lines: 'x = a' and 'y = a'

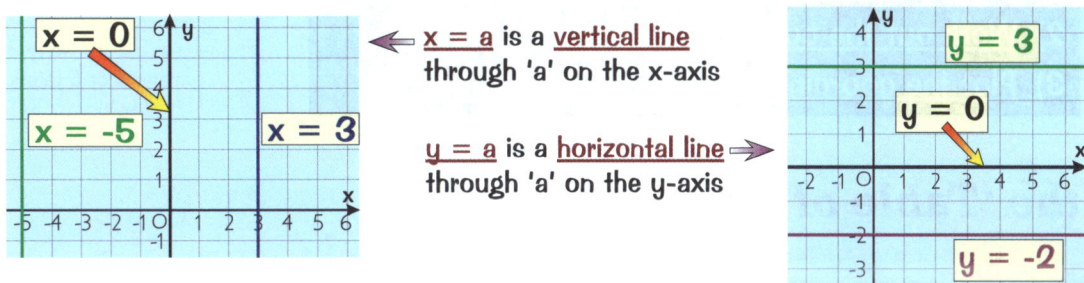

← $x = a$ is a vertical line through 'a' on the x-axis

$y = a$ is a horizontal line → through 'a' on the y-axis

The Main Diagonals: 'y = x' and 'y = –x'

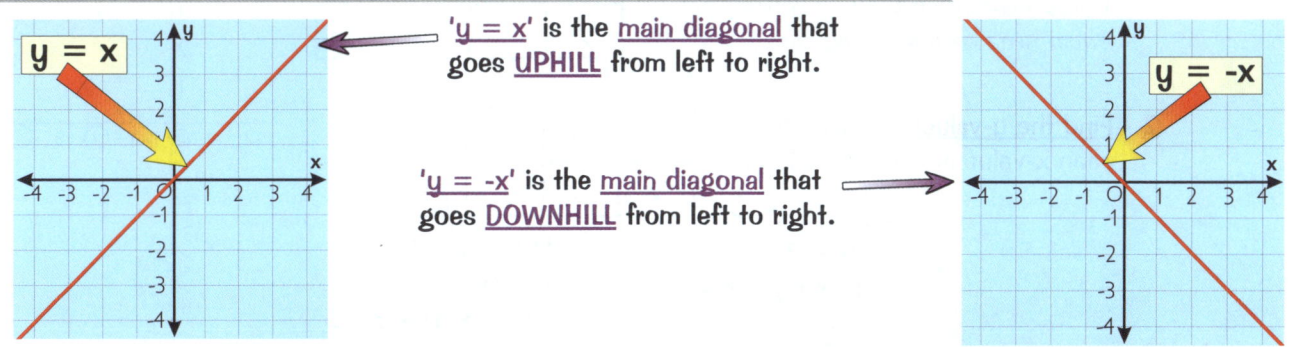

'$y = x$' is the main diagonal that goes UPHILL from left to right.

'$y = -x$' is the main diagonal that goes DOWNHILL from left to right.

Other Lines Through the Origin: 'y = ax' and 'y = –ax'

$y = ax$ and $y = -ax$ are the equations for
A SLOPING LINE THROUGH THE ORIGIN.

The value of 'a' (known as the gradient) tells you the steepness of the line. The bigger 'a' is, the steeper the slope. A MINUS SIGN tells you it slopes DOWNHILL.

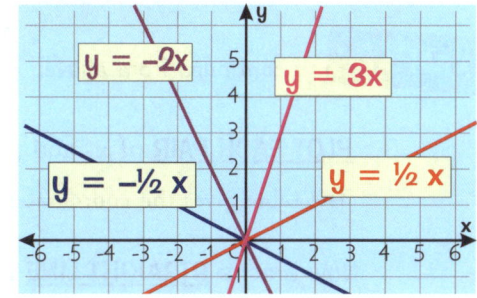

Learn to Spot Straight Lines from their Equations

All straight-line equations just contain 'something x, something y and a number'.

There's more on x^2 graphs on page 58.

Straight lines:		NOT straight lines:	
$x - y = 0$	$y = 2 + 3x$	$y = x^3 + 3$	$\frac{1}{y} + \frac{1}{x} = 2$
$2y - 4x = 7$	$4x - 3 = 5y$	$x^2 = 4 - y$	$xy + 3 = 0$

It's no Shakespeare, but my favourite line is y = 3x...

It's worth learning all the graphs above. Once you've done that, test yourself with this question.

Q1   On a grid with x-axis from –5 to 5 and y-axis from –5 to 5, draw these lines:
    a) $y = -1$ b) $y = -x$ c) $x = 2$ [3 marks]

Drawing Straight-Line Graphs

You might be asked to DRAW THE GRAPH of an equation in the exam.
This EASY METHOD will net you the marks every time:

> 1) Choose 3 values of x and draw up a wee table.
> 2) Work out the corresponding y-values.
> 3) Plot the coordinates, and draw the line.

You might get lucky and be given a table in an exam question. Don't worry if it contains 5 or 6 values.

Doing the 'Table of Values'

   Draw the graph of $y = 2x - 3$ for values of x from −2 to 4.

1. **Choose 3 easy x-values for your table:**
   Use x-values from the grid you're given.
   Avoid negative ones if you can.

x	0	2	4
y			

2. **Find the y-values** by putting each x-value into the equation:

x	0	2	4
y	−3	1	5

   When $x = 0$,
   $y = 2x - 3$
   $= (2 \times 0) - 3 = -3$

   When $x = 4$,
   $y = 2x - 3$
   $= (2 \times 4) - 3 = 5$

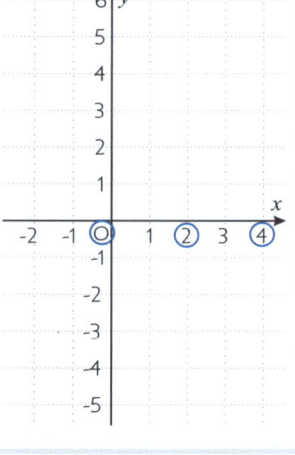

Plotting the Points and Drawing the Graph

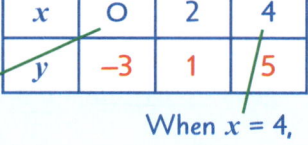 ...continued from above.

3. **PLOT EACH PAIR** of x- and y- values from your table.

   The table gives the coordinates (0, −3), (2, 1) and (4, 5).

   Now draw a **STRAIGHT LINE** through your points.
   Make sure that the line goes at least from $x = -2$ to $x = 4$, because that's what the question asked you to do.

   > If one point looks a bit wacky, check 2 things:
   > – the y-values you worked out in the table
   > – that you've plotted the points properly.

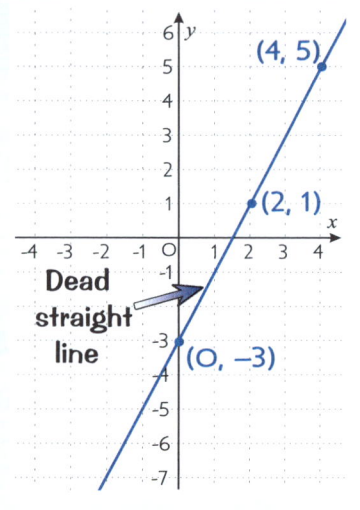

Dead straight line

Careful plotting — the key to straight lines and world domination...

If the examiners are feeling mean, they'll give you an equation like $3x + y = 5$ to plot, making finding the y-values a tad trickier. Substitute the x-value and find the y-value that makes the equation true.
E.g. when $x = 1$, $3x + y = 5 \rightarrow (3 \times 1) + y = 5 \rightarrow 3 + y = 5 \rightarrow y = 2$.

Q1 Draw the graph of $y = x + 4$ for values of x from −6 to 2. [3 marks]

Q2 Draw the graph of $y + 3x = 2$ for values of x from −2 to 2. [3 marks]

Section Four — Graphs

Straight-Line Graphs — Gradients

Time to hit the slopes. Well, find them anyway...

Finding the Gradient

The gradient of a line is a measure of its slope. The bigger the number, the steeper the line.

EXAMPLE: Find the gradient of the straight line shown.

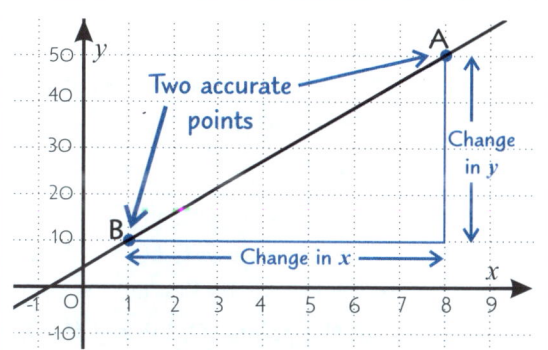

1. **Find two accurate points and complete the triangle.**

   Choose easy points with positive coordinates.
   Two points that can be read accurately are:
   Point A: (8, 50)   Point B: (1, 10)

2. **Find the change in y and the change in x.**

   Change in $y = 50 - 10 = 40$
   Change in $x = 8 - 1 = 7$

   Make sure you subtract the x-coordinates the SAME WAY ROUND as you do the y-coordinates.
   E.g. y-coord. of pt A − y-coord. of pt B and x-coord. of pt A − x-coord. of pt B

3. **LEARN this formula, and use it:**

   $$\text{GRADIENT} = \frac{\text{CHANGE IN Y}}{\text{CHANGE IN X}}$$

   Gradient $= \frac{40}{7} = 5.71$ (to 2 d.p.)

   Make sure you get the formula the right way up.
   Remember it's VERy HOt — VERtical over HOrizontal.

4. **Check the sign's right.**

   If it slopes uphill left → right (↗) then it's positive.
   If it slopes downhill left → right (↘) then it's negative.

   As the graph goes uphill, the gradient is positive. So the gradient is 5.71 (not −5.71).

Finding gradients is often an uphill battle...

Learn the four steps for finding a gradient then have a bash at this Exam Practice Question. Take care — you might not be able to pick two points with nice, positive coordinates. Fun times ahoy.

Q1 Find the gradient of the line shown.   [2 marks]

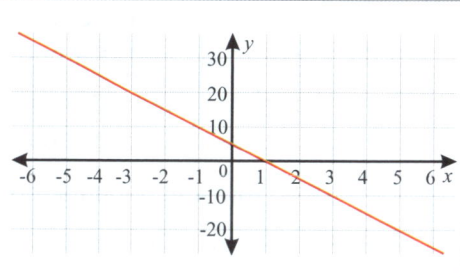

Real-Life Graphs

Graphs aren't just something you need to know for your Maths exam. They're actually used in **real life** too...

Graphs are Used to Show Information

If you're given information on how two things are related, you might be able to draw a graph to show the relationship between them.

EXAMPLE: Radha buys carrots for £0.80 per kg.

Plot a graph using the axes on the right to show the price of carrots compared to the weight of the carrots.

Plot the weight of the carrots on the x-axis and the price of the carrots on the y-axis.

0 kg of carrots costs £0 and 1 kg of carrots costs £0.80, so the line will go through the points (0, 0) and (1, 0.8).

Plot the points (0, 0) and (1, 0.8). Then draw a line that goes through both of them.

The equation for this line is $y = 0.8x$.

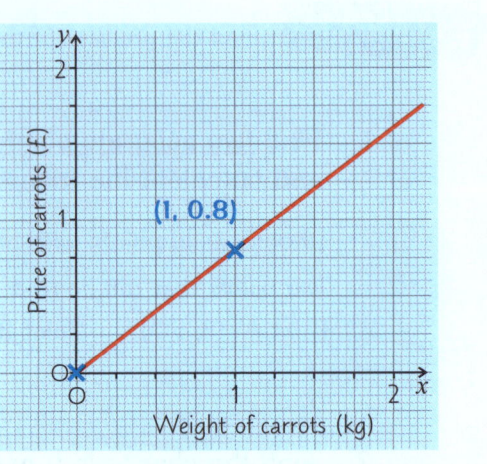

Interpreting Information from Graphs

You can grab one quick bit of information from a graph's intercepts.

1) For a line on a graph, the x-intercept is the point where the line crosses the x-axis (and $y = 0$) and the y-intercept is the point where the line crosses the y-axis (and $x = 0$).

2) They are useful to look at because they tell you the value of one variable (x or y) while the other is 0.

There is other information you can grab from a graph too — just take a look at the example below.

EXAMPLE: BeyondSpaceInvaders hires out computer games to its members. The graph shows how much it charges.

a) What is the basic annual cost?

The basic annual cost is the amount it costs even if you don't hire any games (when x = 0). This is the cost at the y-intercept.

y-intercept = basic annual cost = £15

b) How many games are included in the basic annual cost?

20 The first section of the graph is horizontal. It's only if you hire more than 20 games that you pay more.

c) Estimate the cost per game for additional games.

Gradient of sloped section = cost per game = $\dfrac{\text{change in } y}{\text{change in } x}$ = $\dfrac{25}{20}$ = **£1.25 per game**

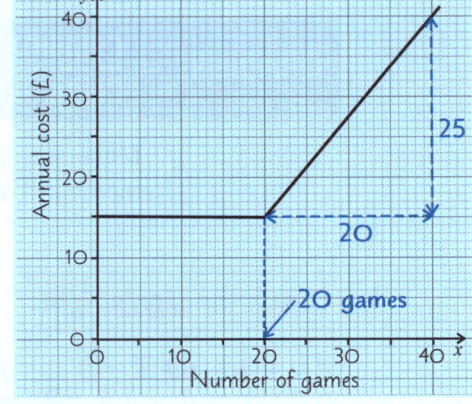

What do you call a giraffe with no eyes? A graph...

Real-life graphs are a bit wordier than normal graphs, but the maths is the same for both.

Q1 Shaughna weighed her puppy once a week until it was ten weeks old. Her results are shown on the graph.

  a) How much did the puppy weigh when it was born? [1 mark]

  b) Estimate how much weight the puppy gained each week. [2 marks]

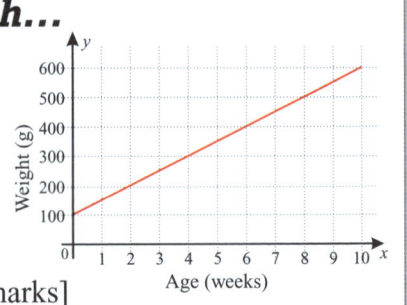

Conversion Graphs

Sometimes you'll be given a graph which converts something like £ to dollars or mph to km/h.

Conversion Graphs are Easy to Use

METHOD FOR USING CONVERSION GRAPHS:
1. Draw a line from a value on one axis.
2. When you hit the LINE, change direction and go straight to the other axis.
3. Read off the value from this axis. The two values are equivalent.

Here's a straightforward example:

This graph converts between miles and kilometres

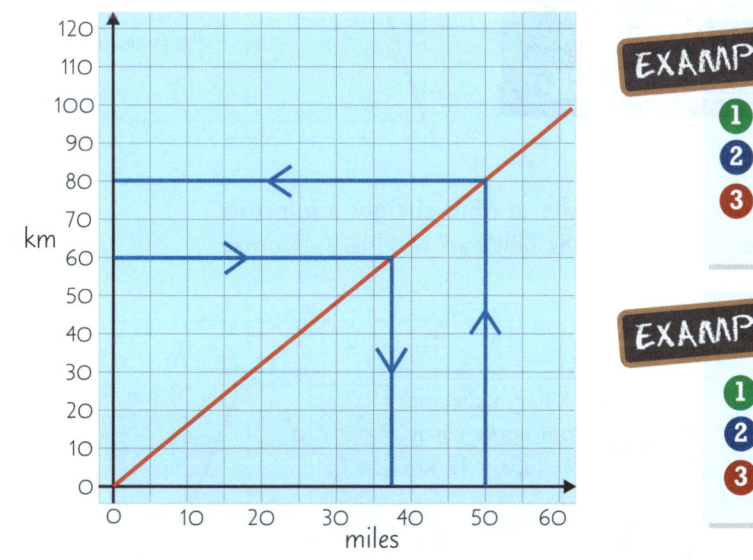

EXAMPLE: How many miles is 60 km?
1. Draw a line across from '60' on the 'km' axis.
2. When it hits the line, go down to the 'miles' axis.
3. Read off the answer: **37.5 miles**

EXAMPLE: How many km is 50 miles?
1. Draw a line up from '50' on the 'miles' axis.
2. When it hits the line, go across to the 'km' axis.
3. Read off the answer: **80 km**

Using Conversion Graphs to Answer Harder Questions

Conversion graphs are so simple to use that examiners might want to wrap one up into a tricky question.

EXAMPLE: Sam went on holiday to Florida and paid $360 for a camera. The same camera in Coleraine costs £250. Where was the camera cheaper? Show your working.

$360 is way off the graph, so find a point which will make calculating easy. The easiest way is to read off the value for $36 and multiply by 10.

Reading off the graph, $36 = £22
So $360 = £22 × 10 = £220

Now compare the values and add your conclusion.
£220 is less than £250, so the camera was cheaper in Florida.

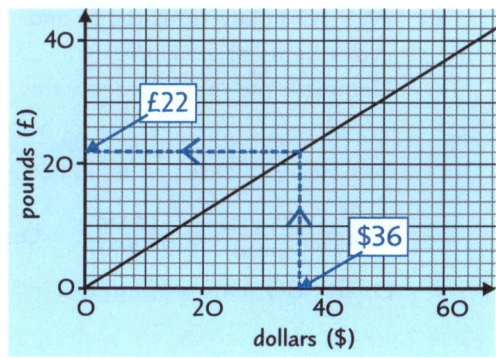

Learn how to convert graph questions into marks...

Draw your conversion lines on the graph in the exam. If all else fails, this might get you a mark.

Q1   The distance between Tokyo and Belfast is about 6000 miles.
Use the graph at the top of the page to estimate this distance in km.   [2 marks]

Distance-Time Graphs

Ah, what could be better than some nice D/T graphs? OK, so a slap-up meal with Hugh Jackman might be better. Unfortunately this section isn't called 'Tea With The Stars' so a D/T graph will have to do...

Distance-Time Graphs

Distance-time graphs can look a bit awkward at first, but they're not too bad once you get your head around them.

Just remember these 4 important points:

1) At any point, <u>GRADIENT = SPEED</u>.
2) The <u>STEEPER</u> the graph, the <u>FASTER</u> it's going.
3) <u>FLAT SECTIONS</u> are where it is <u>STOPPED</u>.
4) If the gradient's negative, it's <u>COMING BACK</u>.

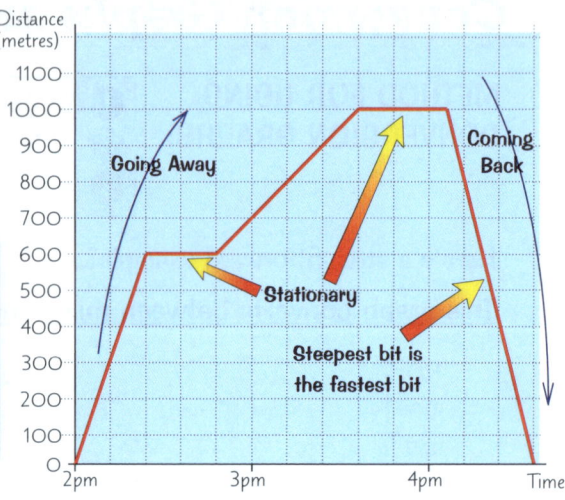

EXAMPLE: Hilary went out for a ride on her bike. After a while she got a puncture and stopped to fix it. This graph shows the first part of Hilary's journey.

a) What time did Hilary leave home?

She left home at the point where the line starts. **At 8:15**

b) How far did Hilary cycle before getting a puncture?

The horizontal part of the graph is where Hilary stopped. **12 km**

c) What was Hilary's speed before getting a puncture?

Using the speed formula (p65) is the same as finding the gradient.

speed = $\frac{\text{distance}}{\text{time}}$ = $\frac{12 \text{ km}}{0.5 \text{ hours}}$
= **24 km/h**

d) At 9:30 Hilary turns round and cycles home at 24 km/h. Complete the graph to show this.

You have to work out how long it will take Hilary to cycle the 18 km home:

time = $\frac{\text{distance}}{\text{speed}}$ = $\frac{18 \text{ km}}{24 \text{ km/h}}$ = **0.75 hours**
0.75 × 60 mins = **45 mins**

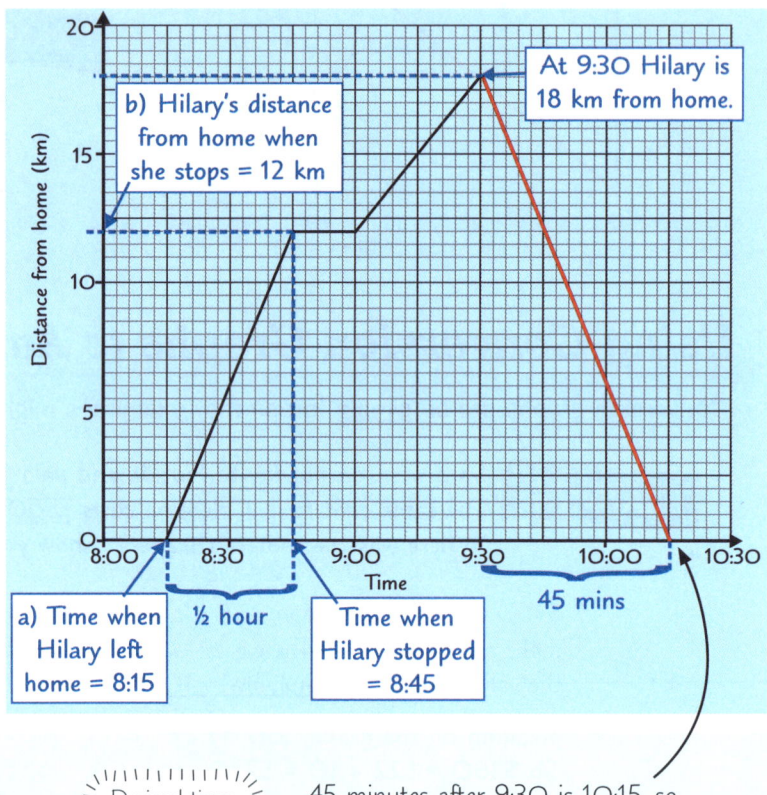

Decimal times are yuck, so convert it to minutes.

45 minutes after 9:30 is 10:15, so that's the time Hilary gets home. Now you can complete the graph.

D-T Graphs — filled with highs and lows...

... like my bungee jumping career. The way to get good at distance-time graphs is to practise using them.

Q1 a) Using the graph above, how long did Hilary stop for? [1 mark]

b) What was Hilary's speed after she had repaired the puncture, before she turned back home? [2 marks]

Section Four — Graphs

Solving Equations Using Graphs

You can plot graphs to find <u>solutions</u> (or <u>approximate</u> solutions) to simultaneous equations.
Plot the equations you want to solve and the solution lies where the lines <u>intersect</u>.

Solving Simultaneous Equations

Simultaneous equations are a <u>pair of equations</u> that you have to solve at the <u>same time</u>.
To solve them, you have to find values of x and y <u>that work in both equations</u>.

> E.g. $2x + y = 6$ and $6x + y = 10$ are a pair of simultaneous equations.
> $x = 2$, $y = 2$ works in the first equation but <u>not</u> the second — so these values <u>don't</u> solve the equations.
> $x = 1$, $y = 4$ works in <u>both</u> equations — so these values solve the equations.

If you want to solve a pair of simultaneous equations with a graph, it's just a matter of plotting them both on a graph and writing down <u>where they cross</u>.

1. Use the graph to the right to solve the simultaneous equations $y = 3x - 3$ and $y = x + 1$.

   Read off the x and y values where the two lines intersect.

   $x = 2$, $y = 3$

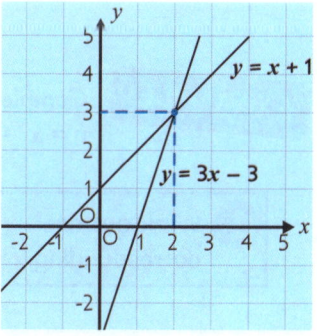

2. Draw and use a graph to solve the simultaneous equations $y = \frac{1}{2}x$ and $y = -2x + 5$

   Use the 3-point method to draw the two lines.

x	0	2	4
y	0	1	2

x	0	1	2
y	5	3	1

   You don't need to pick the same three values for x for both lines.

   Read off the x and y values where the two lines cross.

   The solution is $x = 2$, $y = 1$.

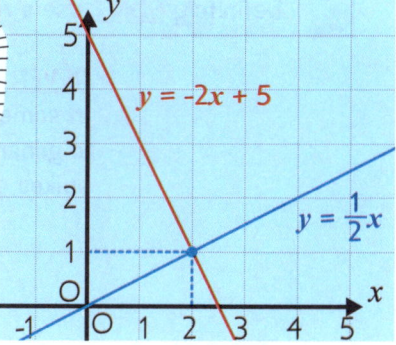

3. The graph of $y = 4 - x$ is shown to the right.
   Use the graph to find the solution to $4 - x = x$.

   Each side of the equation $4 - x = x$ <u>represents a line</u>.
   These lines are $y = 4 - x$ and $y = x$.

   Draw the line $y = x$ on the graph, then read off the <u>x-coordinate</u> where it crosses $y = 4 - x$.

   The solution is $x = 2$.

   At the point where the lines cross, both sides of the equation are equal, so this is the <u>solution</u>.

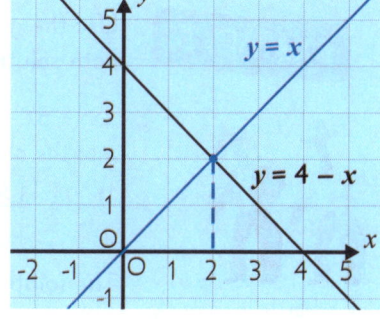

I'll do equations, but graphs are where I draw the line...

Make sure you take care when drawing your lines.
A small mistake can cause a big difference in where the two lines cross.

Q1 The line $y = 2x - 3$ is plotted on the grid on the right.
Plot $y = -x + 3$ on the same grid and use your line to solve
the simultaneous equations $y = 2x - 3$ and $y = -x + 3$. [4 marks]

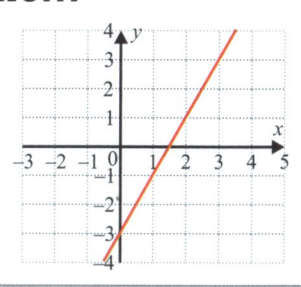

Quadratic Graphs

Enough of straight lines. You now get to graduate to lovely, smooth curves. Quadratic ones, to be precise.

Drawing a *Quadratic Graph*

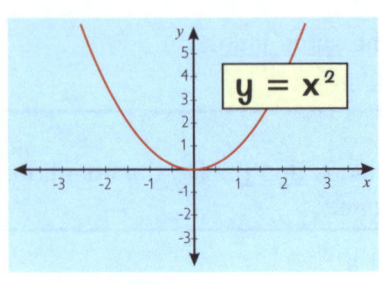

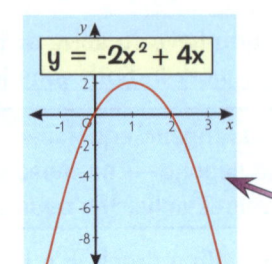

Quadratic graphs are of the form y = anything with x^2 (but not higher powers of x).

They all have the same symmetrical bucket shape.

If the x^2 bit has a '−' in front of it then the bucket is upside down.

EXAMPLE: Complete the table of values for the equation $y = x^2 - 5$ and then draw the graph.

x	-3	-2	-1	0	1	2	3
y	4	-1	-4	-5	-4	-1	4

1) Work out each y-value by substituting the corresponding x-value into the equation.

$y = (-3)^2 - 5$
$= 9 - 5 = 4$

$y = (2)^2 - 5$
$= 4 - 5 = -1$

2) Plot the points and join them with a completely smooth curve. Definitely DON'T use a ruler.

NEVER EVER let one point drag your line off in some ridiculous direction. When a graph is generated from an equation, you never get spikes or lumps — only MISTAKES.

This point is obviously wrong

Solving *Quadratic Equations*

A quadratic equation is one where the highest power is x^2.

EXAMPLE: Use the graph of $y = 2x^2 - 3x$ (on the right) to estimate both solutions to the equation $2x^2 - 3x = 5$.

$2x^2 - 3x = 5$ is what you get when you put $y = 5$ into the graph's equation, so:

1) Draw a line at $y = 5$.
2) Read the x-values where the curve crosses this line.

The solutions are about $x = -1$ and $x = 2.5$.

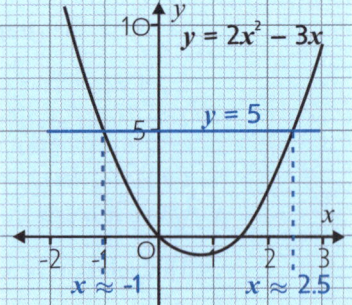

Now celebrate the only way graphs know how: line dancing.

Quadratic equations usually have 2 solutions.

How refreshing — a page on graphs. Not seen one in a while...

You know the deal by now — learn what's on this page, then treat yourself to the question below.

Q1 a) Draw the graph of $y = x^2 - 1$ for values of x between −3 and 3. [4 marks]

  b) Use your graph to estimate the solutions to $5 = x^2 - 1$. [2 marks]

Section Four — Graphs

Revision Questions for Section Four

Well, that wraps up Section Four — time to put yourself to the test and find out how much you really know.
- Try these questions and tick off each one when you get it right.
- When you've done all the questions for a topic and are completely happy with it, tick off the topic.

Coordinates and Line Segments (p49-50) ☐

1) Give the coordinates of points A to E in the diagram on the right.
2) Find the midpoint of a line segment with endpoints B and C.
3) Use Pythagoras' theorem to find the length of the line BD to 2 decimal places.

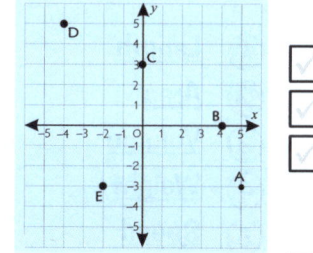

Straight-Line Graphs (p51-53) ☐

4) Draw these lines on a grid: a) $y = x$, b) $y = -4$, c) $x = -1$.
5) Which of the following equations gives a straight-line graph:
$y = x^2 - 2$, $x + y = 4$ or $y = 3 - \frac{1}{x}$?
6) By making a table of values, draw the graph of $y = -4x - 2$.
7) a) Find the gradient of line A on the right.
   b) Find the gradient of line B on the right.
8) Find the gradient of the straight line passing through (3, –6) and (6, –3).

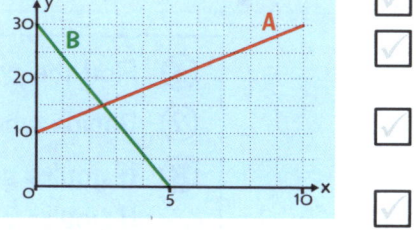

Real-Life and Conversion Graphs (p54-55) ☐

9) This graph shows the monthly cost of a mobile phone contract.
   a) What is the basic monthly fee?
   b) How many minutes does the monthly fee include?
   c) Mary uses her phone for 35 minutes one month. What will her bill be?
   d) Bilal is charged £14 one month. How long did he use his phone for?
   e) Estimate the cost per minute for additional minutes. Give your answer to the nearest 1 p.
10) Describe how to use a conversion graph.

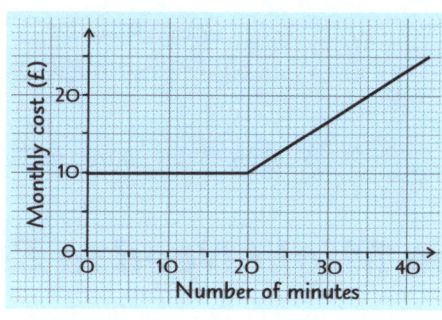

Distance-Time Graphs (p56) ☐

11) What does a horizontal line mean on a distance-time graph?
12) The graph on the right shows Beth's car journey to the supermarket and home again.
    a) Did she drive faster on her way to the supermarket or on her way home?
    b) How long did she spend at the supermarket?

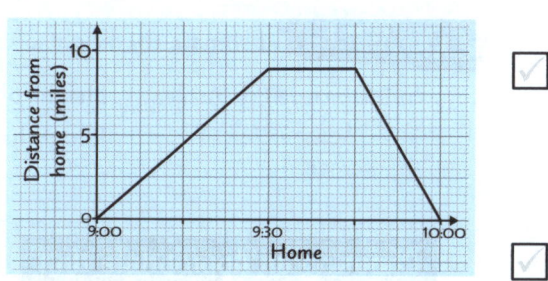

Solving Equations and Quadratic Graphs (p57-58) ☐

13) The graphs $y = x + 2$ and $y = 2x + 4$ are shown on the right. Use the graphs to solve the simultaneous equations $y = x + 2$ and $y = 2x + 4$.
14) Plot the graph of $y = 2x - 1$ and use it to find the solution to $5 = 2x - 1$.
15) Describe the shapes of the graphs $y = x^2 - 8$ and $y = -x^2 + 2$.
16) Plot the graph $y = x^2 + 2x$ for values of x between –3 and 3, and use it to solve $2 = x^2 + 2x$.

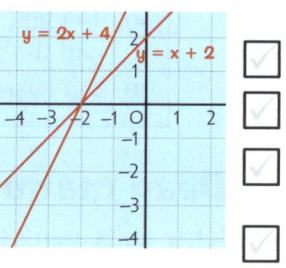

Section Five — Measures and Angles

Metric Units

From the dawn of civilisation, humans have tried to find how far or wide or tall or deep things are*. And they like to have set things to measure them with. So here's a page to tell you all about <u>metric units</u>. Hooray!

*I assume.

Metric Units

① <u>Length</u> — mm, cm, m, km
② <u>Area</u> — mm², cm², m², km²,
③ <u>Volume</u> — mm³, cm³, m³, ml, litres
④ <u>Weight</u> — g, kg, tonnes
⑤ <u>Speed</u> — km/h, m/s

MEMORISE THESE KEY FACTS:

1 cm = 10 mm	1 tonne = 1000 kg
1 m = 100 cm	1 litre = 1000 ml
1 km = 1000 m	1 litre = 1000 cm³
1 kg = 1000 g	1 cm³ = 1 ml
1 g = 1000 mg	1 litre = 100 cl

You should learn these off by heart for the exam.

3-Step Method for Converting Units

① Find the <u>conversion factor</u> (always easy).
② Decide whether to <u>MULTIPLY</u> or <u>DIVIDE</u> by it.
③ If you're going from a <u>smaller unit</u> to a <u>bigger unit</u>, <u>DIVIDE</u>.
   If you're going from a <u>bigger unit</u> to a <u>smaller unit</u>, <u>MULTIPLY</u>.

EXAMPLE: Convert 7 litres into ml.

1) Find the <u>conversion factor</u>.   1 litre = 1000 ml, so conversion factor = 1000
2) Work out whether to <u>multiply</u> or <u>divide</u>.   You're going from a bigger unit to a smaller unit, so you need to multiply.
3) <u>Multiply</u> by the <u>conversion factor</u>.   7 litres = 7 × 1000 = **7000 ml**

You Might Need to Estimate a Measurement

If you need to estimate a measurement, start with a measurement you know and <u>compare it</u> with the thing you're estimating.

EXAMPLE: Estimate the height of the baby giraffe in the picture.

In the picture the giraffe's about <u>twice</u> as tall as the woman.

Height of a woman is about 1.8 m
Rough height of giraffe = 2 × height of woman
= 2 × 1.8 = **3.6 m**

Use <u>1.8 m</u> as an estimate for the <u>height of a person</u>.

Choosing an Appropriate Unit

1) You might be asked to <u>choose an appropriate unit</u> to measure something in.
2) The <u>unit</u> you choose will depend on <u>what it is</u> you're measuring (e.g. a length/weight) and the <u>size</u> of the thing you're measuring.
3) For example, the <u>weight of a lorry</u> would be best measured in <u>tonnes</u> as it would be <u>very heavy</u>.

'Dead mammoth how heavy?' 'Hmm, about 3 boulders...'

Metric units aren't too bad. Just don't get caught out when handling the conversion factors... Now try:

Q1 Kendrick's dog weighs 9.3 kg and is 284 mm tall.
    a) How much does his dog weigh in grams? [1 mark]   b) How tall is his dog in cm? [1 mark]

Imperial Units

So now you know all about metric units, here are some more units — imperial this time. A lot of stuff is measured in metric units nowadays, but imperial units are still used sometimes, so you need to know them.

Imperial Units

1) Length — Inches, feet, yards, miles
2) Area — Square inches, square feet, square miles
3) Volume — Cubic inches, cubic feet, pints, gallons
4) Weight — Ounces, pounds, stones, tons
5) Speed — mph

IMPERIAL UNIT CONVERSIONS
1 Foot = 12 Inches
1 Yard = 3 Feet
1 Gallon = 8 Pints
1 Stone = 14 Pounds (lb)
1 Pound = 16 Ounces (oz)

EXAMPLE: Neil's jet ski can hold 116 pints of fuel. How many gallons is this? (1 gallon = 8 pints)

1) Find the conversion factor. — 1 gallon = 8 pints, so conversion factor = 8
2) Work out whether to multiply or divide by it. — You're going from a smaller unit to a bigger unit, so you need to divide.
3) Divide by the conversion factor. — 116 pints = 116 ÷ 8 = **14.5 gallons**

Metric-Imperial Conversions

APPROXIMATE CONVERSIONS
1 kg ≈ 2.2 pounds (lb)
1 foot ≈ 30 cm
1 litre ≈ 1¾ pints
1 gallon ≈ 4.5 litres
1 mile ≈ 1.6 km (or 5 miles ≈ 8 km)

≈ means roughly equal to

Make sure you know these two off by heart for your exam.

EXAMPLE: Iris unicycles 8 miles to work. How far is this in km? (1 mile ≈ 1.6 km)

1) Find the conversion factor. — 1 mile ≈ 1.6 km, so conversion factor = 1.6
2) Work out whether to multiply or divide by it. — You're going from a bigger unit to a smaller unit, so you need to multiply.
3) Multiply by the conversion factor. — 8 miles ≈ 8 × 1.6 = **12.8 km**

If 1 mile is 1.6 km, 1 mile is longer than 1 km.

Learn how to convert these questions into marks...

Hmm, I don't know about you, but I quite fancy a conversion-based question after all that.

Q1 A squash court is 32 feet long. 1 foot ≈ 30 cm and 1 foot = 12 inches.
   a) How long is the court in inches? [1 mark]   b) How long is the court in metres? [2 marks]

Area and Volume Conversion

Time for some trickier conversions to sink your teeth into. There are a couple of methods for you to remember so that when it comes to the exam you can feel confident converting areas and volumes.

Converting Areas

You need to be really careful when converting areas — just because 1 m = 100 cm DOES NOT mean 1 m² = 100 cm².
Follow this method to guarantee success:

$1 m^2 = 100 cm \times 100 cm = 10\,000 cm^2$
$1 cm^2 = 10 mm \times 10 mm = 100 mm^2$

1) Find the conversion factor — it'll be the same as for converting units (see p60).
2) Decide whether to MULTIPLY or DIVIDE by the conversion factor.
3) Smaller unit to a bigger unit → DIVIDE TWICE. Bigger unit to a smaller unit → MULTIPLY TWICE.
4) Don't forget that the units come with a power of 2, e.g. mm², cm².

EXAMPLE: The area of the top of a table is 0.6 m². Find its area in cm².

1) Find the conversion factor: 1 m = 100 cm, so conversion factor = 100
2) Decide whether to multiply or divide by the conversion factor. You're going from a bigger unit to a smaller unit, so you need to multiply.
3) It's an area, so multiply TWICE by the conversion factor.
$0.6 m^2 = 0.6 \times 100 \times 100 = 6000 cm^2$

Converting Volumes

This is very similar to converting areas, except you use the conversion factor THREE TIMES instead of twice.

$1 m^3 = 100 cm \times 100 cm \times 100 cm = 1\,000\,000 cm^3$
$1 cm^3 = 10 mm \times 10 mm \times 10 mm = 1000 mm^3$

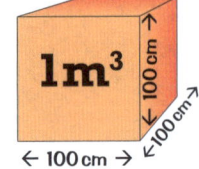

1) Find the conversion factor — it'll be the same as for converting units (see p60).
2) Decide whether to MULTIPLY or DIVIDE by the conversion factor.
3) Smaller unit to a bigger unit → DIVIDE THREE TIMES.
   Bigger unit to a smaller unit → MULTIPLY THREE TIMES.
4) Don't forget that the units come with a power of 3, e.g. mm³, cm³.

EXAMPLE: A glass has a volume of 72 000 mm³. What is its volume in cm³?

1) Find the conversion factor: 1 cm = 10 mm, so conversion factor = 10
2) Decide whether to multiply or divide by the conversion factor. You're going from a smaller unit to a bigger unit, so you need to divide.
3) It's a volume, so divide THREE TIMES by the conversion factor.
$72\,000 mm^3 = 72\,000 \div 10 \div 10 \div 10 = 72 cm^3$

That's it, you've converted me, I love maths...

For areas, use the conversion factor twice, for volumes use it three times. Have a go at these questions:

Q1 The area of a forest is 6 km². What is its area in m²? [2 marks]

Q2 The volume of a golf ball is 40 cm³. What is its volume in mm³? [2 marks]

Reading Scales

You can pick up some easy marks on questions that ask you to read a scale. The same rules apply to scales measuring lengths, weights, volumes, speeds and temperatures, so learn them and those marks will be yours.

How to Read a Scale

All scales consist of a line divided into intervals like this:

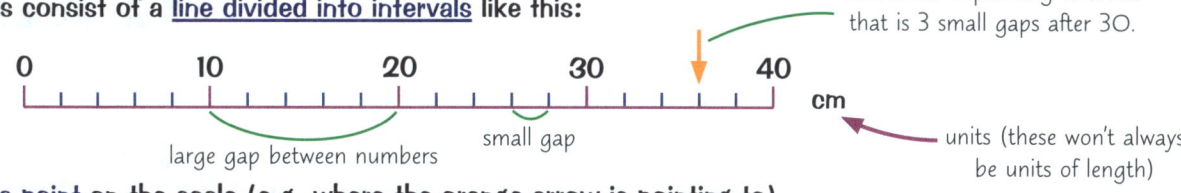

To read a point on the scale (e.g. where the orange arrow is pointing to), you need to know what each small gap represents:

$$\text{Small gap} = \frac{\text{Size of large gap between numbers}}{\text{Number of small gaps between numbers}}$$

Make sure you count the GAPS — NOT the marks.

1) On the scale above there's a difference of 10 between the numbers, and 5 small gaps between them, so each small gap is worth 10 ÷ 5 = 2 cm.

2) The orange arrow is 3 small gaps after 30. 3 small gaps = 3 × 2 = 6, so the arrow is pointing to 30 + 6 = 36 cm.

EXAMPLE: What is the weight of the miniature frog on the right?

1) Work out what each small gap represents.
   Large gap = 5   No. of small gaps = 10
   Small gap = 5 ÷ 10 = 0.5 g

2) The arrow points to 7 small gaps after 10.
   7 small gaps = 7 × 0.5 = 3.5   Weight of frog = 10 + 3.5 = 13.5 g

Measurements are Only Approximate

1) When you measure something, you actually round it to the number on the scale that it's nearest to.

2) Take this slimy grey slug for example:
   If you look closely, you'll see its length lies somewhere between 5.7 cm and 5.8 cm. You'd record it as 5.8 cm, because that's the number on the scale that it's nearest to. But even if the slug's length was just over 5.8 cm, you'd still record it as 5.8 cm, as long as that was still the number on the scale that it was nearest to.

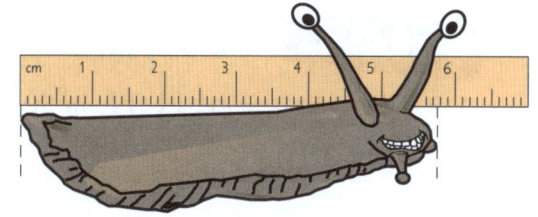

3) So whenever you're given a measurement that has been rounded off, the actual measurement could be up to half a unit bigger or smaller.

4) For example, if an object is measured as 13.5 g to 1 decimal place, the object's weight could actually be anywhere between 13.45 g and 13.55 g. Another way of writing this is that the object's weight (W) lies in the range: 13.45 g ≤ W < 13.55 g.

≤ means "less than or equal to". < just means "less than".

Nothing beats curling up on the sofa and reading a good scale...

You need to be comfortable reading any sort of scale, so give these Exam Practice Questions a try.

Q1 What temperature does the thermometer show?   [1 mark]

Q2 A room is 9 m long to the nearest metre.
    What is the minimum length the room could be?   [1 mark]

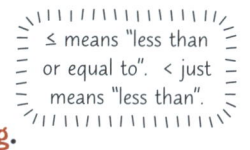

Section Five — Measures and Angles

Time Intervals

Make sure you can convert between <u>time units</u> — it's <u>simple</u> and might grab you a mark or two in the exam.

Converting Time Units

1) You ought to know the standard <u>time unit conversions</u> by now.
2) Use these standard conversions to change the units of <u>other times</u>.

> 1 day = 24 hours
> 1 hour = 60 minutes
> 1 minute = 60 seconds

EXAMPLES:

1. How many seconds are there in an hour?
1) First convert <u>hours</u> into <u>minutes</u>.   1 hour = 60 minutes
2) Then convert <u>minutes</u> into <u>seconds</u>.   60 minutes = 60 × 60 = **3600** seconds

Be <u>careful</u> when using <u>calculators</u> — the decimal answers they give can be confusing, e.g. <u>2.5 hours = 2 hours 30 mins</u>, <u>NOT 2 hours 50 mins</u>.

2. Write 186 minutes in hours and minutes.
1) Work out how many <u>complete hours</u> there are in 186 minutes.
   2 hours = 2 × 60 = 120 minutes
   3 hours = 3 × 60 = 180 minutes ✓
   4 hours = 4 × 60 = 240 minutes — too many
2) Find how many <u>minutes over 3 hours</u> it is.
   186 − 180 = <u>6 minutes</u>
   So 186 minutes = **3 hours 6 minutes**

Break Time Calculations into Simple Stages

EXAMPLE: Jahea watched a film that started at 7.20 pm and finished at 10.05 pm. How long was the film in minutes?

1) Split the time between 7.20 pm and 10.05 pm into <u>simple stages</u>.

   7.20 pm → 9.20 pm → 10.00 pm → 10.05 pm
   + 2 hours   + 40 minutes   + 5 minutes

2) <u>Convert</u> the hours to minutes.   2 hours = 2 × 60 = 120 minutes
3) <u>Add</u> to get the total minutes.   120 + 40 + 5 = **165 minutes**

Timetables

EXAMPLE: Use the timetable to answer this question.

Ciara wants to get a bus from the <u>bus station</u> to the <u>train station</u> in time for a train that leaves at <u>19:30</u>. What is the latest bus she can catch?

Bus Timetable				
Bus Station	18 45	19 00	19 15	19 30
Market Street	18 52	19 07	19 22	19 37
Long Lane	19 01	19 16	19 31	19 46
Train Station	19 11	19 26	19 41	19 56

1) Read along the <u>train station</u> row.   19 11 (19 26) 19 41 19 56
   This is the latest time she could arrive before 19:30.
2) Move up this column to the <u>bus station</u> row and read off the entry.
   The bus that gets to the train station at 19:26 leaves the bus station at **19:00**.

Got a friend who's always late? Show them this page...

Calculators can be a nightmare when it comes to working with time intervals. Practise with these:

Q1 a) How many minutes are there in 2 days?   [1 mark]
   b) Write 265 seconds in minutes and seconds.   [2 marks]

Q2 Zoe works 4 days a week at an owl sanctuary. She starts work at 6.20 am and finishes at 12.50 pm. She earns £7.20 per hour. How much does she earn in a week?   [3 marks]

Compound Units

A compound unit is a unit that involves two different measurements — e.g. speed measured in m/s is a compound unit as it involves distance (m) and time (s). Now, let's see if you can speed through this page...

Speed = Distance ÷ Time

Speed is the distance travelled per unit time — e.g. the number of km per hour or metres per second.

$$\text{SPEED} = \frac{\text{DISTANCE}}{\text{TIME}} \qquad \text{TIME} = \frac{\text{DISTANCE}}{\text{SPEED}} \qquad \text{DISTANCE} = \text{SPEED} \times \text{TIME}$$

A formula triangle is a mighty handy tool for remembering formulas. Here's the one for speed. To remember the order of the letters (S^DT) we have the words SaD Times. So if it's a question on speed, distance and time, just say SAD TIMES.

HOW DO YOU USE FORMULA TRIANGLES?
1) COVER UP the thing you want to find and WRITE DOWN what's left.
2) Now PUT IN THE VALUES for the other two things and WORK IT OUT.

E.g. to get the formula for speed from the triangle, cover up S and you're left with $\frac{D}{T}$.

EXAMPLES:

1. Rob cycles 18 miles in 2 hours. What is his average speed?
1) You want speed so covering S gives: $S = \frac{D}{T}$
2) Put in the numbers — and don't forget the units. $S = 18 \div 2 = 9$ mph

CHECK YOUR UNITS MATCH
If the distance is in miles and the time is in hours then you'll get a speed in mph.

2. A cheetah runs at a constant speed of 27 m/s for 20 s. What distance does it cover?
1) You want distance so covering D gives: $D = S \times T$
2) Put in the numbers — and don't forget the units. $D = 27 \times 20 = 540$ m

UNITS CHECK: m/s and s go in so m comes out.

More Compound Units

There are other compound units that you may come across such as:
1) bpm (beats per minute) which measures how many times your heart beats per minute.
2) mpg (miles per gallon) which measures the number of miles driven in a vehicle for each gallon of fuel the vehicle uses.

$$\text{BPM} = \frac{\text{NO. OF HEARTBEATS}}{\text{MINUTES}}$$

$$\text{MPG} = \frac{\text{NO. OF MILES DRIVEN}}{\text{GALLONS USED}}$$

EXAMPLE:
Saoirse's heart beats 360 times in 5 minutes. What is her heart rate in beats per minute (bpm)?
1) You want beats per minute, so you need to divide the number of beats by the number of minutes: $\text{bpm} = \frac{\text{no. of heartbeats}}{\text{minutes}}$
2) Put in the numbers — and don't forget the units. $\text{bpm} = 360 \div 5 = 72$ bpm

No need to get your bpm up with this page...

The units you put into the calculation determine what units you get out of the calculation. Try:

Q1 a) Ian drives 210 miles at an average speed of 60 mph. How many hours will this take? [2 marks]
b) His car uses 4.2 gallons of fuel for the whole journey. How many miles per gallon did his car do? [2 marks]

Section Five — Measures and Angles

Compound Units

Density, like speed, is a measurement that's a combination of two units...

Density = Mass ÷ Volume

Density is the mass per unit volume of a substance. It's usually measured in kg/m³ or g/cm³.

$$\text{DENSITY} = \frac{\text{MASS}}{\text{VOLUME}} \qquad \text{VOLUME} = \frac{\text{MASS}}{\text{DENSITY}} \qquad \text{MASS} = \text{DENSITY} \times \text{VOLUME}$$

Here's the formula triangle for density. To remember the order of the letters in the formula triangle think D^M V or DiMoV (the Russian agent).

EXAMPLES:

1. A giant chocolate bar has a density of 1.3 g/cm³ and a volume of 1800 cm³. What is the mass of the bar in grams?
   1) You want the mass, so covering M gives: M = D × V
   2) Put in the numbers — and remember the units.   M = 1.3 g/cm³ × 1800 cm³ = **2340 g**

2. A plate of glass has a density of 2500 kg/m³ and a mass of 11.25 kg. What is its volume?
   1) You want the volume, so covering V gives: V = M ÷ D
   2) Put in the numbers — and remember the units.   V = 11.25 kg ÷ 2500 kg/m³ = **0.0045 m³**

Converting Density

1) Units of density are made up of two measures — a mass and a volume.
2) So to convert units for density, you might need to do two conversions — one for each measure.
3) If you need to convert volume, remember to use the conversion factor three times (see p62).

EXAMPLE: The density of silver is 10.5 g/cm³. What is this in kg/m³?

1) First convert from g/cm³ to kg/cm³:
   1 kg = 1000 g, so conversion factor = 1000
   Smaller units to bigger units, so divide.
   10.5 g/cm³ = 10.5 ÷ 1000
   = 0.0105 kg/cm³

2) Now convert from kg/cm³ to kg/m³:
   The units are going from smaller to bigger, but because mass is divided by volume for density, you need to multiply (as dividing by a division means you multiply).

   1 m = 100 cm, so conversion factor = 100
   There'll be more kg/m³ than kg/cm³, so multiply by the conversion factor three times.
   0.0105 kg/cm³ = 0.0105 × 100 × 100 × 100
   = **10 500 kg/m³**

4) You can use this method to convert other compound measures too, such as speed (see p65).

Formula triangles — it's all a big cover-up...

Learn the formula triangle for density and you'll get 3 equations for the price of one. Bargain.

Q1 A marshmallow has a density of 0.5 g/cm³ and a volume of 30 cm³.
    What is its mass in grams?   [2 marks]

Q2 A cube has a mass of 6.9 kg and a volume of 2 m³.
    What is its density? State the units of your answer.   [3 marks]

Section Five — Measures and Angles

Angle Basics

Before we really step foot into the world of angles, there are a few basics you need to know.

Fancy Angle Names

Some angles have special names. You might have to identify these angles in the exam.

This little square means it's a right angle.

ACUTE angles
Sharp pointy ones (less than 90°)

RIGHT angles
Square corners (exactly 90°)

OBTUSE angles
Flatter ones (between 90° and 180°)

REFLEX angles
Ones that bend back on themselves (more than 180°)

Measuring and Drawing Angles with a Protractor

MEASURING

1) ALWAYS position the protractor with the base line of it along one of the lines, as shown on the right.

2) Count the angle in 10° STEPS from the start line right round to the other line.

Make sure you stick to this method so that you read the number off the correct scale — e.g. the angle here is 135°, not 45°.

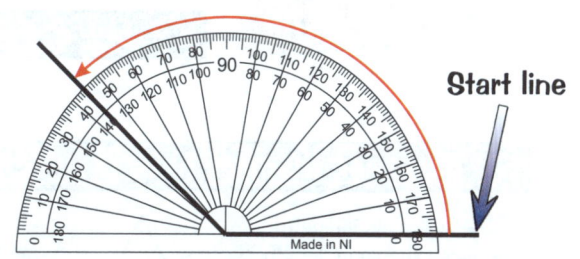
Start line

DRAWING

1) Draw a straight horizontal line to be your base line. Put the protractor on the line so that the middle of the protractor is on one end of the line as shown below.

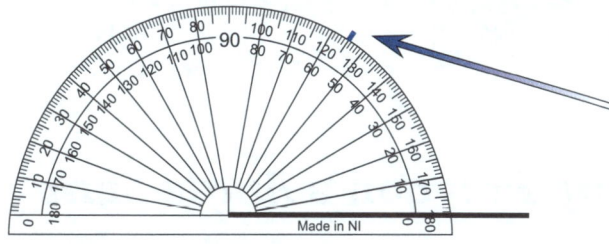

2) Draw a little line or dot next to the angle you're drawing (count up from 0° to make sure you follow the right scale). Here, I'm drawing an angle of 55°, so I'm using the inside scale.

3) Then join your base line to the mark you've just made with a straight line. You must join the end of the base line that was in the middle of the protractor.

55°

Three-Letter Angle Notation

The best way to say which angle you're talking about in a diagram is by using THREE letters.
For example in the diagram, angle ACB = 25°.

1) The middle letter is where the angle is.
2) The other two letters tell you which two lines enclose the angle.

angle ACD = 20°

You might see angles written in other ways as well — ∠ABC and AB̂C are both the same as angle ABC.

If you were an angle you'd be acute one...

As well as measuring angles, you might need to measure the length of lines too. Make sure you line the 0 cm mark on your ruler up with the start of the line you're measuring and measure to the nearest mm.

Q1   An angle measures 66°. What type of angle is this?   [1 mark]

Section Five — Measures and Angles

Five Angle Rules

If you know all these rules thoroughly, you'll at least have a fighting chance of working out problems with lines and angles. If you don't — you've got no chance. Sorry to break it to you like that.

5 Simple Rules — that's all

1) Angles in a triangle add up to 180°.

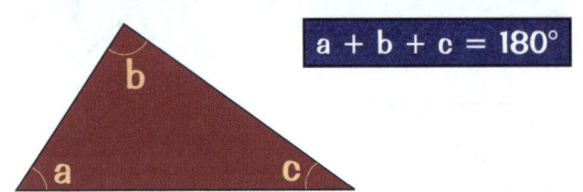

$a + b + c = 180°$

2) Angles on a straight line add up to 180°.

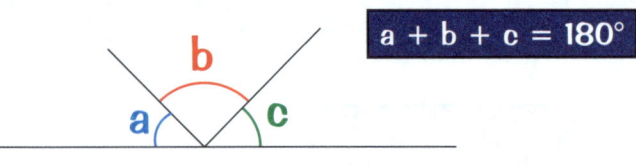

$a + b + c = 180°$

3) Angles in a quadrilateral add up to 360°.

A quadrilateral is a 4-sided shape.

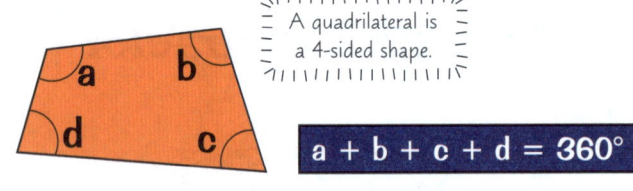

$a + b + c + d = 360°$

4) Angles round a point add up to 360°.

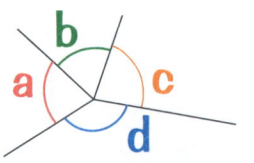

$a + b + c + d = 360°$

5) Isosceles triangles have 2 sides the same and 2 angles the same.

In an isosceles triangle, you only need to know one angle to be able to find the other two.

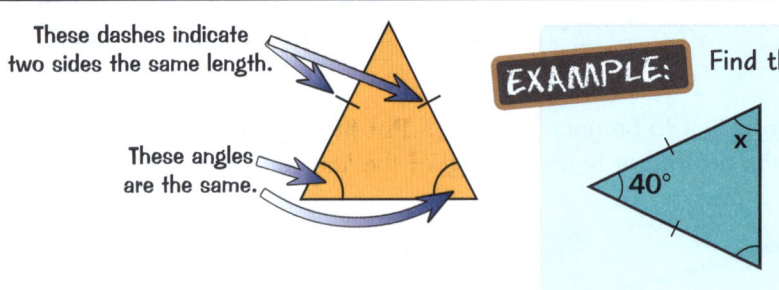

These dashes indicate two sides the same length.

These angles are the same.

EXAMPLE: Find the size of angle x.

$180° - 40° = 140°$

The two angles on the right are the same (they're both x) and they must add up to 140°, so $2x = 140°$, which means $x = 70°$.

Triangles Help you Find any Polygon's Angle Sum

1) Split any polygon into triangles by drawing as many diagonals as possible from one of its vertices (corners). A diagonal of a polygon is a line joining two vertices that aren't already connected by an edge.

   A polygon is any 2D shape with straight sides. A polygon's angle sum is the total of all of its interior angles.

2) Each triangle has angles adding up to 180°, so the angle sum in the polygon is the number of triangles created multiplied by 180°.

3) For example, only one diagonal can be drawn in a quadrilateral. The diagonal splits the quadrilateral into 2 triangles, so its angle sum is $2 \times 180° = 360°$.

   Angle sum of this polygon = $180° + 180° = 360°$

   Diagonal

4) For more about polygons and their angles, check out page 71.

The first rule of angle club is "you don't talk about angle club"...

Examiners don't like simple. So sometimes they combine the simple rules together and make much harder questions. There are some examples of these on p70, but have a go at this one as a warm-up.

Q1 Find the size of the angle marked x.

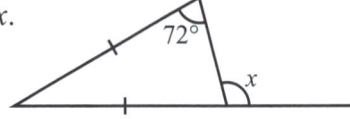

[2 marks]

Parallel Lines

Parallel lines are always the same distance apart. This page is all about them.

Angles Around Parallel Lines

When a line crosses two parallel lines...

1) The two bunches of angles are the same.
2) There are only two different angles: a small one and a big one.
3) These ALWAYS ADD UP TO 180°. E.g. 30° and 150° below.

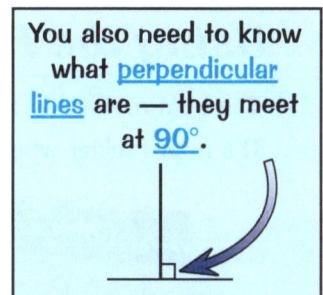

You also need to know what perpendicular lines are — they meet at 90°.

The two lines with the arrows on are parallel:

These are vertically opposite angles. They're equal to each other.

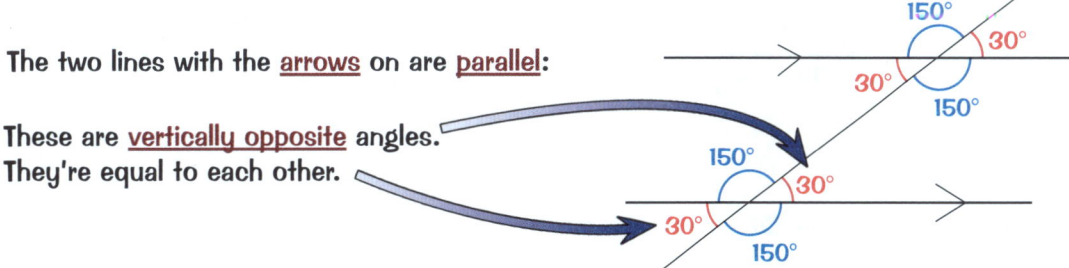

Alternate, Allied, Adjacent and Corresponding Angles

Watch out for 'Z', 'C', 'U' and 'F' shapes popping up.
They're a dead giveaway that you've got a pair of parallel lines.

Don't call them Z, C, U and F angles in the exam — you'll need to use their proper names.

ALTERNATE ANGLES

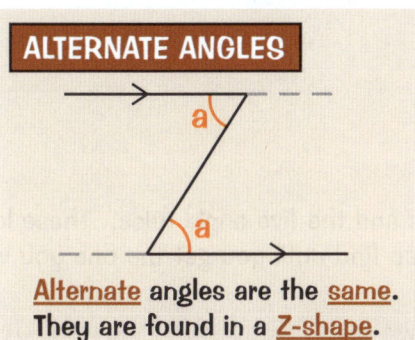

Alternate angles are the same.
They are found in a Z-shape.

ALLIED ANGLES

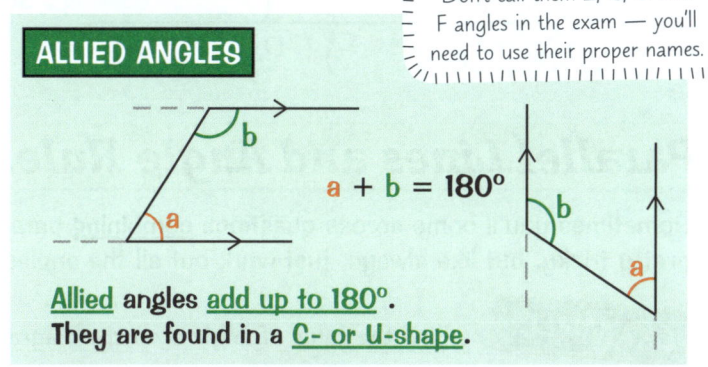

$a + b = 180°$

Allied angles add up to 180°.
They are found in a C- or U-shape.

CORRESPONDING ANGLES

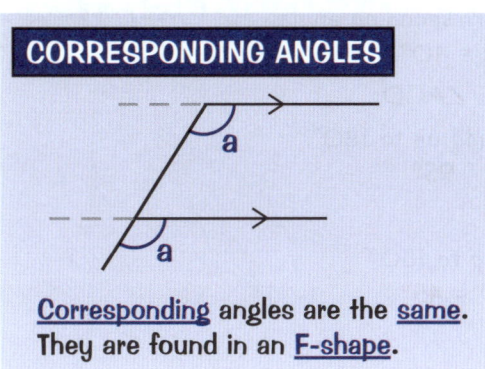

Corresponding angles are the same.
They are found in an F-shape.

ADJACENT ANGLES

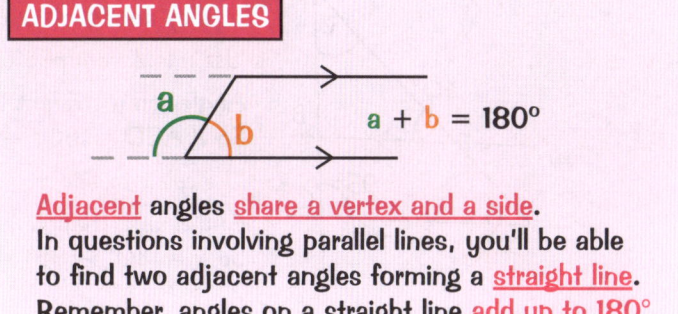

$a + b = 180°$

Adjacent angles share a vertex and a side.
In questions involving parallel lines, you'll be able to find two adjacent angles forming a straight line.
Remember, angles on a straight line add up to 180°.

Looking for Zs isn't a real excuse to sleep in class...

The key to being ace at parallel lines is looking out for those Z, C, U and F shapes.
If you spot one of those, you're onto a winner. When you're ready, try this:

Q1 Find the value of x in the diagram to the right. [2 marks]

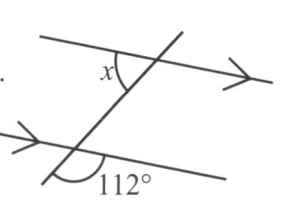

Section Five — Measures and Angles

Geometry Problems

As if geometry wasn't enough of a problem already, here's a page dedicated to geometry problems. Make sure you learn the five angle rules on p68 — they'll help a lot on these questions. Pinky promise.

Using the Five Angle Rules

The best method is to find whatever angles you can until you can work out the ones you're looking for. It's a bit trickier when you have to use more than one rule, but writing them all down is a big help.

EXAMPLES:

1. Find the value of x.   Use rule 4 from p68:

   Angles round a point add up to 360°,
   so $x + 52° + 90° + 167° = 360°$
   $x = 360° - 52° - 90° - 167° = 51°$

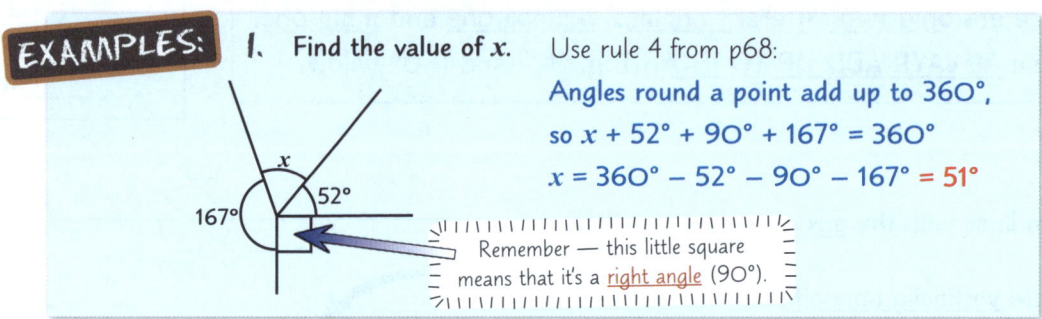

Remember — this little square means that it's a right angle (90°).

2. Find the size of angle CDE.

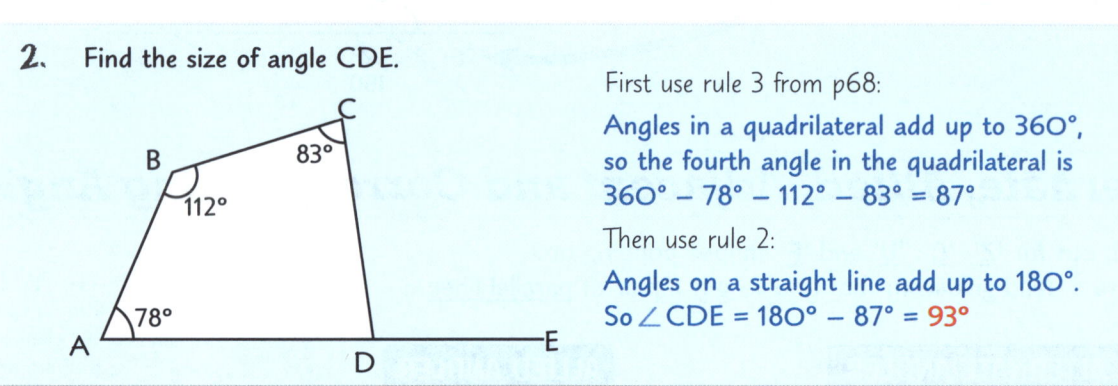

First use rule 3 from p68:

Angles in a quadrilateral add up to 360°, so the fourth angle in the quadrilateral is $360° - 78° - 112° - 83° = 87°$

Then use rule 2:

Angles on a straight line add up to 180°.
So $\angle CDE = 180° - 87° = 93°$

Parallel Lines and Angle Rules

Sometimes you'll come across questions combining parallel lines and the five angle rules. These look pretty tricky, but like always, just work out all the angles you can find until you get the one you want.

EXAMPLE: Find the value of angle x on the diagram below.

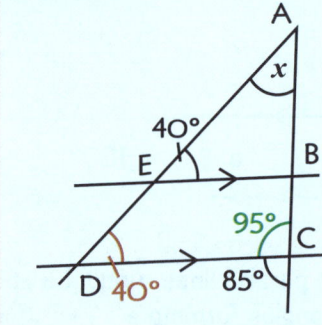

$\angle AEB$ and $\angle ADC$ are corresponding angles, so they are equal. $\angle ADC = 40°$

Use rule 2 from p68 to find $\angle ACD$:

Angles on a straight line add up to 180°.
So $\angle ACD = 180° - 85° = 95°$

Use rule 1 to find x:

Angles in a triangle add up to 180°.
So $x = 180° - 95° - 40° = 45°$

It's always a good idea to label your diagram as you work out each angle.

Heaven must be missing an angle...

Geometry problems often look a lot worse than they are — don't panic, just write down everything you can work out. Watch out for hidden parallel lines and isosceles triangles — they can help you work out angles.

Q1   Find the size of missing angle x.   [2 marks]

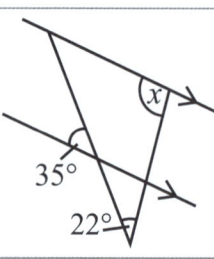

Section Five — Measures and Angles

Angles in Shapes

A polygon is a many-sided shape, and can be regular or irregular. A regular polygon (p77) is one where all the sides are the same length and all the angles are the same size. This page is all about the angles — yippee...

Exterior and Interior Angles

You need to know what exterior and interior angles are and how to find them.

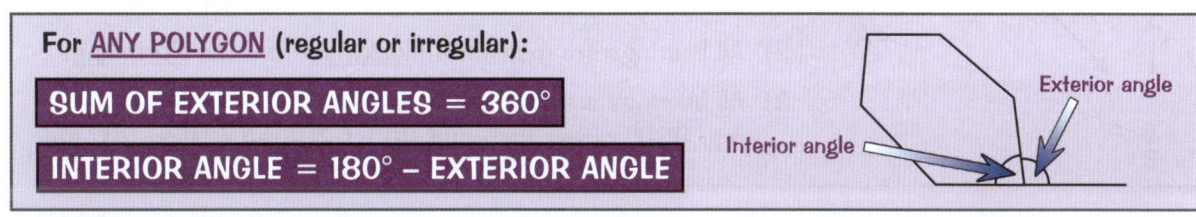

For ANY POLYGON (regular or irregular):
SUM OF EXTERIOR ANGLES = 360°
INTERIOR ANGLE = 180° − EXTERIOR ANGLE

For REGULAR POLYGONS only:
EXTERIOR ANGLE = $\frac{360°}{n}$
(n is the number of sides)

Each sector triangle is ISOSCELES (see p84).

This angle is always the same as the exterior angles.

EXAMPLE: Find the size of the exterior and interior angles of a regular octagon.

Octagons have 8 sides: exterior angle = $\frac{360°}{n}$ = $\frac{360°}{8}$ = **45°**

Use the exterior angle to find the interior angle: interior angle = 180° − exterior angle
= 180° − 45° = **135°**

The Tricky One — Sum of Interior Angles

This formula for the sum of the interior angles works for ALL polygons, even irregular ones:

SUM OF INTERIOR ANGLES = (n − 2) × 180°

EXAMPLE: Find the sum of the interior angles of the polygon on the right.

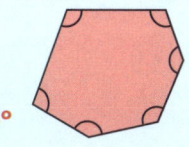

The polygon is a hexagon, so n = 6: Sum of interior angles = (n − 2) × 180°
= (6 − 2) × 180° = **720°**

Don't panic if those pesky examiners put algebra in an interior angle question. It looks worse than it is.

EXAMPLE: Find the value of x in the diagram on the right.

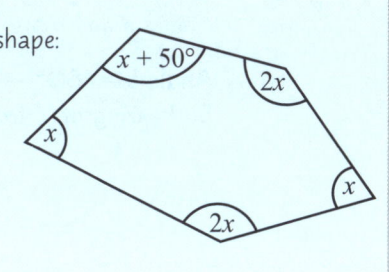

First, find the sum of the interior angles of the 5-sided shape:

Sum of interior angles = (n − 2) × 180°
= (5 − 2) × 180° = 540°

Now write an equation and solve it to find x:
$2x + x + 2x + x + (x + 50°) = 540°$
$7x + 50° = 540°$ → $7x = 490°$ → $x = $ **70°**

EXCLUSIVE: Heptagon lottery winner — "I'm just a regular guy"...

Learn all the formulas above, and remember whether they go with regular or irregular polygons.

Q1 Find the size of the interior angle of a regular 10-sided shape. [2 marks]

Q2 A regular polygon has exterior angles of 72°. What is the name of the polygon? [2 marks]

Section Five — Measures and Angles

Bearings

Bearings. They'll be useful next time you're off sailing… And in your maths exam.

Bearings

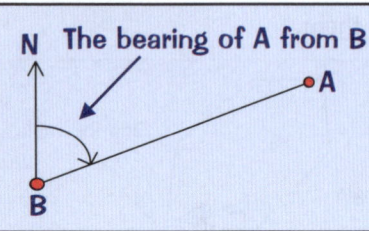

1) A bearing is just a <u>direction</u> given as an <u>angle</u> in degrees.
2) All bearings are measured <u>clockwise</u> from the <u>North line</u>.
3) All bearings are given as <u>3 figures</u>:
   e.g. 060° rather than just 60°, 020° rather than 20° etc.

The 3 Key Words

To find or draw a bearing you must remember <u>three key words</u>:

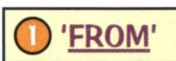 <u>Find the word 'FROM' in the question</u>, and put your pencil on the diagram at the point you are going '<u>from</u>'.

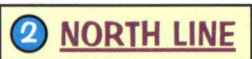 At the point you are going <u>FROM</u>, draw in a <u>NORTH LINE</u>.

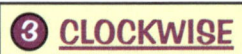 Now draw in the angle <u>CLOCKWISE</u> from the <u>NORTH LINE</u> to the <u>line joining the two points</u> — this angle is the <u>bearing</u>.

EXAMPLES:

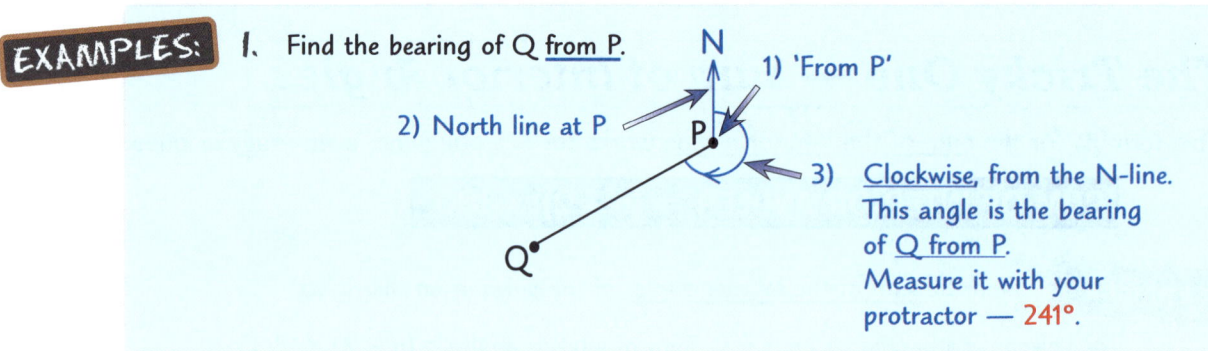

2. The bearing of Z from Y is 110°.
   Find the bearing of Y from Z.

   First sketch a diagram so you can see what's going on.
   Angles a and b are <u>allied</u>, so they add up to <u>180°</u>.
   (See p69 for allied angles.)

   Angle b = 180° − 110° = 70°
   So bearing of Y from Z = 360° − 70° = **290°**.

Please bear with me while I figure out where we are…

Learn the three key points above and scribble them out from memory. Now try these practice questions.

Q1 Measure the bearing of T from H. [1 mark]

Q2 A man walks in a straight line from A to B on a bearing of 210°.
    What bearing should he travel on to walk straight from B to A? [2 marks]

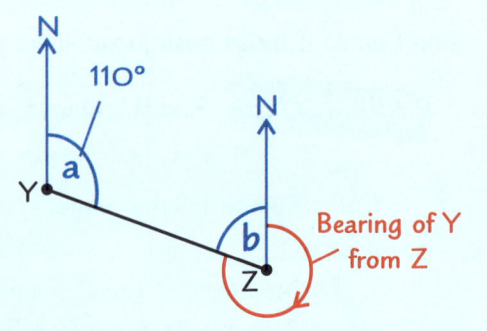

Maps

To know your way around a map, you should be familiar with <u>compass directions</u>. You'll also need to know about <u>scales</u> — they tell you what a <u>distance</u> on a <u>map</u> represents in <u>real life</u>.

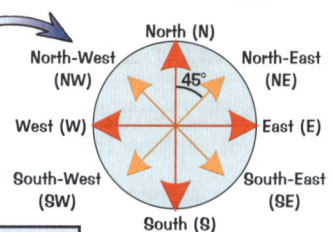

Map Scales

1 cm = 3 km — "1 cm represents 3 km"

1 : 2000 — 1 cm on the map means 2000 cm in real life. The 2000 tells you the <u>scale factor</u> — the number you have to multiply by to get the distance in real life. Converting to m gives: "1 cm represents 20 m"

 Use a ruler — the line's 2 cm long, so 2 cm means 1 km.
Dividing by 2 gives "1 cm represents 0.5 km"

To <u>convert</u> between <u>maps</u> and <u>real life</u>, <u>learn</u> these rules:
- Make sure your map scale is of the form "<u>1 cm = ...</u>"
- To find <u>REAL-LIFE</u> distances, <u>MULTIPLY</u> by the <u>MAP SCALE</u>.
- To find <u>MAP</u> distances, <u>DIVIDE</u> by the <u>MAP SCALE</u>.
- Always check your answer looks <u>sensible</u>.

Converting from Map Distance to Real Life — Multiply

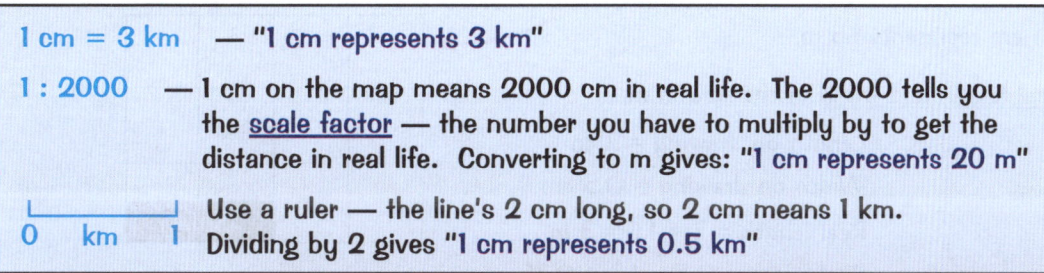

EXAMPLE: This map shows an area around Belfast. Work out the distance between Belfast and Lisburn in km.

1) Measure with a <u>ruler</u>: Distance on map = 2 cm
2) Read off the <u>scale</u>: Scale is 1 cm = 6 km
3) For <u>real life</u>, <u>multiply</u>: Real distance is: 2 × 6 = 12 km

This looks <u>sensible</u>. ✓

Converting from Real Life to Map Distance — Divide

EXAMPLE: Coleraine is approximately 21 km west of Armoy.

a) How far apart would they be on this map?
Real-life distance = 21 km
Scale is 1 cm = 7 km
Distance on map = 21 ÷ 7 = 3 cm

<u>Divide</u> for a <u>map distance</u>.

This looks <u>sensible</u>. ✓

b) Mark Coleraine on the map.
<u>Measure</u> 3 cm to the <u>west</u> (left) of Armoy:

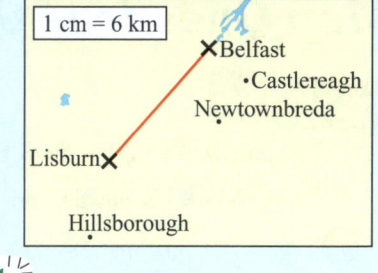

Follow this map of the road to exam glory...What?... Cheesy?... Me?

Once you're happy converting between maps and real life, try out these questions:

Q1 Use this map to find the distance between Kesh and Killadeas in miles. [2 marks]

Q2 Sarah's house is 2.25 km away from Qiang's house. How far apart in cm would they be on a map where 1 cm represents 500 m? [2 marks]

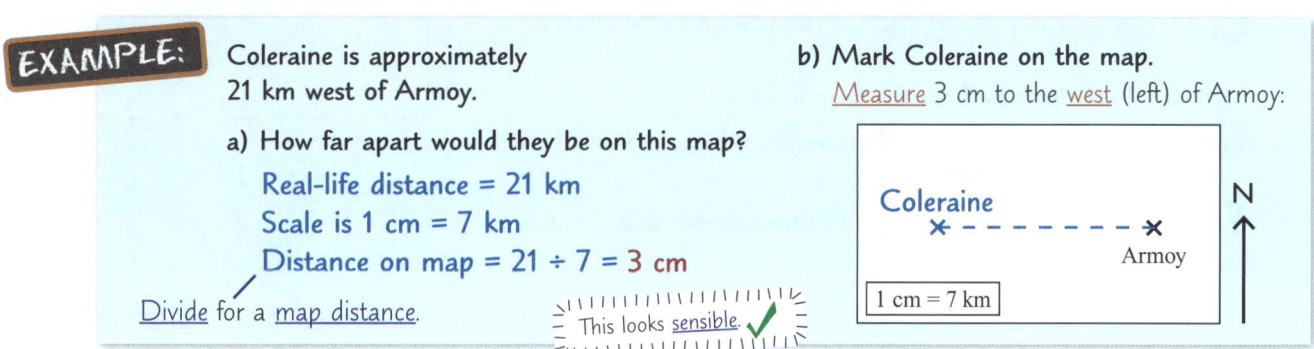

Section Five — Measures and Angles

Maps and Scale Drawings

Scale Drawings

Scale drawings work just like maps. To convert between real life and scale drawings, just replace the word 'map' with 'drawing' in the rules on the previous page.

Scale drawings will often be shown on a grid.

EXAMPLE: This is a scale drawing of a room in Clare's house. 1 cm represents 1.5 m.

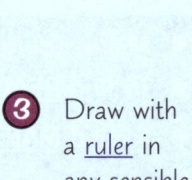

a) Find the real length and width of the sofa in m.

① Measure with a ruler.   Length on drawing = 2 cm
                          Width on drawing = 0.5 cm

② Multiply to get real-life length.   Real length = 2 × 1.5 = 3 m
                                       Real width = 0.5 × 1.5 = 0.75 m

b) Clare's dining table is 90 cm wide and 180 cm long. Draw the table on the scale drawing.

① Scale uses m, so convert cm to m.   Width = 90 cm = 0.9 m
                                       Length = 180 cm = 1.8 m

② Divide to get scale drawing length.   Width on drawing = 0.9 ÷ 1.5 = 0.6 cm
                                         Length on drawing = 1.8 ÷ 1.5 = 1.2 cm

③ Draw with a ruler in any sensible position and label.

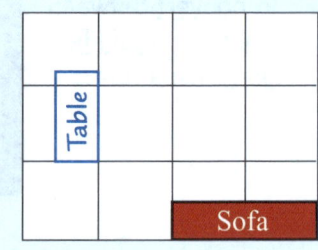

Map Questions Using Bearings

EXAMPLE:

Liam walks 1.2 km from the car park on a bearing of 120°.

a) Mark his position on the map.

① Work out how many km 1 cm represents.   1 cm = 20 000 cm
                                           = 200 m = 0.2 km. So 1 cm = 0.2 km

② Divide to get distance on map.   Distance walked on map = 1.2 ÷ 0.2
                                    = 6 cm

③ Mark a point 6 cm away, 120° clockwise from the North line.

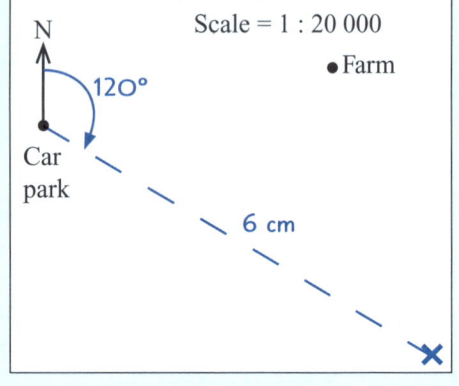

b) How far is he from the farm in km?

① Measure distance between Liam and farm.   Distance between Liam and farm = 4 cm

② For real life, multiply: Real distance = 4 × 0.2 = 0.8 km

Well, you should have got your bearings on map scales by now...

Keep your ruler and protractor handy when you're doing map and scale-drawing questions.

Q1 This is a scale drawing of a park. What does 1 cm represent? Mark on an area of woodland with dimensions 250 m × 300 m. [3 marks]

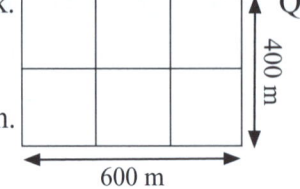

Q2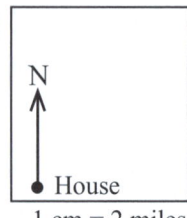
1 cm = 2 miles

A cinema is on a bearing of 035° from Ellie's house and is 5 miles away. Mark the cinema on this map. [3 marks]

Section Five — Measures and Angles

Pythagoras' Theorem

Once upon a time there lived a clever chap called Pythagoras. He made famous a clever theorem...

Pythagoras' Theorem is Used on Right-Angled Triangles

Pythagoras' theorem only works for RIGHT-ANGLED TRIANGLES.
It uses two sides to find the third side.

The formula for Pythagoras' theorem is: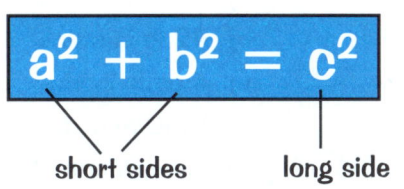

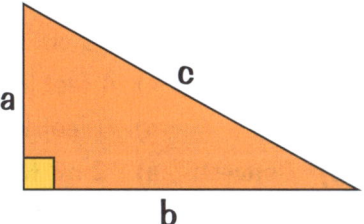

The formula can be quite tricky to use, so below it's been broken down into three simple steps. Follow these steps, and you won't go far wrong.

1) **SQUARE THEM** — SQUARE THE TWO NUMBERS that you are given, (use the x^2 button if you've got your calculator).

2) **ADD or SUBTRACT** — To find the longest side, ADD the two squared numbers. $a^2 + b^2 = c^2$
To find a shorter side, SUBTRACT the smaller from the larger. $c^2 - b^2 = a^2$

3) **SQUARE ROOT** — Once you've got your answer, take the SQUARE ROOT (use the $\sqrt{}$ button on your calculator). $c = \sqrt{a^2 + b^2}$
$a = \sqrt{c^2 - b^2}$

EXAMPLES:

1. Find the length of side PQ in this triangle.
   1) Square them: $a^2 = 5^2 = 25$, $b^2 = 12^2 = 144$
   2) You want to find the longest side, so ADD: $a^2 + b^2 = c^2$
      $25 + 144 = 169$
   3) Square root: $c = \sqrt{169} = 13$, so PQ = **13 cm**

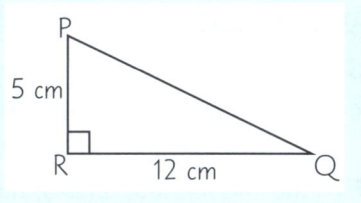

Always check the answer's sensible — 13 cm is longer than the other two sides, but not too much longer, so it seems OK.

2. Find the length of SU to 1 decimal place.
   1) Square them: $b^2 = 3^2 = 9$, $c^2 = 6^2 = 36$
   2) You want to find a shorter side, so SUBTRACT: $c^2 - b^2 = a^2$
      $36 - 9 = 27$
   3) Square root: $a = \sqrt{27} = 5.196...$,
      so SU = **5.2 m (to 1 d.p.)**

Check the answer is sensible — yes, it's a bit shorter than the longest side.

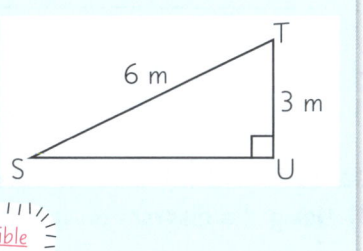

Remember, if it's not a right angle, it's a wrong angle...

Once you've learned all the Pythagoras facts, try these Exam Practice Questions.

Q1 Find the length of AC correct to 1 decimal place. [3 marks]

Q2 A 4 m long ladder leans against a wall. Its base is 1.2 m from the wall. How far up the wall does the ladder reach? Give your answer in metres to 1 decimal place. [3 marks]

Revision Questions for Section Five

There are lots of opportunities to show off your artistic skills here (as long as you use them to answer the questions).
- Try these questions and tick off each one when you get it right.
- When you've done all the questions for a topic and are completely happy with it, tick off the topic.

Conversions and Reading Scales (p60-63)

1) Convert: a) 38 cm to mm   b) 5.6 litres to cm³   c) 731 g to kg
2) Work out: a) 4 feet in inches b) 42 lb in stone   c) 2 gallons in pints
              d) 8 feet to cm   e) 4 pints in litres   f) 10 miles in km
3) Convert: a) 12 m³ to cm³   b) 1280 mm² to cm²   c) 2.75 cm³ to mm³
4) How do you work out what a small gap on a scale stands for?
5) How much orange juice is in the jug on the right?
6) An elephant weighs 6 tonnes to the nearest tonne. What is the range of possible weights that the elephant could be?

Time Intervals and Compound Units (p64-66)

7) Work out: a) 1 day in minutes   b) 2 weeks in hours   c) 14 400 seconds in hours
8) A musical production starts at 19:30. The musical is 118 minutes long plus a 20 minute interval. What time does the musical finish? Give your answer in 12-hour time.
9) Write down the formula triangle linking speed, distance and time.
10) Keerat's car uses 0.3 gallons of fuel over a 12-mile drive. How many miles per gallon can her car do?
11) A slab of concrete has a mass of 96 kg and a volume of 0.04 m³. What is its density?
12) What is 5 m/s in km/h?

Angles and Geometry Problems (p67-71)

13) What is the name for an angle larger than 90° but smaller than 180°?
14) The hexagon on the right has been split into 4 triangles. Use this information to find the sum of the hexagon's angles.
15) Find the missing angles, marked x, y and z, in the diagrams below.

    a) 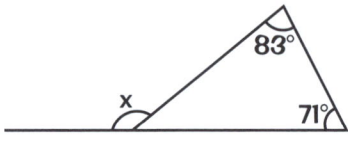   b) 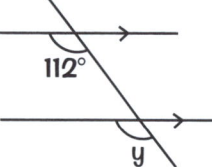   c)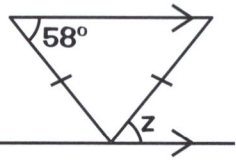

16) Find the exterior angle of a regular 9-sided shape.
17) Find the sum of the interior angles in a regular octagon.

Bearings, Maps and Scale Drawings (p72-74)

18) Using the diagram on the right, find the bearing of Y from X.

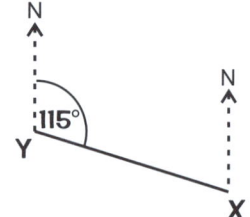

19) The scale on a map is 1 cm = 4 km. On the map, Ballycity is 6.5 cm away from Waterleg. How far is this in real life?
20) Jane travels on a bearing of 180° for 3 km. She then travels on a bearing of 145° from her new position for 6 km. Using a scale of 1 cm = 1.5 km, draw an accurate diagram to represent this.

Pythagoras' Theorem (p75)

21) Look at the triangle on the right. Find the length of YZ in cm to 1 d.p.
22) A rectangle has a diagonal of 15 cm. Its short side is 4 cm. Calculate the length of the rectangle's long side in cm to 1 d.p.

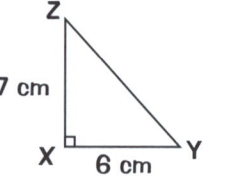

Section Six — Shapes and Area

Properties of 2D Shapes

Here's a nice easy page to get you started on 2D shapes.

Line Symmetry

This is where you draw one or more MIRROR LINES across a shape and both sides fold exactly together.

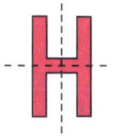  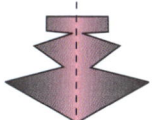 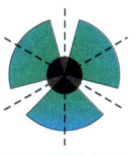  

| 2 LINES OF SYMMETRY | 1 LINE OF SYMMETRY | 1 LINE OF SYMMETRY | 3 LINES OF SYMMETRY | NO LINES OF SYMMETRY | 1 LINE OF SYMMETRY |

Rotational Symmetry

This is where you can rotate the shape into different positions that look exactly the same.

   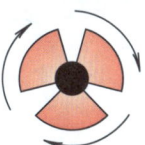 

Order 1   Order 2   Order 2   Order 3   Order 4

The ORDER OF ROTATIONAL SYMMETRY is the posh way of saying: 'how many different positions look the same'. You should say the Z-shape above has 'rotational symmetry of order 2'.

When a shape has only 1 position you can either say that it has 'rotational symmetry of order 1' or that it has 'NO rotational symmetry'.

Regular Polygons

All the sides and angles in a regular polygon are the same.
Learn the names of these regular polygons and how many sides they have.
(An equilateral triangle and a square are both regular polygons — see the next page for their properties.)

In an irregular polygon, the sides and angles aren't all equal.

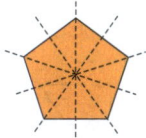
REGULAR PENTAGON
5 sides
5 lines of symmetry
Rotational symmetry of order 5

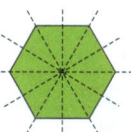
REGULAR HEXAGON
6 sides
6 lines of symmetry
Rotational symmetry of order 6

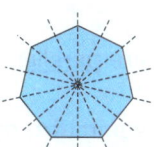
REGULAR HEPTAGON
7 sides
7 lines of symmetry
Rotational symmetry of order 7

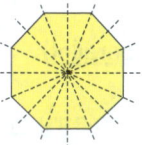
REGULAR OCTAGON
8 sides
8 lines of symmetry
Rotational symmetry of order 8

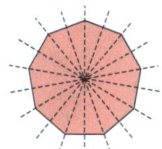
REGULAR NONAGON
9 sides
9 lines of symmetry
Rotational symmetry of order 9

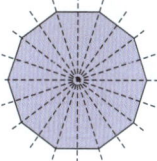
REGULAR DECAGON
10 sides
10 lines of symmetry
Rotational symmetry of order 10

Mirror line, mirror line on the wall...

Make sure you learn the two different types of symmetry, and dazzle your friends by spotting them in everyday shapes like road signs, warning signs and letters.

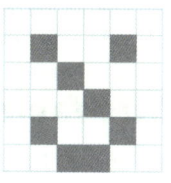

Q1 Make two copies of the pattern to the right.
   a) Shade two squares to make a pattern with one line of symmetry. [1 mark]
   b) Shade two squares to make a pattern with rotational symmetry of order 2. [1 mark]

Properties of 2D Shapes

This page is jam-packed with details about triangles and quadrilaterals — and you need to learn them all.

Triangles

1) **EQUILATERAL TRIANGLES**
   3 equal sides and
   3 equal angles of 60°.
   3 lines of symmetry,
   rotational symmetry order 3.

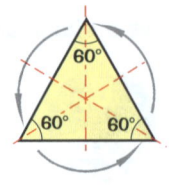

2) **RIGHT-ANGLED TRIANGLES**
   1 right angle (90°).
   No lines of symmetry
   (unless it's also isosceles).
   No rotational symmetry.

   The little square means it's a right angle.

3) **ISOSCELES TRIANGLES**
   2 sides the same.
   2 angles the same.
   1 line of symmetry.
   No rotational symmetry.

   These dashes mean that the two sides are the same length.

4) **SCALENE TRIANGLES**
   All three sides different.
   All three angles different.
   No symmetry (pretty obviously).

An acute-angled triangle has 3 acute angles, and an obtuse-angled triangle has one obtuse angle (see p67).

Quadrilaterals

1) **SQUARE**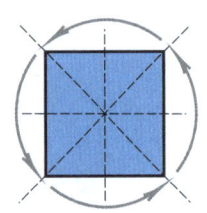
   4 equal angles of 90° (right angles).
   4 lines of symmetry, rotational symmetry order 4.

2) **RECTANGLE**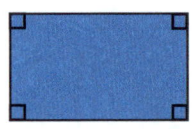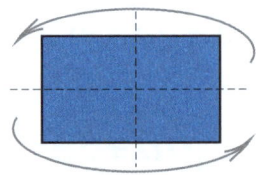
   4 equal angles of 90° (right angles).
   2 lines of symmetry, rotational symmetry order 2.

3) **RHOMBUS** (A square pushed over)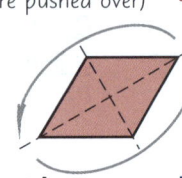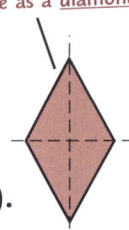
   A rhombus is the same as a diamond.
   Matching arrows show parallel sides.
   4 equal sides (opposite sides are parallel).
   2 pairs of equal angles.
   2 lines of symmetry, rotational symmetry order 2.

4) **PARALLELOGRAM** (A rectangle pushed over)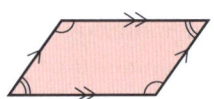
   2 pairs of equal sides (each pair are parallel).
   2 pairs of equal angles.
   NO lines of symmetry, rotational symmetry order 2.

5) **TRAPEZIUM**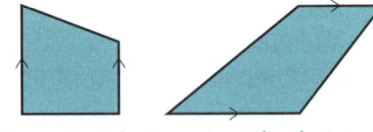
   1 pair of parallel sides.
   NO lines of symmetry*.
   No rotational symmetry.

6) **KITE**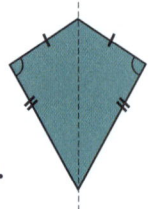
   2 pairs of equal sides.
   1 pair of equal angles.
   1 line of symmetry.
   No rotational symmetry.

*In an isosceles trapezium, the sloping sides are the same length. An isosceles trapezium has 1 line of symmetry.

Kite facts — 2 pairs of equal sides, 1 line of symmetry, Gemini...

Learn the names (and spellings) and properties of all the shapes on this page, then try this question:

Q1 A quadrilateral has all 4 sides the same length and two pairs of equal angles.
    Identify the quadrilateral, and write down its order of rotational symmetry. [2 marks]

Section Six — Shapes and Area

Perimeter and Area

Perimeter is the distance around the outside of a shape. Area is trickier — you need to learn some formulas.

Area Formulas for Triangles and Rectangles

Learn these formulas:

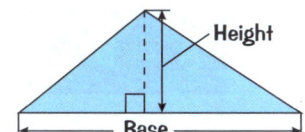

Area of triangle = ½ × base × vertical height

Area of rectangle = base × height

$A = ½ \times b \times h$

$A = b \times h$

The formula for the area of a rectangle and a square are the same, but the base and height of a square are equal.

EXAMPLE: For the triangle shown on the right:

a) Find the perimeter.
   Make sure all the side lengths are labelled, then add them up:
   17 cm + 20 cm + 21 cm = **58 cm**

b) Find the area.
   Use the formula for the area of a triangle:
   Area of triangle = $\frac{1}{2}$ × base × height = $\frac{1}{2}$ × 21 × 12 = **126 cm²**

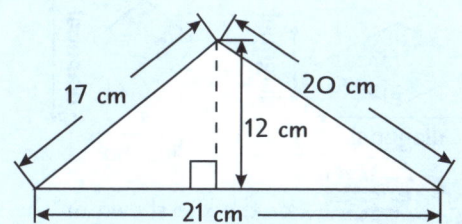

Perimeter and Area Problems

You might have to use the perimeter or area of a shape to answer a slightly more complicated question (e.g. find the area of a wall, then work out how many rolls of wallpaper you need to wallpaper it).

EXAMPLE: Logan is making a stained-glass window in the shape shown below.

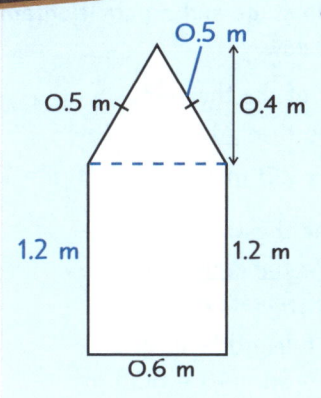

a) Find the perimeter of the window.
   Label all the side lengths, then add them up:
   0.5 m + 1.2 m + 0.6 m + 1.2 m + 0.5 m = **4 m**

When you're adding side lengths it's a good idea to mark them off as you go along to make sure you don't repeat or miss any.

b) Coloured glass costs £82 per m². Work out the cost of the glass needed for the window.
   Split the shape into a triangle and a rectangle (as shown) to find the area:
   Area of rectangle = length × width = 0.6 × 1.2 = 0.72 m²
   Area of triangle = $\frac{1}{2}$ × base × height = $\frac{1}{2}$ × 0.6 × 0.4 = 0.12 m²
   Total area of shape = 0.72 + 0.12 = **0.84 m²**

   Then multiply the area by the price to work out the cost:
   Cost = area × price per m² = 0.84 × 82 = **£68.88**

No jokes about my vertical height please...

If you have a compound shape (a shape made up of different shapes stuck together), split it into triangles and quadrilaterals, work out the area of each bit and add them together.

Q1 The triangle and rectangle shown on the right have the same area. Find the value of x. [2 marks]

Perimeter and Area

If you love perimeter and area stuff then celebrate now — because there's another page of it...

Area Formulas for Quadrilaterals

The formulas for the areas of parallelograms and trapeziums are:

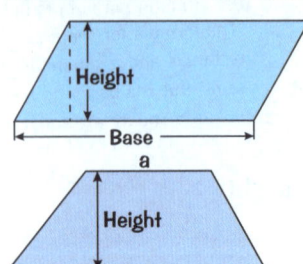

Area of parallelogram = base × vertical height

$A = b \times h$

Area of trapezium = average of parallel sides × distance between them (vertical height)

$A = \frac{1}{2}(a + b) \times h$

The formula for the area of a rhombus or a kite is the same:

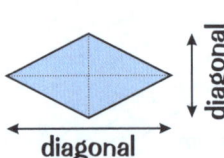 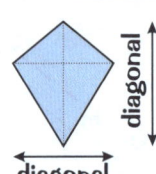

Area of rhombus or kite = ½ × diagonal × diagonal

$A = \frac{1}{2} \times d \times d$

EXAMPLE: For the kite shown on the right:
a) Find the perimeter.
Label all the side lengths, then add them up:
10 cm + 14 cm + 14 cm + 10 cm = **48 cm**

b) Find the area.
Use the formula for the area of a kite:
Area of a kite = $\frac{1}{2}$ × diagonal × diagonal = $\frac{1}{2}$ × 15 × 18 = **135 cm²**

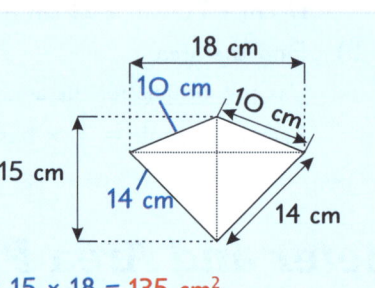

Perimeter and Area for Composite Shapes

You might be asked to find the perimeter or area of shapes made up of different shapes stuck together.

EXAMPLE: An open-air theatre is made up of a trapezium-shaped main stage and a parallelogram-shaped backstage. The floor plan of the theatre is shown below.

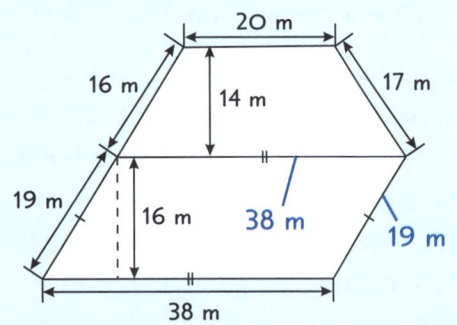

a) What is the perimeter of the theatre?
Label all the side lengths, then add them up:
38 m + 19 m + 16 m + 20 m + 17 m + 19 m = **129 m**

b) What is the area of the theatre?
Work out the area of the trapezium stage and parallelogram stage separately:
Area of parallelogram = length × height
= 38 × 16 = 608 m²

Area of trapezium = $\frac{1}{2}$ × (base + top) × height = $\frac{1}{2}$ × (38 + 20) × 14 = 29 × 14 = 406 m²

Then add them together: Total area of the theatre = 608 + 406 = **1014 m²**

The area of a trapezium guitar = bass × vertical height...

Don't forget the factor of ½ when calculating the area of trapeziums, rhombuses and kites (and triangles).

Q1 A shape is made up of a triangle and a parallelogram. The triangle has base length 3 cm and the parallelogram has base length 11 cm. They both have a vertical height of 6 cm. Find the total area of the shape. [3 marks]

Circles

There are a surprising number of circle terms you need to know — don't mix them up.

Radius, Diameter and Chord

The DIAMETER goes right across the circle, passing through the centre.
The RADIUS goes from the centre of the circle to any point on the edge.

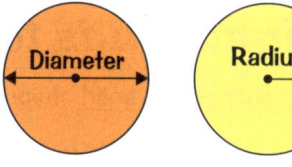

The DIAMETER IS EXACTLY DOUBLE THE RADIUS

So if the radius is 4 cm, the diameter is 8 cm.

A CHORD is just a line between two points on the edge of a circle.

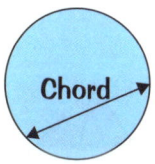

Area, Circumference and π

There are two more important formulas for you to learn here — circumference and area. The circumference is the distance round the outside of the circle (its perimeter).

1) **CIRCUMFERENCE** = π × diameter
   = π × radius × 2
   (as diameter = 2 × radius)

   $C = \pi \times D$ or $C = 2 \times \pi \times r$

   π = 3.141592.... = 3.142 (approx.)
   The big thing to remember is that π (called "pi") is just an ordinary number (3.14159...) which is sometimes rounded off to 3.142. You should try to use the unrounded version in calculations where possible — your calculator will have a π button.

2) **AREA** = π × (radius)² 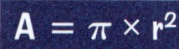 $A = \pi \times r^2$

Area and Perimeter of Semicircles

There are some extra steps when you're finding the area and perimeter of a semicircle (half circle).
1) **AREA**: find the area of the whole circle then divide by 2.
2) **PERIMETER**: divide the circumference by 2 and add on the straight edge (i.e. the diameter of the circle).

For the area or perimeter of a quarter circle you divide by 4 instead of dividing by 2.

EXAMPLE: Find the area and perimeter of the semicircle shown on the right. Give your answers to 2 decimal places.

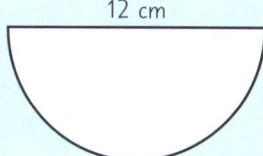

First find the area of the whole circle then divide by 2:
Radius = 12 ÷ 2 = 6 cm
Area of whole circle = π × r² = π × 6² = π × 36 = 113.097...
So area of semicircle = 113.097... ÷ 2 = 56.548... = **56.55 cm² (2 d.p.)**

Find the circumference of the circle and divide by 2 to find the curved edge...
Circumference of whole circle = π × D = π × 12 = 37.699...
So curved edge = 37.699... ÷ 2 = 18.849...

Then add on the diameter to find the total perimeter:
Perimeter = curved edge + diameter = 18.849... + 12 = 30.849... = **30.85 cm (2 d.p.)**

Mmm — pi...

Circles can also crop up in composite shape questions (see pages 79 and 80), but use the formulas in the usual way and it should all work out fine. You can always draw a sketch to help you figure it out if you're not given a diagram in the question.

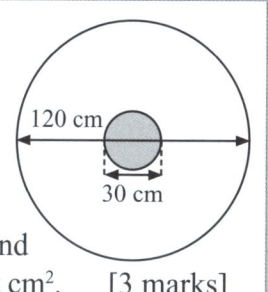

Q1 Safiya is making a tutu out of a circle of netting with diameter 120 cm. She cuts a circular hole with diameter 30 cm out of the middle of the netting and puts this away. Find the area of netting that she keeps for the tutu to the nearest cm². **[3 marks]**

Section Six — Shapes and Area

3D Shapes

I was going to make some pop-out 3D shapes to put on this page, but I couldn't find the scissors and sticky tape. Sorry. Still, you need to learn it all though — so chin up and learn the page.

Eight Solids to Learn

3D shapes are solid shapes. These are the ones you need to know:

There's more about prisms on p84.

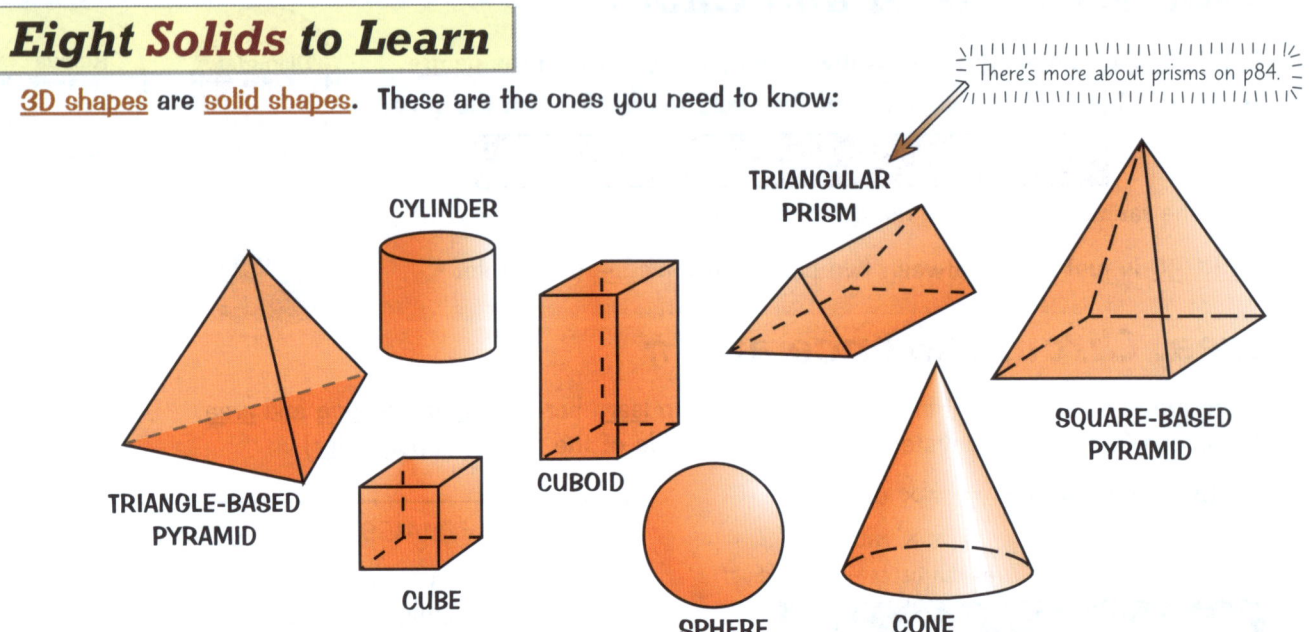

Different Parts of Solids

There are different parts of 3D shapes you need to be able to spot. These are vertices (corners), faces (the flat bits) and edges. You might be asked for the number of vertices, faces and edges in the exam — just count them up, and don't forget the hidden ones.

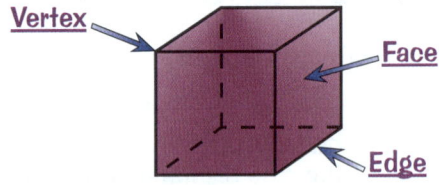

Faces (especially curved faces) are sometimes called surfaces.

EXAMPLE: For the triangular prism on the right, write down the number of faces, the number of edges and the number of vertices.

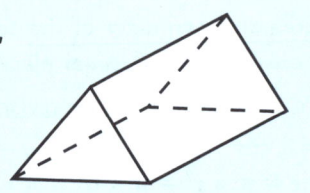

A triangular prism has **5 faces** (there are three rectangular faces and two triangular ones).

It has **9 edges** (there are 3 hidden ones — the dotted lines in the diagram).

It has **6 vertices** (there's one hidden at the back).

Edge, vertex, face and toes, face and toes. Edge, vertex...

Remember — 1 vertex, 2 vertices. They're funny words, designed to confuse you, so don't let them catch you out. Now have a go at this Exam Practice Question.

Q1   a) Write down the mathematical name of the shape on the right.   [1 mark]
       b) Write down: (i)   the number of faces   [1 mark]
                        (ii)   the number of edges   [1 mark]
                        (iii)   the number of vertices   [1 mark]

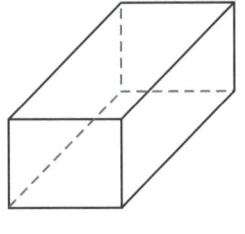

Section Six — Shapes and Area

Cubes and Cuboids

Nets aren't just used to catch fish — they're used to help find the surface area of cubes and cuboids.

Nets and Surface Area

1) A NET is just a hollow 3D shape folded out flat.
2) There's often more than one net that can be drawn for a 3D shape (see the cube example below).
3) SURFACE AREA only applies to solid 3D objects — it's the total area of all the faces added together.
4) There are two ways to find the surface area:

> 1) Work out the area of each face and add them all together (don't forget the hidden faces).
> 2) Sketch the net, then find the area of the net (this is the method we'll use on these pages).

Remember — SURFACE AREA OF SOLID = AREA OF NET.

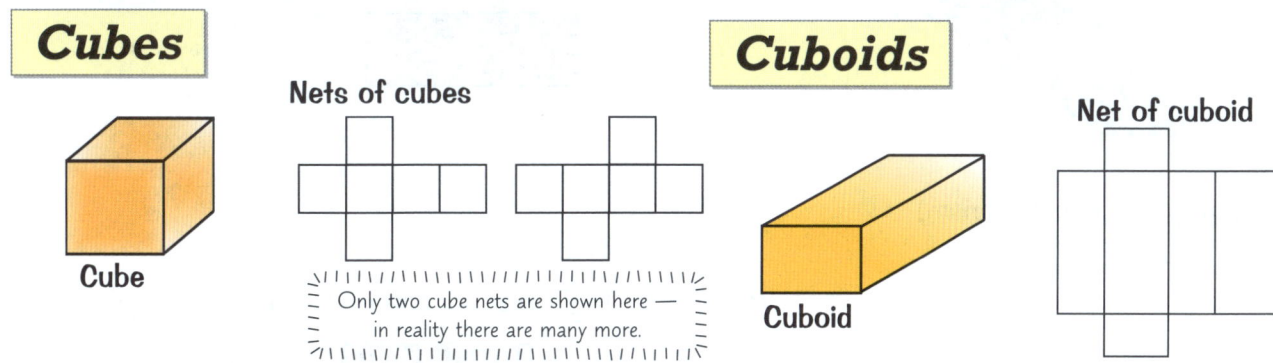

Cubes
Cube

Nets of cubes

Only two cube nets are shown here — in reality there are many more.

Cuboids
Cuboid

Net of cuboid

Volumes of Cuboids

A cuboid is a rectangular block. Finding its volume is dead easy:

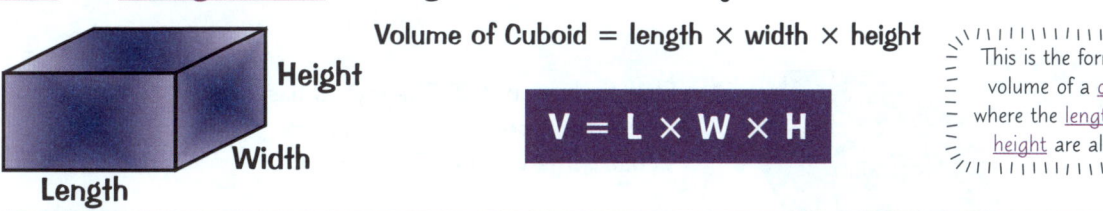

Volume of Cuboid = length × width × height

$$V = L \times W \times H$$

This is the formula for the volume of a cube too — where the length, width and height are all the same.

 **EXAMPLE:**

a) Find the surface area of this cuboid:

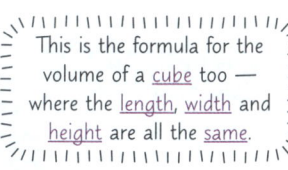

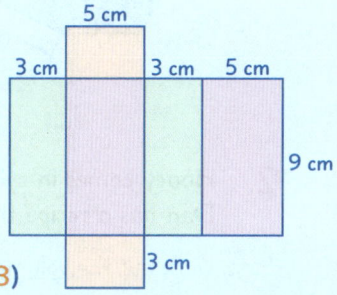

Sketch the net of the shape, and label all the measurements:

Then work out the surface area of each face and add them up (note there are 2 each of 3 different rectangles).

Surface area = 2(3 × 9) + 2(5 × 9) + 2(5 × 3)
= 54 + 90 + 30 = **174 cm²**

b) Find the volume of the cuboid.

The formula for the volume is just length × width × height. Make sure you've got all three of these, then multiply them together.

Volume = 5 × 9 × 3 = **135 cm³**

Net yourself some extra marks...

When finding the surface area of a cube or cuboid, it's probably best to draw out its net. This way you won't miss out any sneaky, hidden faces.

Q1 A cuboid has length 12 cm, width 4 cm and height 6 cm. Find its volume. [1 mark]

Q2 Draw an accurate net for a cube with side length 1.5 cm. [2 marks]

Section Six — Shapes and Area

Prisms

Where do mathematicians go when they commit a crime? Prism.

Volumes of Prisms

> A PRISM is a solid (3D) object which is the same shape all the way through — i.e. it has a CONSTANT AREA OF CROSS-SECTION.

Triangular Prism

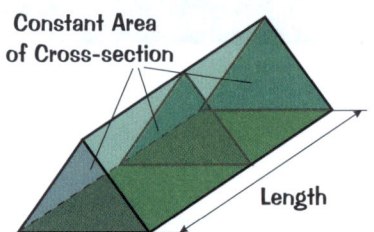

Volume of Prism = cross-sectional area × length

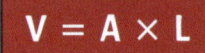

This formula works for any prism.

Cylinder (circular prism)

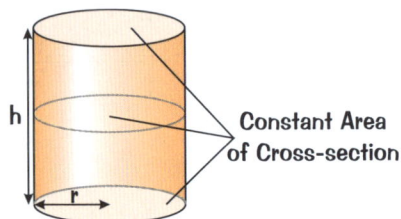

Volume of Cylinder = area of circle × height

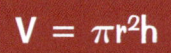

$V = \pi r^2 h$

This is still V = A × L, where A = πr^2 and L = h.

EXAMPLES:

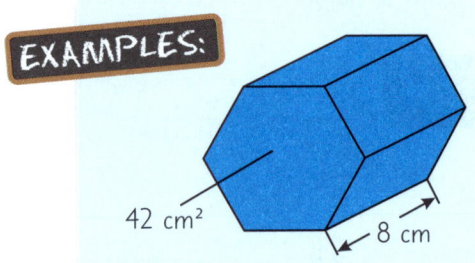

1. Elsie finds a crystal. The crystal has a hexagonal prism shape as shown. What is the volume of the crystal?

   Use the formula for prisms:
   V = A × L = 42 × 8 = **336 cm³**

2. Honey comes in cylindrical jars with radius 4.5 cm and height 12 cm. Dan has a recipe that needs 1 litre of honey. How many jars should he buy?

   First, work out the volume of the jar — just use the formula above:
   $V = \pi r^2 h = \pi \times 4.5^2 \times 12 = 763.4070...$ cm³
   1 litre = 1000 cm³ (see p60), so he needs to buy **2 jars of honey**.

   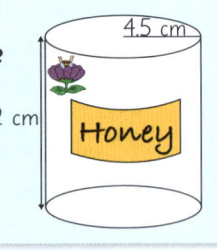

Don't make it any more angry — it's already a cross-section…

Prisms can be any sort of shape — rectangular, pentagonal, circular or any other — as long as it's the same shape all the way through. Cubes and cuboids (see p83) are both the same shape all the way through, so they are also prisms — rectangular prisms. Have a go at this Exam Practice Question — you'll need your area formulas from p79.

Q1 Find the volume of the triangular prism on the right.
    Give your answer in the correct units.   [3 marks]

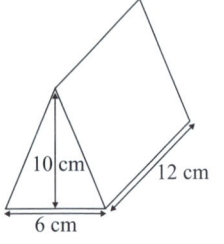

Section Six — Shapes and Area

Plans and Elevations

Plans and elevations are just different views of a 3D solid shape — looking at it from the front, side and top.

The Three Different Views

There are three different types of view — front elevations, side elevations and plans (these three types can also be called projections).

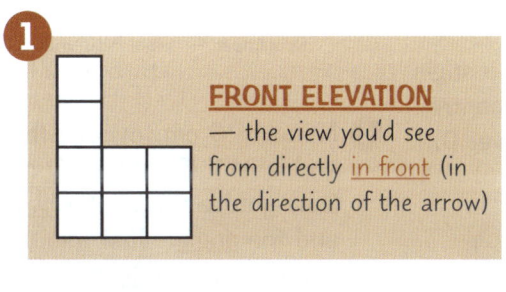

① FRONT ELEVATION — the view you'd see from directly in front (in the direction of the arrow)

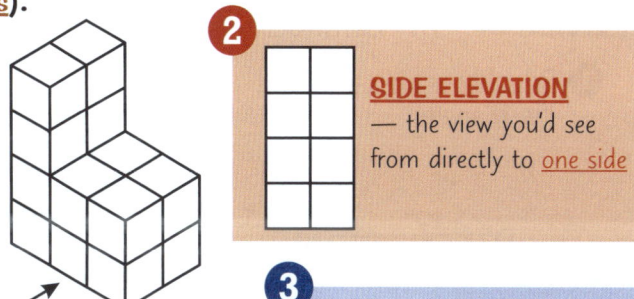

② SIDE ELEVATION — the view you'd see from directly to one side

③ PLAN — the view you'd see from directly above

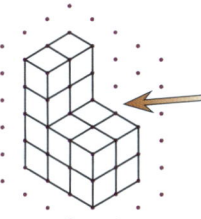

Don't be thrown if you're given a diagram on isometric (dotty) paper like this — it works in just the same way. If you have to draw shapes on isometric paper, just join the dots. You should only draw vertical and diagonal lines (no horizontal lines).

Drawing Elevations

EXAMPLES:

1. The front elevation and plan view of a shape are shown below. Sketch the solid shape.

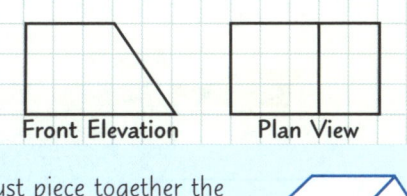

Front Elevation   Plan View

Just piece together the original shape from the information given — here you get a prism in the shape of the front elevation.

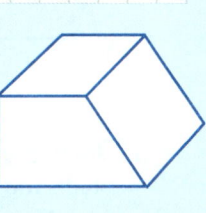

2. a) On the cm square grid, draw the front elevation of the prism from the direction of the arrow.
   b) Draw a plan of the prism on the grid.

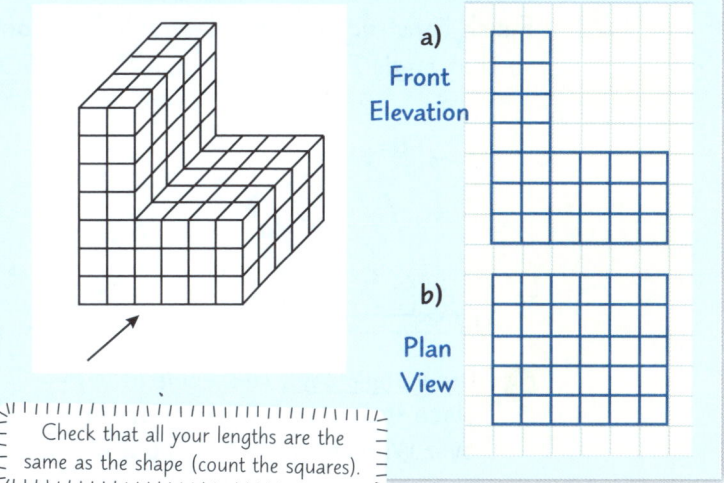

a) Front Elevation

b) Plan View

Check that all your lengths are the same as the shape (count the squares).

Elevations — enough to send you dotty...

This type of question's not too bad — just take your time and sketch the diagrams carefully. Watch out for questions on isometric paper — they might look confusing, but they can actually be easier than other questions.

Q1 For the shape on the right, draw:
    a) The front elevation (from the direction of the arrow),   [1 mark]
    b) The side elevation,   [1 mark]
    c) The plan view.   [1 mark]

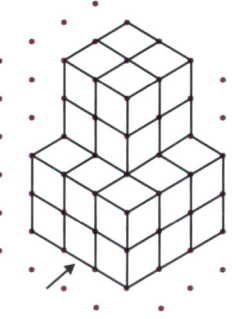

Section Six — Shapes and Area

Construction

How you construct triangles and quadrilaterals depends on what info you're given. If you've got enough sides and angles you can use a ruler and a protractor. Otherwise you might need to use compasses (p87).

Constructing using a Ruler and a Protractor

EXAMPLES:

1. Construct triangle DEF. DE = 5 cm, DF = 3 cm, and angle EDF = 40°.

① Roughly sketch and label the triangle.

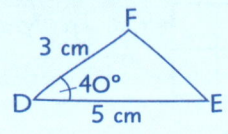

② Draw the base line.

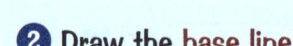

③ Draw angle EDF (the angle at D) — place the centre of the protractor over D, measure 40° and put a dot.

Remember — angle ABC means the angle between lines AB and BC.

④ Measure 3 cm towards the dot and label it F. Join up D and F. Now you've drawn the two sides and the angle. Just join up F and E to complete the triangle.

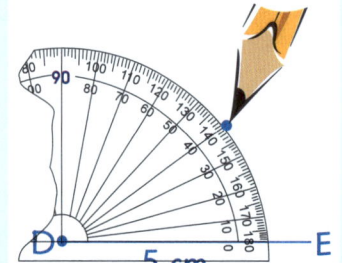

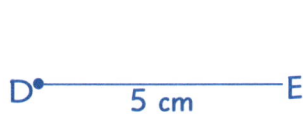

If you're given two angles and one side the method for constructing a triangle is similar:

1) First draw the side you have, make it the base and make it the right length. Then use your protractor to measure the two angles at each end of the line (marking them out with dots).
2) Use a ruler to draw from each end towards the dots you've marked out.
3) The point where these lines meet is the third corner of the triangle.

2. Finish constructing quadrilateral WXYZ on the right, so that angle ZWX = 30° and XYZ = 160°.

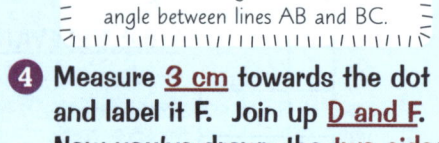

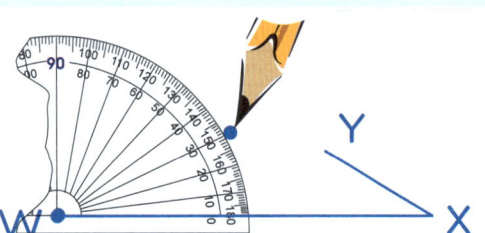

① Draw angle ZWX (the angle at W) — place the centre of the protractor over W, measure 30° and put a dot.

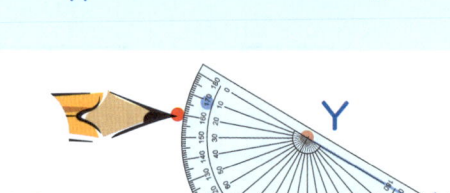

② Draw angle XYZ (the angle at Y) — place the centre of the protractor over Y, measure 160° and put a dot.

③ Draw from W towards the blue dot and from Y towards the red dot. The point at which both lines meet completes the quadrilateral.

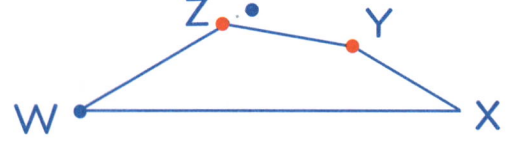

Pencils at the ready — three, two, one... Construct...

Constructions are always better when drawn with a nice sharp pencil. So remember to get that sharpener out and make sure your pencils, like your brain, are sharp before the exam.

Q1 Construct triangle PQR where PQ = 6 cm, angle RPQ = 70° and angle PQR = 30°. [2 marks]

Section Six — Shapes and Area

Construction

Don't just read the page through once and hope you'll remember it — get your ruler, compasses and pencil out and have a go. It's the only way of testing whether you really know this stuff.

Constructing Triangles Using Compasses

EXAMPLE: Construct the triangle ABC where AB = 6 cm, BC = 4 cm, AC = 5 cm.

① First, sketch and label a triangle so you know roughly what's needed. It doesn't matter which line you make the base line.

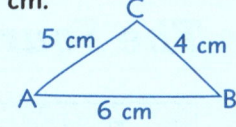

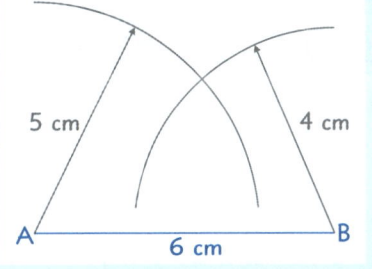

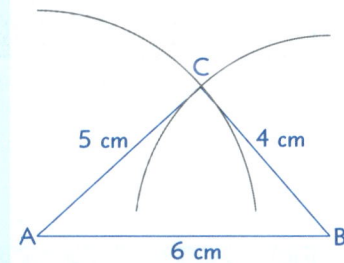

② Draw the base line. Label the ends A and B.

③ For AC, set the compasses to 5 cm, put the point at A and draw an arc. For BC, set the compasses to 4 cm, put the point at B and draw an arc.

④ Where the arcs cross is point C. Now you can finish your triangle.

Constructing Equilateral Triangles

1) You might be asked to draw an accurate equilateral triangle without a protractor.

2) Follow the method shown in this diagram (make sure you leave the compass settings the same for each step).

3) If you just want a 60° angle, you can ignore Step 3 where you join up the triangle.

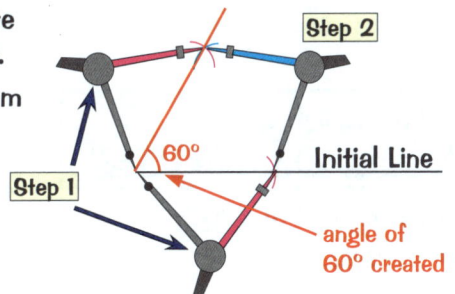
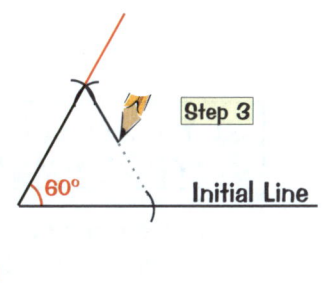

Construct Right Angles to Draw the Perpendicular

1) If you're asked to draw a perpendicular from a point to a line, you'll be given a line and a point, like this: A——————B   •

2) Follow the method in the diagram to draw the perpendicular. This is the shortest distance between the point and the line.

3) You can use this method if you just want an accurate 90° angle — simply put the initial point on the line itself, where you want the angle to be.

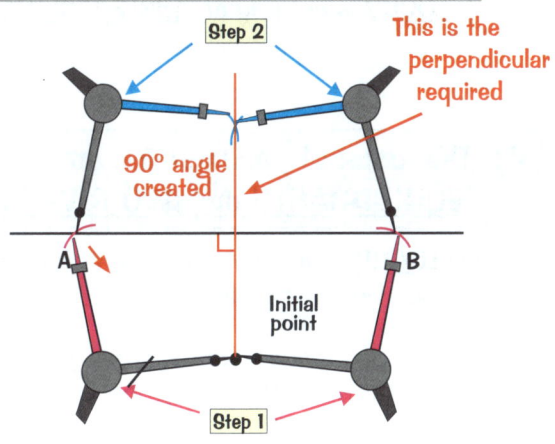

My compasses don't construct anything — they just point north...

You can't do these constructions 'by eye' or with a protractor. You've got to do them with compasses — so don't rub out your compass marks, or the examiner won't know you used the proper method.

Q1   Construct an equilateral triangle with sides of 5 cm. Leave visible construction marks. [2 marks]

Section Six — Shapes and Area

Loci and Construction

A LOCUS (another ridiculous maths word) is simply:

A LINE or REGION that shows all the points which fit a given rule.

Make sure you learn how to do these PROPERLY using a ruler and compasses as shown below.

The Four Different Types of Loci

Loci is just the plural of locus.

1) The locus of points which are 'A FIXED DISTANCE from a given POINT'.

This locus is simply a CIRCLE.

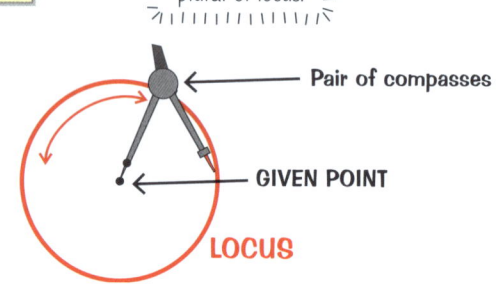

2) The locus of points which are 'A FIXED DISTANCE from a given LINE'.

This locus is a SAUSAGE SHAPE.

It has straight sides (drawn with a ruler) and ends which are perfect semicircles (drawn with compasses).

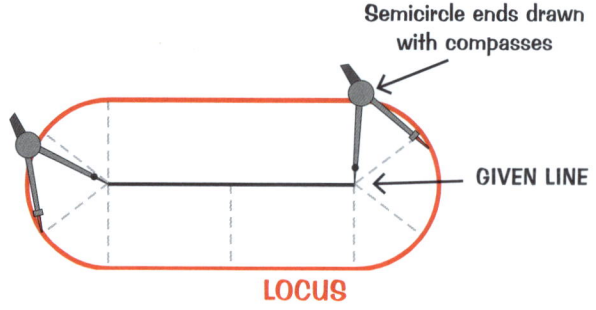

3) The locus of points which are 'EQUIDISTANT from TWO GIVEN LINES'.

1) Keep the compass setting THE SAME while you make all four marks.
2) Make sure you leave your compass marks showing.
3) You get two equal angles — i.e. this LOCUS is actually an ANGLE BISECTOR.

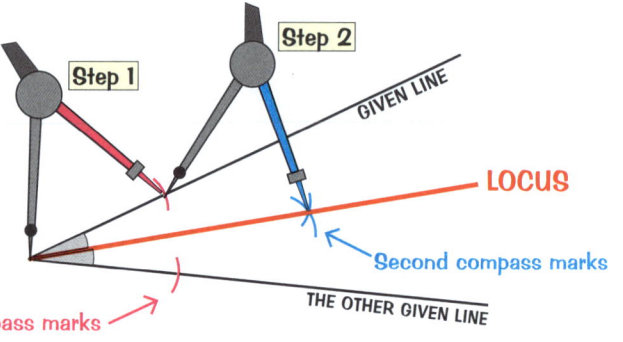

4) The locus of points which are 'EQUIDISTANT from TWO GIVEN POINTS'.

This LOCUS is all points which are the same distance from A as they are from B.

This time the locus is actually the PERPENDICULAR BISECTOR of the line joining the two points.

(In the diagram below, A and B are the two given points.)

Keep the compass setting THE SAME for all of these arcs.

The perpendicular bisector of line segment AB is a line at right angles to AB, passing through the midpoint of AB. This is the method to use if you're asked to draw it.

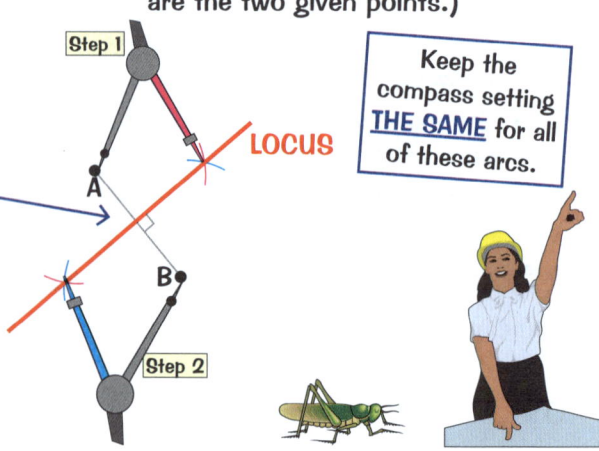

Section Six — Shapes and Area

Loci and Construction — Examples

After all that learning it must be time for a break, right? Wrong. There will be time for tea and biscuits later. For now it's all about learning how to put all that crazy loci knowledge to good use.

EXAMPLES:

1. A farmer wants to place a fence around his chicken coop. It should be exactly 2 m from the coop on all sides. Using a scale of 1 cm = 1 m, draw where the fence should go.

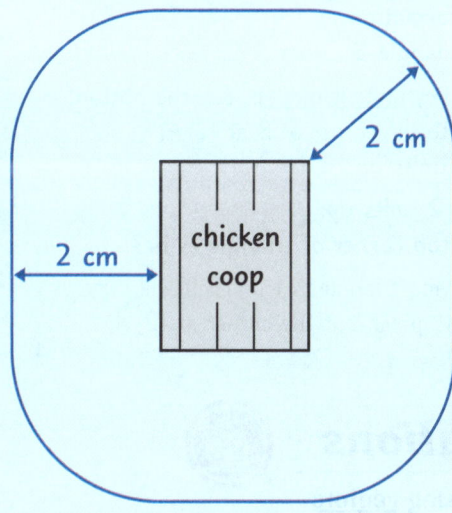

1) 1 cm = 1 m, so 2 m = 2 cm.

2) Set your compasses to 2 cm.

3) Place the point on each corner and draw a quarter-circle at each one.

4) Draw lines parallel to each edge of the chicken coop 2 cm away, joining up the ends of the quarter-circles.

2. Point P lies somewhere in triangle ABC. Shade the area in which P could lie, given that:

P is at least 4 cm away from A.
P is closer to B than C.

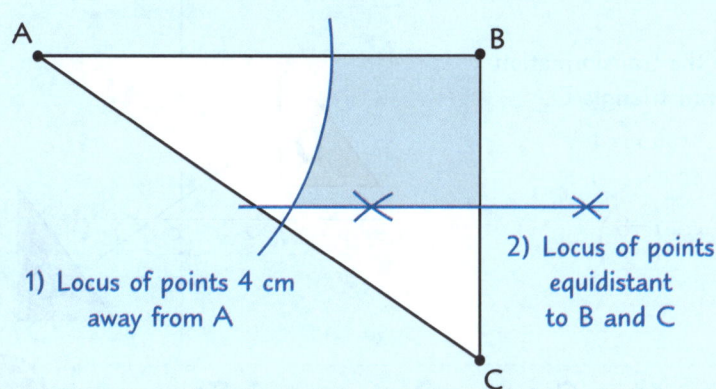

1) Set your compasses to 4 cm. Place the point on A and draw an arc.

2) Draw the perpendicular bisector of line BC using the method given on page 88.

3) Shade the area that's at least 4 cm away from A and closer to B than C.

Always leave your construction lines showing.
They show the examiner that you used the proper method.

Stay at least 3 m away from point C — or I'll release the hounds...

I can't stress this enough — make sure you draw your diagrams ACCURATELY (using a ruler and a pair of compasses). Now try this practice question:

Q1 In an art gallery, visitors must stay at least 2 m away from the portrait and at least 2 m away from the statue. Make a copy of the diagram using a scale of 1 cm = 1 m and indicate the area where visitors can go. [4 marks]

Section Six — Shapes and Area

Translation

The next few pages cover the four transformations you need to know. The first one is translation...

Translations Move Shapes

A translation is just a SLIDE around the page.
You can describe a translation in words by saying how many units a shape has moved.

EXAMPLE:

a) Describe in words the transformation that maps triangle A onto triangle B.

Pick a corner of the triangle and see how many units it moves. E.g. the bottom left corner of A is at (2, 1) and corresponds to the corner of B at (2, 4). So the transformation is **a translation of 3 units up**.

b) Triangle A is translated 1 unit left and 2 units up. What will the new coordinates of the top corner of triangle A be?

The corner starts at coordinates (3, 2). Moving triangle A 1 unit left will put the corner at (2, 2). Then moving it 2 units up will put the corner at **(2, 4)**.

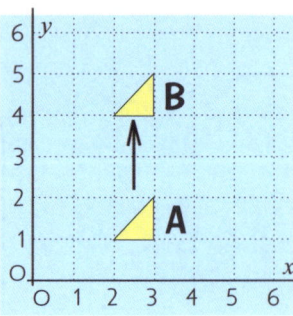

Vectors Describe Translations

A lot of the time, translations are described using vectors.

Vectors describing translations look like this.
x is the number of spaces right,
y is the number of spaces up.
$\begin{pmatrix} x \\ y \end{pmatrix}$

If the shape moves left, x will be negative. If it moves down, y will be negative.

EXAMPLE: Use vectors to describe the transformation that maps triangle C onto triangle D.

To get from triangle C to triangle D you need to move 8 units left and 4 units up, so it's:

A translation by the vector $\begin{pmatrix} -8 \\ 4 \end{pmatrix}$

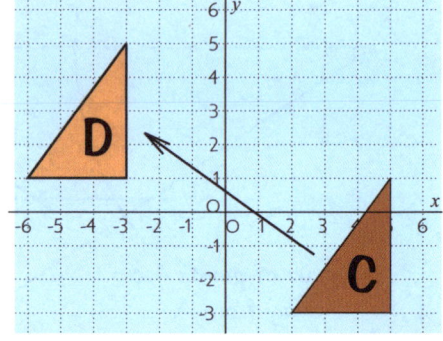

Congruent Shapes are the Same Size and Shape

1) Congruent means identical in size and shape. Shapes that have been rotated or reflected can still be congruent.
2) When a shape is translated, the lengths and angles of the shape DO NOT change. So it is said that length and angle are PRESERVED (stay the same) under translations.
3) This means a translated shape is congruent with its original shape.

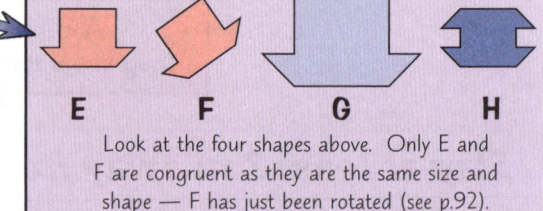

Look at the four shapes above. Only E and F are congruent as they are the same size and shape — F has just been rotated (see p.92).

Moving eet to ze left — a perfect translation...

Remember, translations don't change size or shape — they just move the shape somewhere else.

Q1 Triangle D in the example above is translated by the vector $\begin{pmatrix} 2 \\ -2 \end{pmatrix}$. What coordinates will its bottom right corner be at after the translation? [2 marks]

Section Six — Shapes and Area

Reflection

The second transformation is reflection. And no this isn't a chance to check yourself out in the mirror.

Reflections in the x- and y-axes

A mirror line is a line in which a shape is reflected.

When the mirror line is the x- or y-axis:
1) The reflection of a shape is the same distance away from the axis as the original shape.
2) To describe a reflection, you must give the axis that the shape has been reflected in.

EXAMPLE:
a) Describe the transformation that maps shape A onto shape B.

Shape A and shape B are both the same distance away from the x-axis. So the transformation is **a reflection in the x-axis**.

b) Shape B is reflected in the y-axis. What will the coordinates of this corner be after the shape is reflected?

The labelled corner is at (−4, −1) so it is 4 units left of the y-axis. So the reflected corner will be 4 units right of the y-axis, at **(4, −1)**.

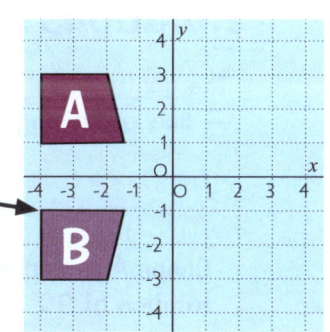

Reflections in Lines Parallel to the x- or y-axis

1) Shapes can also be reflected in lines other than the x- and y-axes — you need to know about those that are parallel to the axes.
2) To describe a reflection (when it's not in the x- or y-axis), you must give the equation of the mirror line.
3) E.g. triangle C is mapped onto triangle D by a reflection in the line $x = 1$.

The matching corners are equal distances from the mirror line.

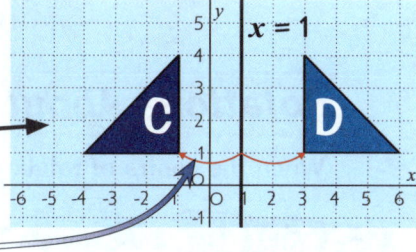

EXAMPLE: Reflect shape E in the line $y = 3$

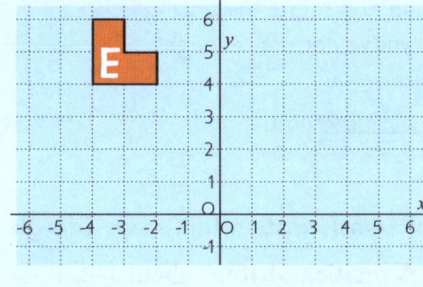

① Draw the line $y = 3$.

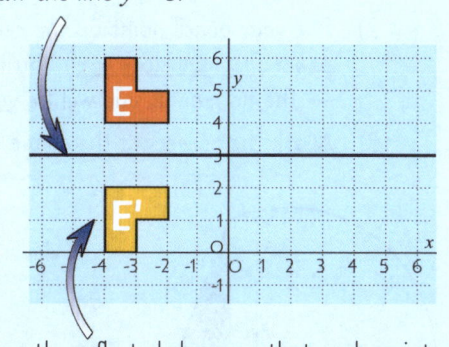

② Draw the reflected shape so that each point of it is the same distance from $y = 3$ as the original shape.

Like translations (see p90), length and angle are preserved under reflections.

Learn this stuff and reflections will become clear...

You're allowed to use tracing paper in the exam — use it to check your answers to reflection questions. Trace the original shape and the mirror line, then flip the tracing paper over and line up the mirror lines. If you've done the reflection correctly, the shapes will match up perfectly.

Q1 On a grid, copy shape A above and reflect it in the line $x = −1$. Label the new shape A′. [2 marks]

Section Six — Shapes and Area

Rotation

Say hello to transformation number 3 — rotation.

Rotation is When a Shape Turns About a Point

To describe a rotation, you must give 3 details:
1) The angle of rotation (usually 90° or 180°).
2) The direction of rotation (clockwise or anticlockwise).
3) The centre of rotation.

Rotations About the Origin

The centre of rotation is sometimes the origin (0, 0) — like in the diagram to the right.

Have a look at Example 1 below to see how to perform a rotation — just put the centre at (0, 0) whenever you're asked to rotate around the origin.

Shape A is mapped onto Shape B by a rotation of 90° clockwise about the origin.

Shape A is mapped onto Shape C by a rotation of 180° about the origin.

For a rotation of 180°, it doesn't matter whether you go clockwise or anticlockwise.

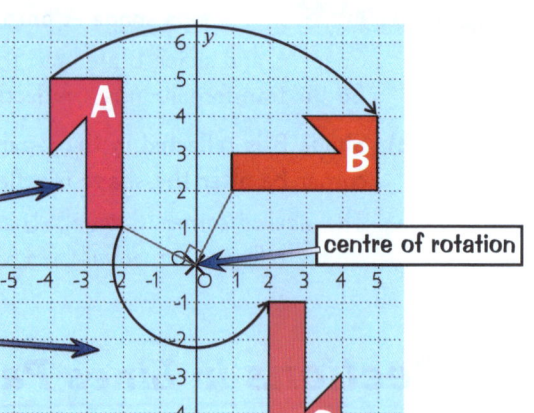

Rotations About Any Point

When the centre of rotation isn't the origin, things get a little trickier.

EXAMPLES:

1. Rotate Triangle D 90° anticlockwise about (1, 1).

   The best way to tackle this is with tracing paper:
   1) Trace the shape and mark the centre of rotation at (1, 1).
   2) Put your pencil point on the centre of rotation and rotate the tracing paper 90° anticlockwise. You'll know when you've gone far enough — the horizontal side will be vertical, and vice versa.
   3) Mark the corners of the shape in their new positions on the grid.

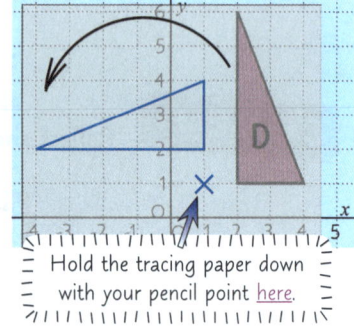

Hold the tracing paper down with your pencil point here.

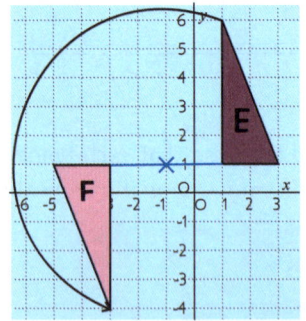

2. Describe the transformation that maps Triangle E onto Triangle F.

   A rotation of 180° about (−1, 1).

   You can use tracing paper to help you find the centre of rotation. Trace the original shape and then try putting your pencil on different points until the traced shape rotates onto the image. When this happens your pencil must be on the centre of rotation.

Like translations and reflections (see pages 90 and 91), length and angle are preserved under rotations.

Rotate this page 180° twice and then you've finished...

... the third type of transformation — only one to go. Have a go at this question before moving on:

Q1 On a grid, copy shape B and rotate it 90° anticlockwise about (2, 1). Label it B´. [2 marks]

Section Six — Shapes and Area

Enlargement

One last transformation coming up — enlargements. They're the trickiest, but also the most fun (honest).

Enlargements Change the Size of a Shape

For an enlargement, you must specify:
1) The scale factor.
2) The centre of enlargement.

scale factor = $\dfrac{\text{new length}}{\text{old length}}$

1) The scale factor for an enlargement tells you how long the sides of the new shape are compared to the old shape. E.g. a scale factor of 3 means you multiply each side length by 3.
2) If you're given the centre of enlargement, then it's vitally important where your new shape is on the grid.

> The scale factor tells you the RELATIVE DISTANCE of the old points and new points from the centre of enlargement.

So, a scale factor of 2 means the corners of the enlarged shape are twice as far from the centre of enlargement as the corners of the original shape.

If you're not given the centre of enlargement in a question, it doesn't matter where you draw the new shape.

Describing Enlargements

EXAMPLE: Describe the transformation that maps Triangle A onto Triangle B.

Use the formula to find the scale factor. (Just do this for one pair of sides.)
Old length of triangle base = 3 units. New length of triangle base = 6 units.

Scale factor = $\dfrac{\text{new length}}{\text{old length}} = \dfrac{6}{3} = 2$

To find the centre of enlargement, draw lines that go through matching corners of both shapes and see where they cross.

So the transformation is an enlargement of scale factor 2, centre (2, 6).

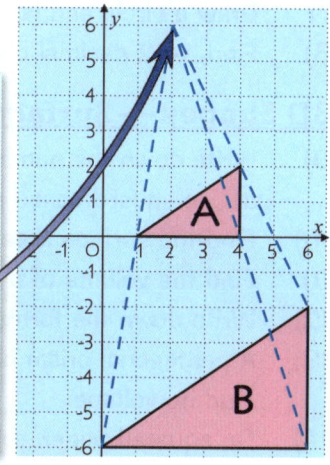

Enlargement Affects Perimeter and Area

If a 2D shape is enlarged by a scale factor, its perimeter and area will change.

> **For a SCALE FACTOR k:**
> The PERIMETER will be k times bigger.
> The AREA will be k^2 times bigger.
> And: $k = \dfrac{\text{new length}}{\text{old length}}$ $k^2 = \dfrac{\text{new area}}{\text{old area}}$

So if the scale factor is 2, the perimeter will be twice as big and the area will be 2^2 = 4 times as big.

EXAMPLE: The perimeter of a rectangle is 12 cm. The rectangle is enlarged so that its perimeter is now 36 cm. How many times larger will the area of the new rectangle be?

The perimeter is k times bigger, so k = 36 ÷ 12 = 3.
This means the area will be $k^2 = 3^2$ = 9 times larger.

Enlargements DO preserve angle (as the shape itself doesn't change).
However, unlike the other transformations, they DON'T preserve length (as the size of the shape changes).

Scale factors — they're enough to put the fear of cod into you...

Shapes are not congruent under enlargement as their size changes (even though their shape doesn't).

Q1 On a grid, draw triangle A with vertices (2, 1), (4, 1) and (4, 3), and triangle B with vertices (3, 1), (7, 1) and (7, 5). Describe the transformation that maps A to B. [4 marks]

Section Six — Shapes and Area

Revision Questions for Section Six

There were lots of facts and formulas in that section — time to see if it's all sunk in...
- Try these questions and tick off each one when you get it right.
- When you've done all the questions for a topic and are completely happy with it, tick off the topic.

2D Shapes (p77-78)
1) For each of the letters shown, write down how many lines of symmetry they have and their order of rotational symmetry.   H Z T N E X S
2) Write down four properties of an isosceles triangle.
3) How many pairs of equal sides does a parallelogram have? What is its order of rotational symmetry?

Perimeter and Area (p79-80)
4) Find the area of a triangle with base 6 cm and vertical height 12 cm.
5) Write down the formula for finding the area of a trapezium.
6) One side of a rhombus is 8 cm long. What is its perimeter?

Circles (p81)
7) Draw a circle and label its radius, diameter and a chord.
8) Find, to 2 decimal places, the area and circumference of a circle with radius 7 cm.

3D Shapes — Surface Area, Volume and Elevations (p82-85)
9) Write down the number of faces, edges and vertices for the following 3D shapes:
   a) a square-based pyramid   b) a cone   c) a triangular prism.
10) Find the surface area of a cube with side length 5 cm.
11) Find the volume of a cuboid with length 4 cm, width 8 cm and height 11 cm.
12) Write down the formula for the volume of a cylinder with radius r and height h.
13) A pentagonal prism has a cross-sectional area of 24 cm² and a length of 15 cm. Find its volume.
14) On squared paper, draw the front elevation (from the direction of the arrow), side elevation and plan view of the shape on the right.

Construction and Loci (p86-89)
15) Construct triangle XYZ, where XY = 5.6 cm, XZ = 7.2 cm and angle YXZ = 55°.
16) Construct an accurate 90° angle.
17) What shape does the locus of points that are a fixed distance from a given point make?
18) Draw a horizontal line with a length of 8 cm. Draw the locus of points exactly 2 cm away from the line.
19) Draw a square with sides of length 6 cm and label it ABCD. Shade the region that is nearer to AB than CD and less than 4 cm from vertex A.

Transformations (p90-93)
20) Describe the transformation that maps shape A onto shape B:
    a) using words   b) using a vector
21) Are shapes A and B congruent? Are shapes B and C congruent?
22) Describe the transformation that maps shape A onto shape C.
23) Write down the properties that are preserved when a shape is transformed by:
    a) translation   b) reflection   c) rotation   d) enlargement
24) Carry out the following transformations on the triangle X, which has vertices (1, 1), (4, 1) and (2, 3):
    a) a translation by the vector $\begin{pmatrix} -3 \\ -4 \end{pmatrix}$ b) a reflection in $y = -1$
    c) a rotation of 90° clockwise about (1, 1)   d) an enlargement of scale factor 2, centre (1, 1)
25) Find the area of an 8 cm² triangle that is enlarged by a scale factor of 3.

Section Six — Shapes and Area

Section Seven — Statistics and Probability

Planning an Investigation

Statistics is all about <u>data</u> — you've got to <u>collect</u> it, <u>process</u> it and <u>interpret</u> it. But before you can get on with any of that, you need to know precisely what you're <u>investigating</u>. That's where a <u>hypothesis</u> comes in...

An Investigation starts with a Hypothesis

> A HYPOTHESIS is a <u>statement</u> that might be <u>true</u> or <u>false</u>, but you haven't got enough <u>evidence</u> to support it either way yet. A hypothesis must be <u>testable</u>.

 A tourist board wants to investigate whether more people go to a particular beach when the weather is warm. Suggest a suitable hypothesis for the tourist board to test.

You'd expect more people to go to the beach when it's warmer, so a <u>testable hypothesis</u> could be:
'<u>The higher the temperature, the more people go to the beach.</u>'

Once you've chosen a <u>hypothesis</u>, you should <u>plan</u> your investigation to <u>test</u> it. That means planning how you'll <u>collect</u> and <u>analyse</u> suitable <u>data</u>, and how you'll use it to draw <u>conclusions</u> about your hypothesis.

An Investigation has Several Stages

When <u>planning</u> an investigation, you should consider the <u>five stages</u> of the <u>handling data cycle</u> (see the example below) and plan what you'll do at each stage. In the exam you might be asked to give <u>examples</u> of things to include in a plan and to <u>explain</u> why they're <u>appropriate</u>.

 A tourist board is planning to investigate the popularity of a particular beach. Their hypothesis is 'the higher the temperature, the more people go to the beach'. Give five examples of other details they should include in their plan, and say why each is appropriate.

1. **<u>Planning</u>** — choose your hypothesis, what data to collect and how to record and use it

   E.g. Measure air temperature at the beach to the <u>nearest degree</u> and observe the number of people there every Saturday at the <u>same time of day</u> for a <u>year</u>, so that data is recorded for <u>all seasons</u> and is <u>consistent</u>.

2. **<u>Collecting data</u>** — choose data sources and collection methods, identifying any constraints

   E.g. Collect your own data (<u>primary data</u>). This should be <u>reliable</u> because you can <u>control</u> how the data is collected (e.g. you can record the temperature at the same time each day).

   Constraints are limitations due to availability and reliability of data, practicalities of methods, etc.

3. **<u>Processing and presenting data</u>** — choose diagrams and measures, considering use of technology

   E.g. Put the data in a <u>spreadsheet</u>, so that a scatter diagram and calculations can be produced <u>easily</u> and <u>accurately</u>.

4. **<u>Interpreting results</u>** — plan analysis in order to draw conclusions and make predictions

   E.g. Interpret a <u>scatter diagram</u> to see if there's a <u>relationship</u> between temperature and number of people.

5. **<u>Communicating results clearly and evaluating methods</u>** — being aware of the target audience

   E.g. Describe what the scatter diagram shows to suit the <u>target audience</u> — this will be a <u>clear</u> visual representation of the results.

   <u>Evaluating</u> could involve planning <u>more analysis</u> — e.g. looking at the summer months separately.

Most people hate novelty ringtones — a detestable hypothesis...

Knowing the stages of the handling data cycle is pretty important, so check you do with this question.

Q1 A researcher plans to investigate whether children can solve a logic puzzle faster than adults.
   a) Suggest a suitable hypothesis for the researcher to test. [1 mark]
   b) Using your hypothesis, explain three other details she could include in her plan. [3 marks]

Sampling and Bias

Sampling is about using what you know about smaller groups to tell you about bigger groups. Simple, or is it...

Use a Sample to Find Out About a Population

1) For any statistical project, you need to find out about a group of people or things. E.g. all the pupils in a school, or all the trees in a forest. This whole group is called the POPULATION.
2) Often you can't collect information about every member of the population because there are too many. So you select a smaller group from the population, called a SAMPLE, instead.
3) It's really important that your sample fairly represents the WHOLE population. This allows you to apply any conclusions about your sample to the whole population.

E.g. if you find that ¾ of the people in your sample like cheese, you can estimate that ¾ of the people in the whole population like cheese.

An effort to collect information about every member of a population is called a census.

You Need to Spot Problems with Sampling Methods

A BIASED sample (or survey) is one that doesn't properly represent the whole population.

To SPOT BIAS, you need to think about:
1) WHEN, WHERE and HOW the sample is taken.
2) HOW MANY members are in it.

If certain groups are left out of the sample, there can be BIAS in things like age, gender, or different interests.

If the sample is too small, it's also likely to be biased.

Bigger populations need bigger samples to represent them.

Samir's school has 800 pupils. Samir is interested in whether these pupils would like to have more music lessons. For his sample he selects 5 members of the school orchestra to ask. Explain why the opinions Samir collects from his sample might not represent the whole school.

Only members of the orchestra are included, so the opinions are likely to be biased in favour of more music lessons. And a sample of 5 is too small to represent the whole school.

If possible, the best way to AVOID BIAS is to select a large sample at random from the whole population.

Simple Random Sampling — choosing at Random

One way to get a random sample is to use 'simple random sampling'.

To SELECT a SIMPLE RANDOM SAMPLE...
1. Assign a number to every member of the population.
2. Create a list of random numbers.
3. Match the random numbers to members of the population.

E.g. by using a computer, calculator or picking numbers out of a bag.

If you ask me, I love this page — but I'm biased...

Make sure you understand why samples should be representative and how to spot when they're not. Then you'll be ready to take on this Exam Practice Question.

Q1 Tina wants to find out how often people in Northern Ireland travel by train. She decides to ask 20 people waiting for trains at her local train station one morning. Comment on whether Tina can use the results of her survey to draw conclusions about the whole population. [2 marks]

Section Seven — Statistics and Probability

Collecting Data

Data you <u>collect yourself</u> is called <u>primary</u> data. If you use data that <u>someone else has collected</u>, e.g. you get it from a website, it's called <u>secondary</u> data. You need to <u>record</u> primary data in a way that's <u>easy to analyse</u> and <u>suitable</u> for the <u>type</u> of data you've got.

There are Different Types of Data

QUALITATIVE DATA is <u>descriptive</u>. It uses <u>words</u>, not numbers.
E.g. <u>pets' names</u> — Smudge, Snowy, Dave, etc. <u>Favourite flavours of ice cream</u> — 'vanilla', 'caramel-marshmallow-ripple', etc.

QUANTITATIVE DATA measures <u>quantities</u> using <u>numbers</u>.
E.g. <u>heights</u> of people, <u>times taken</u> to finish a race, <u>numbers of goals</u> scored in football matches, and so on.

There are two types of <u>quantitative</u> data.

DISCRETE DATA
1) It's <u>discrete</u> if the numbers can only take certain <u>exact</u> values.
2) E.g. the number of customers in a shop each day has to be a whole number — you can't have half a person.

CONTINUOUS DATA
1) If the numbers can take <u>any value</u> in a range, it's called <u>continuous</u> data.
2) E.g. heights and weights are continuous measurements.

Design Your Questionnaire Carefully

You need to be able to <u>say what's wrong</u> with questionnaire <u>questions</u> and <u>write</u> your own <u>good questions</u>.

A <u>GOOD</u> question is:

1) CLEAR and EASY TO UNDERSTAND ✓
WATCH OUT FOR: <u>confusing wording</u> or <u>no time frame</u> ✗

How much do you spend on food? ☐ ☐ ☐
a little   average amount   a lot

BAD: Wording is vague and no time frame is specified (e.g. each week or month).
BAD: Response boxes might be interpreted differently by different people.

2) EASY TO ANSWER ✓
WATCH OUT FOR: <u>response boxes</u> that <u>overlap</u>, or <u>don't allow</u> for <u>all possible answers</u> ✗

How many pieces of fruit do you eat a day on average? ☐ ☐ ☐ ☐ ☐
1-2 2-3 3-4 4-5 > 5

BAD: Response boxes overlap and don't allow an answer of zero.

3) FAIR — NOT LEADING or BIASED ✓
WATCH OUT FOR: wording that <u>suggests</u> an answer ✗

Do you agree that potatoes taste better than cabbage? ☐ ☐
Yes No

BAD: This is a leading question — you're more likely to say 'Yes'.

4) EASY TO ANALYSE afterwards ✓
WATCH OUT FOR: <u>open-ended</u> questions, with no limit on the possible answers ✗

What is your favourite food? _____

BAD: Every answer could be different — it would be better to include response boxes to choose from.

✗ Also watch out for questions that people might be <u>embarrassed</u> to answer <u>truthfully</u>. E.g. ones asking for <u>personal</u> information, like someone's exact age.

Who wants to collect a questionnaire — the (not so exciting) quiz spin-off...

Make sure you learn the 4 key points for writing good questions, then try this Exam Practice Question.

Q1 The four questions on the page above are to be included on a questionnaire about food. Design a better version of each question to go on the questionnaire. **[4 marks]**

Section Seven — Statistics and Probability

Collecting Data

Revision tip: take regular dancing breaks — try a quick waltz spin or salsa shimmy... then back to the maths...

You Can Record Your Data in a Table

1) Data-collection tables (or sheets) should look like this table.
2) The first column can contain words (like the table opposite) or numbers. Make sure you include a category to fit every possible data label or value.

Data labels or values → Record how many

Vehicle	Tally	Frequency
Car	‖‖‖ ‖‖	7
Bus	‖‖‖‖	4
Lorry	‖‖‖	3
Other	‖‖‖‖	4

Find totals by adding tally marks

EXAMPLE: Lizzie plans to ask people how many holidays they have been on this year. Design a data-collection sheet she could use to collect her data.

1. Draw and label the 3 columns. The data values are the numbers of holidays.
2. Make sure there's a place to record all the answers Lizzie might get. The category '4 or more' is a good way of doing this without having to add rows for 5, 6, 7, etc.

Number of holidays	Tally	Frequency
0		
1		
2		
3		
4 or more		

You Can Organise Your Data into Classes

1) To record data in a table, you often need to group it into classes to make it more manageable. Discrete data classes should have 'gaps' between them, e.g. '0-1 goals', '2-3 goals' (it jumps from 1 to 2 because there are no values in between). Continuous data classes should have no 'gaps', so are often written using inequalities (see p108).

2) Whatever the data you have, make sure none of the classes overlap and that they cover all the possible values.

When you group data you lose some accuracy because you don't know the exact values any more.

EXAMPLE: Jonty asks a random sample of 30 people to take a general knowledge quiz. The aim is to get as many correct answers as possible in 5 minutes. Each person's score is shown below.

32 9 71 44 59 64 60 14 5 87 75 68 10 25 71
30 55 11 12 91 38 3 65 66 27 42 79 4 18 74

Record Jonty's data in a suitable table.

Include columns for: the data values, 'Tally' to count the data and 'Frequency' to show the totals.

Use non-overlapping classes — with gaps because the data's discrete.

Include classes like '...or over', '...or less' or 'other' to cover all options in a sensible number of classes.

Score	Tally	Frequency
0-19	‖‖‖ ‖‖‖‖	9
20-39	‖‖‖	5
40-59	‖‖‖‖	4
60-79	‖‖‖ ‖‖‖	10
80 or over	‖	2

Go through the list of data values and for each one make a tally mark in the appropriate class.

Find the frequencies by adding the tally marks.

No gaps between classes sounds like no fun at all...

You need to know what type of data you've got so you can record and display it in a suitable way.

Q1 Yu Qi asks some students how many times they went to the cinema in the last year. Say whether this data is discrete or continuous and design a table to record it in. [2 marks]

Mean, Median, Mode and Range

Mean, median, mode and range pop up all the time in stats questions — make sure you know what they are.

The Four Definitions

MODE = MOST common
MEDIAN = MIDDLE value (when values are in order of size)
MEAN = TOTAL of items ÷ NUMBER of items
RANGE = Difference between highest and lowest

REMEMBER:
Mode = most (emphasise the 'mo' in each when you say them)
Median = mid (emphasise the m*d in each when you say them)
Mean is just the average, but it's mean 'cos you have to work it out.

The Golden Rule

There's one vital step for finding the median that lots of people forget:

Always REARRANGE the data in ASCENDING ORDER (and check you have the same number of entries!)

You absolutely must do this when finding the median, but it's also really useful for working out the mode too.

EXAMPLE: Find the median, mode, mean, and range of these numbers:
2, 5, 3, 2, 6, –4, 0, 9, –3, 1, 6, 3, –2, 3

The MEDIAN is the middle value (when they're arranged in order of size) — so first, rearrange the numbers.

When there are two middle numbers, the median is halfway between the two.

–4, –3, –2, 0, 1, 2, (2, 3) 3, 3, 5, 6, 6, 9
← seven numbers this side   seven numbers this side →
Median = 2.5

Check that you still have the same number of entries after you've rearranged them.

An even number of values means there will be two middle numbers.

MODE (or modal value) is the most common value. → Mode = 3

Some data sets have more than one mode, or no mode at all.

MEAN = total of items / number of items
→ $\frac{-4-3-2+0+1+2+2+3+3+3+5+6+6+9}{14}$

= 31 ÷ 14 = 2.214... = **2.21 (2 d.p.)**

RANGE = distance from lowest to highest value, i.e. from –4 up to 9. → 9 – (–4) = **13**

Choose the Best Average

The mean, median and mode all have their advantages and disadvantages — LEARN THEM:

	Advantages	Disadvantages
Mean	Uses all the data. Usually most representative.	Isn't always a data value. May be distorted by extreme data values.
Median	Easy to find in ordered data. Not distorted by extreme data values.	Isn't always a data value. Not always a good representation of the data.
Mode	Easy to find in tallied data. Always a data value (when it exists).	Doesn't always exist or sometimes more than one. Not always a good representation of the data.

The Alps — now there's a mean range...

Learn the four definitions and the extra step you have to do to find the median, then give this a go...

Q1 Find the mean, median, mode and range for these test scores: 6, 15, 12, 12, 11. [4 marks]

Q2 A set of 8 heights has a mean of 1.6 m. A new height of 1.5 m is added.
Explain whether the mean of all 9 heights will be higher or lower than 1.6 m. [1 mark]

Section Seven — Statistics and Probability

 # Frequency Tables — Finding Averages

The word FREQUENCY means HOW MANY, so a frequency table is just a 'How many in each category' table. You saw how to find averages and range on p99 — it's the same ideas here, but with the data in a table.

Find Averages from Frequency Tables

1) The MODE is just the CATEGORY with the MOST ENTRIES.
2) The RANGE is found from the extremes of the first column.
3) The MEDIAN is the CATEGORY of the middle value.
4) To find the MEAN, you have to WORK OUT A THIRD COLUMN yourself.

The MEAN is then: 3rd Column Total ÷ 2nd Column Total

Number of cats	Frequency	
0	17	
1	22	
2	15	
3	7	

Mysterious 3rd column...

EXAMPLE: Some people were asked how many sisters they have. The table opposite shows the results.
Find the mode, the range, the mean and the median of the data.

Number of sisters	Frequency
0	7
1	15
2	12
3	8
4	4
5	0

1 The MODE is the category with the most entries — i.e. the one with the highest frequency:

The highest frequency is 15 for '1 sister', so MODE = 1

2 The RANGE is the difference between the highest and lowest numbers of sisters — that's 4 sisters (no one has 5 sisters) and no sisters, so:

RANGE = 4 − 0 = 4

3 To find the MEAN, add a 3rd column to the table showing 'number of sisters × frequency'. Add up these values to find the total number of sisters of all the people asked.

Number of sisters	Frequency	No. of sisters × Frequency
0	7	0
1	15	15
2	12	24
3	8	24
4	4	16
5	0	0
Total	46	79

MEAN = $\frac{\text{total number of sisters}}{\text{total number of people asked}}$ = $\frac{79}{46}$ = 1.72 (3 s.f.)

4 The MEDIAN is the category of the middle value. Work out its position, then count through the 2nd column to find it.

It helps to imagine the data set out in an ordered list:
0000000111111111111112222222222222333333334444
                              ↑
                           median

The median is in position (n + 1) ÷ 2 = (46 + 1) ÷ 2 = 23.5 — halfway between the 23rd and 24th values. There are a total of (7 + 15) = 22 values in the first two categories, and another 12 in the third category takes you to 34. So the 23rd and 24th values must both be in the category '2 sisters', which means the MEDIAN is 2.

My table has 5 columns, 6 rows and 4 legs...

Learn the four key points about averages, then try this fella.

Q1 50 people were asked how many times a week they play sport. The table opposite shows the results.

a) Find the median. [2 marks]
b) Calculate the mean. [3 marks]

No. of times sport played	Frequency
0	8
1	15
2	17
3	6
4	4
5 or more	0

Two-Way Tables

Get ready for some more data and yet more tables. The fun continues...

Two-Way Tables Divide Data into Categories

1) A two-way table organises data by showing how many people or things fall into different categories.
2) The columns of the table show one set of categories and the rows show a different set. Two-way tables often include totals as well.

EXAMPLE: Complete the two-way table below showing preferred type of music and gender:

Use the given values in the rows and columns to find missing values by adding or subtracting.

1) Either find the number that makes a total of 8 in the Rock column (8 − 5 = 3), or 11 in the Boys row (11 − 7 − 1 = 3)

2) This is the missing value in the Girls row, 13 − 6 − 5 = 2

	Pop	Rock	Classical	Total
Girl	6	5	2	13
Boy	7	3	1	11
Total	13	8	3	24

3) This is the total for the Pop column, 6 + 7 = 13

4) Here you need to work out 2) or 3) first. E.g. if you know 2) you can work out the total for the Classical column, 2 + 1 = 3

You Need to be Able to Read Two-Way Tables

You might be given a completed two-way table and asked questions about reading and interpreting it.

EXAMPLE: An ecologist draws the following two-way table to show the weights and lengths of newts in a local pond:

	Weight (g)		
Length (mm)	$10 \leq w < 40$	$40 \leq w < 70$	$70 \leq w < 100$
$50 \leq l < 70$	7	4	0
$70 \leq l < 90$	3	8	4
$90 \leq l < 120$	0	2	10

The two variables are weight in grams and length in millimetres.

a) How many newts weigh between 10 and 40 g?

The total of the 1st column gives all the newts weighing between 10 and 40 g. So you need to add up all the numbers: 7 + 3 + 0 = 10 newts.

b) How many newts are between 90 and 120 mm long, and weigh between 70 and 100 g?

Follow the row for $90 \leq l < 120$ mm across to where it meets the column for $70 \leq w < 100$ g and that's your answer — 10 newts.

Strangest part of a waitressing job — to weigh tables...

Once you're sure you know how to read data from a two-way table, answer these questions:

Q1 Complete the two-way table showing gender and test result. [3 marks]

Q2 Using the table above showing weights and lengths of newts, find:
a) the number of newts that are between 70 and 90 mm long
b) the number of newts that weigh between 70 and 100 g,
c) the number of newts that were measured altogether. [3 marks]

	Boy	Girl	Total
Pass	13		24
Fail		4	
Total	16		

Section Seven — Statistics and Probability

Venn Diagrams

Venn diagrams are a way of displaying sets of data in intersecting circles — they're very pretty.

Show Groups on Venn Diagrams

1) On a Venn diagram, data is shown divided into groups. Each group is represented by a circle.
2) The diagram can show either the actual data values in each group, or the number of values in each group.

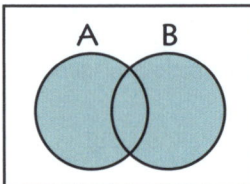

All the data values inside the circles are in either group A or group B.

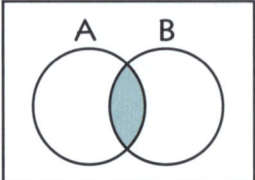

The intersection of the two circles contains all the data values in both group A and group B.

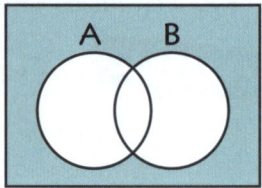

Data values that aren't in group A or group B go in the rectangle outside the circles.

EXAMPLE: In a class of 30 pupils, 8 of them like mustard, 24 of them like ketchup and 5 of them like both mustard and ketchup.

a) Complete the Venn diagram below showing this information.
   Start by filling in the overlap.

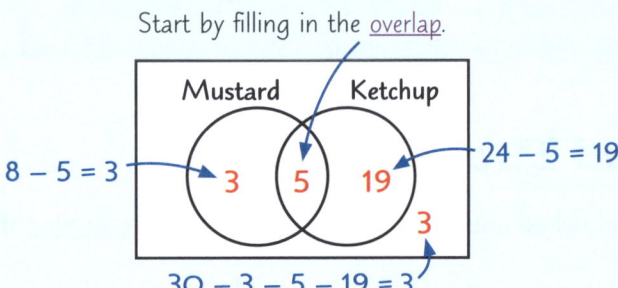

$8 - 5 = 3$
$24 - 5 = 19$
$30 - 3 - 5 - 19 = 3$

b) How many pupils like mustard or ketchup?
   This is the number of pupils who like either just mustard, just ketchup, or both mustard and ketchup. $3 + 5 + 19 = 27$

c) What fraction of the pupils like both mustard and ketchup?
   5 out of 30 pupils are in the intersection. $\frac{5}{30} = \frac{1}{6}$

Venn Diagrams with Three Intersecting Circles

Venn diagrams can have three intersecting circles. The area where all three circles overlap represents the objects that are members of all three groups.

EXAMPLE: A group of 30 children in a nursery each painted a picture. They could use the colours blue, yellow and red. A Venn diagram has been started below. It is also known that 20 children used red, 10 used blue and 3 used only blue. Complete the Venn diagram.

1) 3 used only blue so 3 goes in the part of the blue circle that doesn't overlap with any others.
2) A total of 10 used blue so use this to finish the blue circle: $10 - 5 - 1 - 3 = 1$
3) A total of 20 used red: $20 - 10 - 1 - 1 = 8$
4) There are 30 children in total so use this to complete the diagram: $30 - 10 - 1 - 1 - 8 - 5 - 3 = 2$

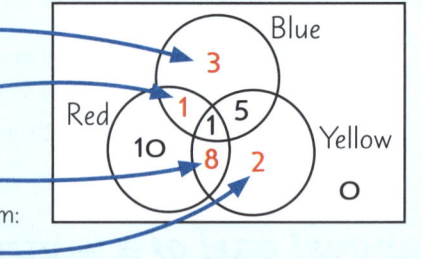

Circles keep falling on my head — it's raining Venn...

Nothing too complicated here — just make sure you check whether a question is asking about values that are in one group only, or whether you need to include the values in the intersection too.

Q1 Group J is the odd numbers, group K is the square numbers and group L is the prime numbers. Draw a Venn diagram showing the numbers 1 to 9 sorted into these groups. [3 marks]

Pictograms and Bar Charts

Pictograms and bar charts both show frequencies. (Remember... frequency = 'how many of something'.)

Pictograms Show Frequencies Using Symbols

Every pictogram has a key telling you what one symbol represents.

With pictograms, you MUST use the KEY.

EXAMPLE: This pictogram shows how many peaches were sold by a greengrocer on different days.

a) How many peaches were sold on Tuesday?
Each circle represents 4 peaches.   2 × 4 = 8 peaches

b) How many peaches were sold on Wednesday?
Three-quarters of a circle = 3 peaches.   (3 × 4) + 3 = 15 peaches

c) 43 peaches were sold altogether. Work out how many peaches were sold on Friday and show this information on the diagram.
1) Add up the peaches for Mon-Thurs.   4 + 8 + 15 + (4 + 2) = 33
2) Subtract this from the total.   Friday = 43 − 33 = 10
3) You need 2 whole circles (= 8), plus another half a circle (= 2).

Half a circle = 2 peaches.

Bar Charts Show Frequencies Using Bars

1) Frequencies on bar charts are shown by the heights of the different bars.
2) Dual bar charts show two things at once — they're good for comparing different sets of data.

EXAMPLE: This dual bar chart shows the number of men and women visiting a coffee shop on different days.

a) How many men visited the coffee shop altogether?
Add up the numbers shown by the heights of the purple bars.   4 + 3 + 6 + 2 = 15 men

b) On which day did the most women visit the coffee shop?
Find the tallest yellow bar.   Tuesday

c) What fraction of the visitors on Wednesday were women? Give your answer in its simplest form.
There were 2 + 6 = 8 visitors on Wednesday — and 2 of them were women. $\frac{2}{8} = \frac{1}{4}$

Bars representing different categories are separated by equal gaps.

Both axes must be labelled.

A sheep's favourite graph — the baaaa chart...

Q1 This pictogram shows the different types of CDs Javier owns, but the key is missing. Javier owns 20 blues CDs.
a) How many jazz CDs does Javier own? [2 marks]
b) He owns 5 opera CDs. Complete the pictogram. [1 mark]

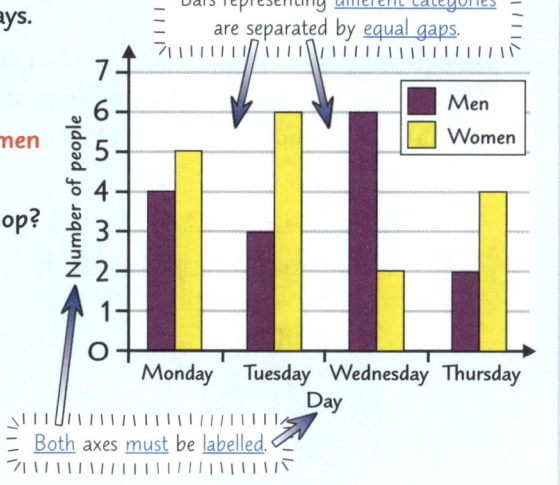

Section Seven — Statistics and Probability

Pie Charts

Unlike other charts, pie charts DON'T tell you numbers of things — they show the proportion in each category. Remember that. And here's another thing to remember... the Golden Pie Chart Rule...

The TOTAL of Everything = 360°

1) Fraction of the Total = Angle ÷ 360°

EXAMPLE:

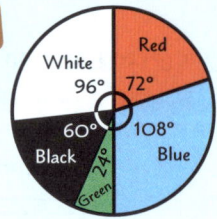

This pie chart shows the colour of all the cars sold by a dealer. What fraction of the cars were red?

Fraction of red cars = $\dfrac{\text{angle of red cars}}{\text{angle of everything}} = \dfrac{72°}{360°} = \dfrac{1}{5}$

2) Find a Multiplier to Calculate Your Angles

EXAMPLE: Draw a pie chart to show this information about the types of animal in a petting zoo.

Animal	Geese	Hamsters	Guinea pigs	Rabbits	Ducks
Number	12	20	17	15	26

1) Find the total by adding.   12 + 20 + 17 + 15 + 26 = 90

2) 'Everything = 360°' — so find the multiplier that turns your total into 360°.   Multiplier = 360 ÷ 90 = 4

3) Multiply every number by 4 to get the angle for each sector.

| Angle | 12 × 4 = 48° | 20 × 4 = 80° | 17 × 4 = 68° | 15 × 4 = 60° | 26 × 4 = 104° |

4) Draw your pie chart accurately using a protractor.

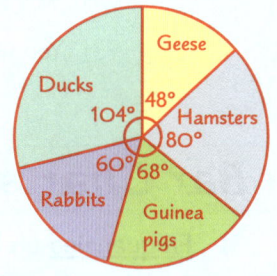

3) Find How Many by Using the Angle for 1 Thing

EXAMPLE: The pie chart on the right shows information about the types of animals liked most by different students. There were 90 students altogether.

a) Work out the number of students who liked dogs most.

1) 'Everything = 360°, so... ⇒ 90 students = 360°
2) Divide by 90 to find... ⇒ 1 student = 4°
3) Divide the angle for dogs by the angle for 1 student to get: ⇒ 160° ÷ 4° = 40 — 40 students liked dogs most

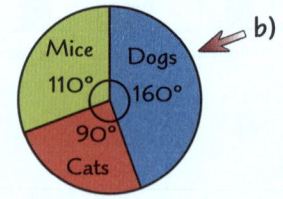

b) The pie chart on the left shows information about the types of animals liked most by a different group of students. Dave says, "This means that 40 students in this group like dogs most." Explain why Dave is not correct.

We don't know how many students in total the pie chart represents, so we can't work out how many students liked dogs most.

I like my pie charts with gravy and mushy peas...

Pie chart questions need a lot of practice. Make a start with this...

Q1 Draw an accurate pie chart to show the information about Rahul's DVD collection given in this bar chart.   [4 marks]

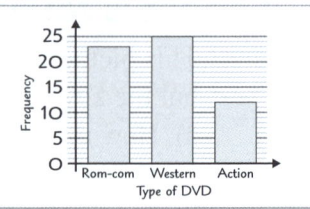

Other Charts and Graphs

Stem and leaf diagrams, frequency trees and flow charts now. Make sure you can draw and/or interpret them.

Stem and Leaf Diagrams put data in Order

An ordered stem and leaf diagram shows a set of data in order of size.
This makes it easy to find things like the median and range (see p99).

EXAMPLE: This stem and leaf diagram shows the ages of some school teachers.

a) How old is the oldest teacher?
   Use the key to help you read off the diagram.   6 | 3 = 63 years old

b) What is the median age?
   The median is the middle value.   There are 11 values, so the median is the 6th value.
   Find its position, then read off the value.   So median age is 4 | 8 = 48 years

```
3 | 3 5
4 | 0 5 7 8
5 | 1 4 9
6 | 1 3
Key: 5|4 = 54 years
```

Record Results in Frequency Trees

When an experiment has two or more steps, you can record the results using a frequency tree.

EXAMPLE: 120 GCSE maths students were asked if they would go on to do A-level maths.
- 45 of them said they would go on to do A-level maths.
- 30 of the students who said they would do A-level maths actually did.
- 9 of the students who said they wouldn't do A-level maths actually did.

Complete the frequency tree:

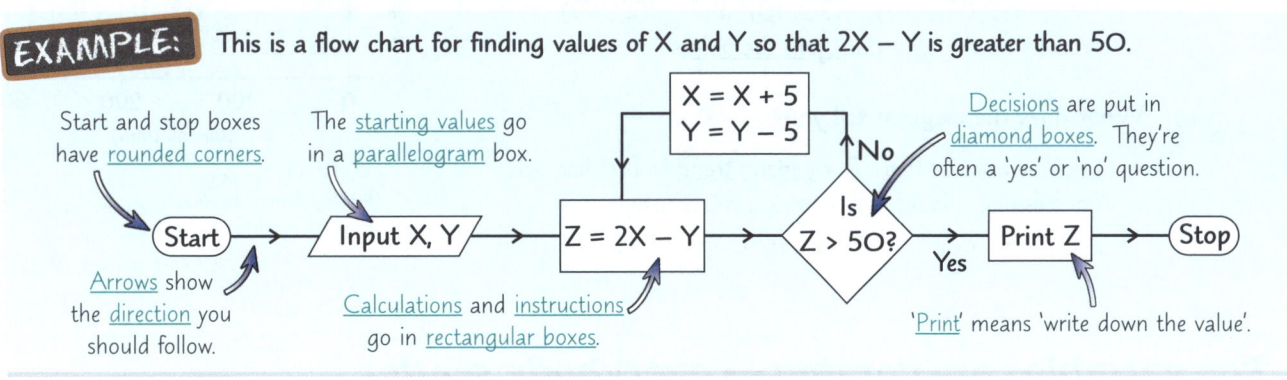

Flow Charts give you a Series of Instructions

EXAMPLE: This is a flow chart for finding values of X and Y so that 2X − Y is greater than 50.

Start and stop boxes have rounded corners. The starting values go in a parallelogram box. Decisions are put in diamond boxes. They're often a 'yes' or 'no' question.

Start → Input X, Y → Z = 2X − Y → Is Z > 50? → (No: X = X + 5, Y = Y − 5, loop back) (Yes:) Print Z → Stop

Arrows show the direction you should follow. Calculations and instructions go in rectangular boxes. 'Print' means 'write down the value'.

Check out my flow, as the words just go, to and fro, yo...

Q1 Use the flow chart above to answer the following questions.

a) What is the result of the flow chart if the values X = 20, Y = 15 are input?   [2 marks]

b) A box containing 'Is Y > 0?' is added to the flow chart. What shape is it?   [1 mark]

Other Charts and Graphs

You didn't think we'd finished with the diagrams just yet did you?

Line Graphs can show Time Series

1) A time series is when you measure the same thing at different times. A line graph of the data has 'time' along the bottom and the thing being measured down the side.
2) A basic pattern often repeats itself — it's called seasonality (but it doesn't have to match the seasons).
3) You can also see the overall trend by looking at the peaks and troughs.

EXAMPLE: The table shows how much Jamie spent on heating during Spring/Summer and Autumn/Winter over 4 years.

6-month period	Spr / Sum	Aut / Win	Spr / Sum	Aut / Win	Spr / Sum	Aut / Win	Spr / Sum	Aut / Win
Amount spent (£)	250	350	300	375	290	400	300	425

a) Draw a line graph of this data on the grid opposite.

   Put 'Time' along the bottom and 'Amount spent' down the side.

   Label your axes at equal intervals.

Plot the points and join them up with straight lines. The pattern repeats itself every 2 points.

b) Describe the trend in the data.

   Look at the trend in the peaks. The data shows an upward trend in the amount Jamie spent.

Scatter Diagrams Compare Different Variables

Scatter diagrams are useful when you've got two different variables that you want to compare. Plotting them in a scatter diagram helps you to see if there might be a link between the variables.

EXAMPLE: The data in this table was collected to investigate the water level of a river after different amounts of rain.

Rainfall (mm)	10	40	120	130	190	260
Height of river (m)	0.7	0.8	1.0	1.2	1.3	1.9

a) Use the data to draw a scatter diagram on the grid provided.

   Check which variable goes on which axis — here the x-axis is rainfall and the y-axis is the height of the river.

   Carefully plot the data points — (10, 0.7), (40, 0.8), (120, 1.0), (130, 1.2), (190, 1.3) and (260, 1.9). Make sure that you don't join the points.

b) What does the diagram tell you?

   Look at whether there is a general trend in the diagram. For this plot it looks like there is a relationship.

   As rainfall gets higher, so does the height of the river.

You might need to draw the axes yourself — you'll need to choose a suitable scale. Pick one that makes it easy to mark on all the points, like the one in this example.

The variables are coming — everybody scatter...

...but before you do, learn the page and answer this question. Arghhhhhhhh...

Q1 a) Use this data to draw and label a scatter diagram. Put the average temperature on the x-axis and the number of cold drinks sold on the y-axis. [2 marks]

Average temperature °C	15	21	16	27	8	14	19
Number of cold drinks sold	15	29	19	38	4	16	24

   b) What does the diagram tell you? [1 mark]

Section Seven — Statistics and Probability

Scatter Diagrams

A <u>scatter graph</u> tells you <u>how closely</u> two things are <u>related</u> — the fancy word is <u>CORRELATION</u>.

Scatter Graphs Show Correlation

1) If you can draw a <u>line of best fit</u> pretty close to <u>most</u> of your data points, the two things are <u>correlated</u>. If the points are <u>randomly scattered</u>, and you <u>can't draw</u> a line of best fit, then there's <u>no correlation</u>.

2) <u>Strong correlation</u> is when your points make a <u>fairly straight line</u> — the two things are <u>closely related</u>. <u>Weak correlation</u> is when your points <u>don't line up</u> so nicely, but you can still draw a line of best fit.

3) If the points form a line sloping <u>uphill</u> from left to right, then there is <u>positive correlation</u>. If the line slopes <u>downhill</u> from left to right, then there is <u>negative correlation</u>.

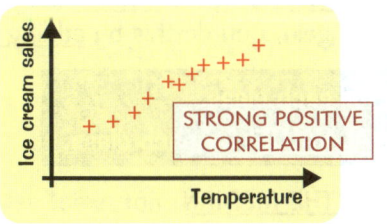
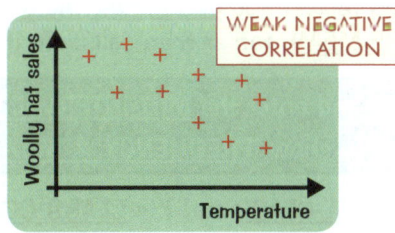
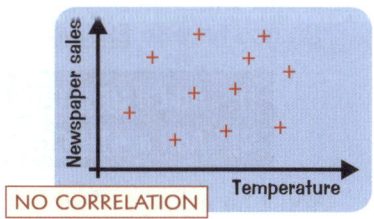

Use a Line of Best Fit to Make Predictions

1) Predicting a value <u>within the range</u> of data you have should be <u>fairly reliable</u>. But if you extend your line <u>outside</u> the range of data your prediction might be <u>unreliable</u>, because the <u>pattern might not continue</u>.

2) Also watch out for <u>outliers</u> — data points that <u>don't fit the general pattern</u>. Outliers can <u>drag</u> your <u>line of best fit</u> away from the other values, so it's best to <u>ignore</u> them when you're drawing the line.

EXAMPLE: This graph shows the number of zoo visitors plotted against the outside temperature for several Sundays.

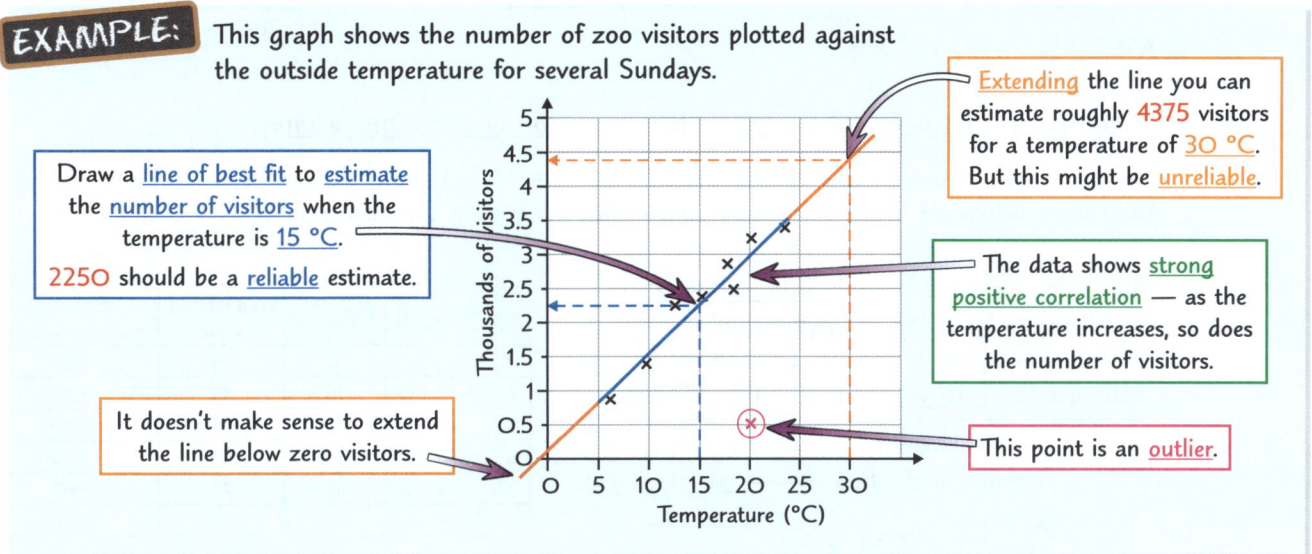

Draw a <u>line of best fit</u> to <u>estimate</u> the <u>number of visitors</u> when the temperature is <u>15 °C</u>. <u>2250</u> should be a <u>reliable</u> estimate.

It doesn't make sense to extend the line below zero visitors.

<u>Extending</u> the line you can estimate roughly <u>4375</u> visitors for a temperature of <u>30 °C</u>. But this might be <u>unreliable</u>.

The data shows <u>strong positive correlation</u> — as the temperature increases, so does the number of visitors.

This point is an <u>outlier</u>.

<u>BE CAREFUL</u> with <u>correlation</u> — if two things are correlated it <u>doesn't mean</u> that one causes the other. There could be a third factor affecting both, or it could just be a coincidence.

Relax and take a trip down Correlation Street...

Q1 This graph shows Sam's average speed on runs of different lengths.
 a) Describe the relationship between length of run and average speed. [1 mark]
 b) Circle the point that doesn't follow the trend. [1 mark]
 c) Estimate Sam's average speed for an 8-mile run. [1 mark]
 d) Comment on the reliability of your estimate in part c). [1 mark]

Section Seven — Statistics and Probability

Grouped Frequency Tables

Grouped frequency tables are like ordinary frequency tables, but they group the data into classes.

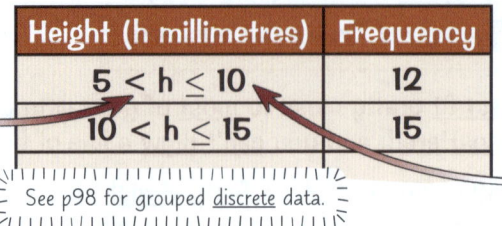

Height (h millimetres)	Frequency
$5 < h \leq 10$	12
$10 < h \leq 15$	15

NO GAPS between classes for **CONTINUOUS** data.
Use inequality symbols to cover all possible values.

See p98 for grouped discrete data.

To find MID-INTERVAL VALUES:
- Add together the end values of the class and divide by 2.
- E.g. $(5 + 10) \div 2 = 7.5$

Find Averages from Grouped Frequency Tables

Unlike with ordinary frequency tables, you don't know the actual data values, only the classes they're in. So you have to **ESTIMATE THE MEAN**, rather than calculate it exactly. Again, you do this by adding columns:

> 1) Add a **3RD COLUMN** and enter the **MID-INTERVAL VALUE** for each class.
> 2) Add a **4TH COLUMN** to show '**FREQUENCY × MID-INTERVAL VALUE**' for each class.

You'll be asked to find the **MODAL CLASS** and the **CLASS CONTAINING THE MEDIAN**, not exact values. And the **RANGE** can only be estimated too — using the class boundaries.

EXAMPLE: This table shows information about the weights, in kilograms, of 60 school children.
a) Write down the modal class.
b) Write down the class containing the median.
c) Calculate an estimate for the mean weight.
d) Estimate the range of weights.

Weight (w kg)	Frequency
$30 < w \leq 40$	8
$40 < w \leq 50$	16
$50 < w \leq 60$	18
$60 < w \leq 70$	12
$70 < w \leq 80$	6

a) The modal class is the one with the highest frequency.

Modal class is $50 < w \leq 60$

b) Work out the position of the median, then count through the 2nd column.

The median is in position $(n + 1) \div 2 = (60 + 1) \div 2 = 30.5$, halfway between the 30th and 31st values. Both these values are in the third class, so the class containing the median is $50 < w \leq 60$.

c) Add extra columns for 'mid-interval value' and 'frequency × mid-interval value'. Add up the values in the 4th column to estimate the total weight of the 60 children.

Weight (w kg)	Frequency	Mid-interval value	Frequency × mid-interval value
$30 < w \leq 40$	8	35	280
$40 < w \leq 50$	16	45	720
$50 < w \leq 60$	18	55	990
$60 < w \leq 70$	12	65	780
$70 < w \leq 80$	6	75	450
Total	60	—	3220

Mean ≈ $\dfrac{\text{total weight}}{\text{number of children}}$ ← 4th column total / 2nd column total

$= \dfrac{3220}{60} = 53.7$ kg (3 s.f.)

d) Find the difference between the highest and lowest class boundaries.

Estimated range = $80 - 30 = 50$ kg

This is the largest possible range. The actual range is likely to be smaller, but you can't tell with grouped data.

Mid-interval value — cheap ice creams...

Q1 a) Find the modal class of the table. [1 mark]
b) Estimate the mean of this data. Give your answer to 3 significant figures. [4 marks]

Length (l cm)	$15.5 \leq l < 16.5$	$16.5 \leq l < 17.5$	$17.5 \leq l < 18.5$	$18.5 \leq l < 19.5$
Frequency	12	18	23	8

Section Seven — Statistics and Probability

Interpreting Data

This page is about getting information from data and recognising when it might be misleading.

You can Find Averages from Diagrams

EXAMPLE: This vertical line graph shows information on the number of pairs of penguin slippers a shop sells each day for 50 consecutive days. Calculate the mean number of pairs sold each day.

Fill in a frequency table and add a third column to find the total number of pairs sold — see p100.

Mean = $\frac{\text{total number of pairs sold}}{\text{total number of days}}$

= $\frac{118}{50}$ = 2.36

Number of pairs	Frequency	No. of pairs × Frequency
0	7	0
1	8	8
2	10	20
3	13	39
4	9	36
5	3	15
Total	50	118

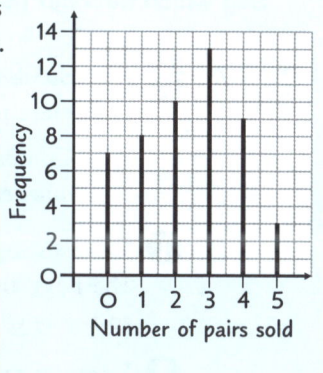

Watch Out for Misleading Diagrams

At first glance, a diagram might look perfectly fine. But at second glance, well, not so fine...

EXAMPLE: This bar chart shows the numbers of dogs of different breeds at a rescue centre.

a) Write down **three** things that are wrong with the bar chart.
   1) The 'number of dogs' axis doesn't start at zero.
   2) The 'number of dogs' axis has inconsistent numbering.
   3) The 'breed of dog' axis has no label.

b) The 'Husky' bar is twice as high as the 'Spaniel' bar. Explain why these bar heights could be misleading in the context of this data.
   The bar heights suggest that there are twice as many Huskies as Spaniels. But reading the scale, there are 6 Huskies and 5 Spaniels.

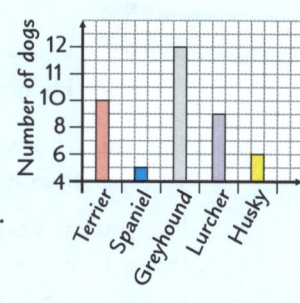

Be Careful with Measures of Average and Range

Outliers are data values that don't fit the general pattern — they're a long way from the rest of the data. Outliers can have a big effect on the mean or range of a data set, so you get a misleading value.

EXAMPLE: The data below shows the number of songs Fred downloads each week for ten weeks.

0, 1, 3, 3, 5, 6, 7, 8, 8, 20

See p99 for averages and range.

a) Fred works out that the range of his data is 20. Comment on this value as a measure of the spread.
   A range of 20 isn't a true reflection of the spread of the whole data set, because most of the data is much closer together. The highest value of 20 has a big effect on increasing the range.

b) Explain why the mode isn't a helpful measure of average for this data.
   The data has two modes, 3 and 8, so this doesn't give you a good idea of the average value.

Don't let data lead you down the garden path...

We should find out more about those penguin slippers. Use the data from the first example above to answer the following:

Q1 a) What is the modal number of pairs of penguin slippers sold? [1 mark]
    b) Give the median and range of the number of pairs of penguin slippers sold. [3 marks]

Section Seven — Statistics and Probability

Comparing Data Sets

You can compare data sets using averages and range, or by drawing suitable diagrams.

Compare Data Sets Using Averages and Range

Say which data set has the higher/lower value and what that means in the context of the data.

EXAMPLE: Some children take part in a 'guess the weight of the baby hippo' competition. Here is some information about the weights they guess.

Compare the distributions of the weights guessed by the boys and the girls.

Boys:
Mean = 40 kg
Median = 43 kg
Range = 42 kg

Girls:
Mean = 34 kg
Median = 33 kg
Range = 30 kg

① Compare averages:
The boys' mean and median values are higher than the girls', so the boys generally guessed heavier weights.

② Compare ranges:
The boys' guesses have a bigger range, so the weights guessed by the boys show more variation.

Compare Data Sets Using Diagrams

The type of diagram you should use depends on what you want to show.

EXAMPLE: Harry carried out a survey into whether or not people like olives. He draws these pie charts to show his results.

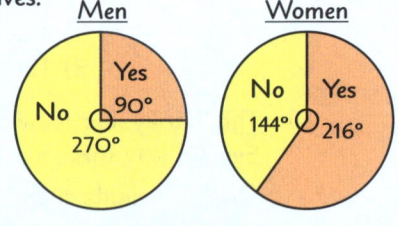

a) Can you tell from the pie charts whether more women said 'yes' than men? Explain your answer.

No, you can't tell whether more women said 'yes'. You can see that a higher proportion of women said 'yes', but you don't know how many men and women the pie charts represent.

b) Harry surveyed 20 men and 20 women. Draw a suitable diagram to compare the numbers of men and women giving each answer.

A dual bar chart is suitable — it shows the numbers of men and women side by side.

Use the pie charts to work out the frequency of each answer. E.g. find the fraction of the total, then multiply by 20.

Men: 'Yes' = $\frac{90}{360} \times 20 = 5$, 'No' = $\frac{270}{360} \times 20 = 15$

Women: 'Yes' = $\frac{216}{360} \times 20 = 12$, 'No' = $\frac{144}{360} \times 20 = 8$

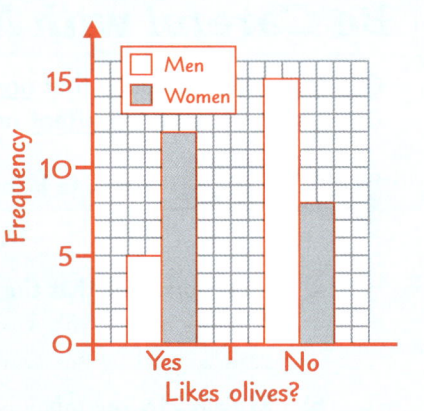

A pie isn't suitable for all occasions — hard to believe, I know...

You might need to work out the values of average and range (see p99) before comparing data sets.

Q1 The data below shows how many football matches two supporters attended in each of the last nine years. Compare the distributions of the number of matches attended. [3 marks]

Hannah: 1, 5, 0, 7, 10, 8, 7, 4, 3
Joseph: 13, 17, 16, 20, 32, 18, 14, 25, 25

Section Seven — Statistics and Probability

Probability Basics

A lot of people think probability is tough. But learn the basics well, and it'll all make sense.

All Probabilities are Between 0 and 1

Random events happen only because of chance — there is no other pattern to them.
The probability of an event is a measure of how high that chance is.

- Probabilities are always between 0 and 1.
- The higher the probability of something, the more likely it is.
- A probability of ZERO means it will NEVER HAPPEN.
- A probability of ONE means it DEFINITELY WILL HAPPEN.

You can show the probability of something happening on a scale from 0 to 1.
Probabilities can be given as fractions, decimals or percentages.

Use This Formula When All Outcomes are Equally Likely

Use this formula to find probabilities for a fair spinner, coin or dice.
A spinner/coin/dice is 'fair' when it's equally likely to land on any of its sides.

$$\text{Probability} = \frac{\text{Number of ways for something to happen}}{\text{Total number of possible outcomes}}$$

Outcomes are just 'things that could happen'.

 The picture on the right shows a fair, 8-sided spinner.

a) Work out the probability of this spinner landing on green.

There are 8 sides so there are 8 possible outcomes.
There are 3 ways for it to land on green.

P(green) means 'The probability of the spinner landing on green'.

$$P(\text{green}) = \frac{\text{number of ways for 'green' to happen}}{\text{total number of possible outcomes}} = \frac{3}{8} \text{ (or 0.375)}$$

b) Which of its four colours is the spinner least likely to land on?

It's least likely to land on the colour that 'can happen in the fewest ways' — this is the one on the fewest sections.

Yellow

The probability of this getting you marks in the exam = 1...

You need to know the facts in the boxes above. You also need to know how to use them.

Q1 Calculate the probability of the fair spinner on the right:
   a) landing on a 4.   [2 marks]   b) landing on an even number.   [2 marks]

Q2 Show the probabilities in Q1 on a scale from 0 to 1.   [1 mark]

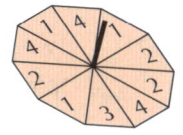

Section Seven — Statistics and Probability

More Probability

Did someone order another page on probability? Coming right up...

Probabilities Add Up To 1

1) If <u>only one</u> possible result can happen at a time, then the probabilities of <u>all</u> the results <u>add up to 1</u>.

> **Probabilities always ADD UP to 1**

2) So since something must either <u>happen</u> or <u>not happen</u> (i.e. <u>only one</u> of these can happen at a time):

> **P(event happens) + P(event doesn't happen) = 1**

EXAMPLE: A spinner has different numbers of red, blue, yellow and green sections.

Colour	red	blue	yellow	green
Probability	0.1	0.4	0.3	

a) What is the probability of spinning green?

All the probabilities must <u>add up to 1</u>.   P(green) = 1 − (0.1 + 0.4 + 0.3) = **0.2**

b) What is the probability of <u>not</u> spinning green?

P(green) + P(not green) = 1   P(not green) = 1 − P(green) = 1 − 0.2 = **0.8**

Listing All Outcomes

A <u>sample space diagram</u> shows all the possible outcomes.

Try to order your lists — here there are 3 choices for the <u>first digit</u>, then the other 2 digits can <u>swap round</u>.

1) It can just be a <u>simple list</u>...

> E.g. Find all the 3-digit numbers that include the digits 1, 2 and 3.   <u>1</u>23, <u>1</u>32, <u>2</u>13, <u>2</u>31, <u>3</u>12, <u>3</u>21

2) Or you can draw a <u>two-way table</u> if there are <u>two activities</u> going on (e.g. two coins being tossed, or a dice being thrown and a spinner being spun).

EXAMPLE: The spinner on the right is spun twice, and the scores added together.

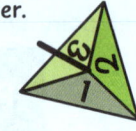

a) Complete this sample space diagram showing all the possible outcomes.

		2nd spin		
+		1	2	3
1st spin	1	2	3	4
	2	3	4	5
	3	4	5	6

There are <u>9 possible outcomes</u> here — even though some of the actual scores are repeated.

b) Find the probability of spinning a total of 3.

$$P(\text{total of 3}) = \frac{\text{ways to score 3}}{\text{total number of possible outcomes}} = \frac{2}{9}$$

There are <u>2 ways</u> to score 3.

c) Find the probability of spinning a total of 4 or more.

$$P(\text{total of 4 or more}) = \frac{\text{ways to score 4 or more}}{\text{total number of possible outcomes}} = \frac{6}{9} = \frac{2}{3}$$

There are <u>6 ways</u> to score either 4, 5 or 6.

Sample space diagrams — they're out of this world...

What is the probability of you acing your exam? A lot higher once you've tackled this question:

Q1 Two fair standard dice are thrown, and their scores added together. By drawing a sample space diagram: a) find the probability of throwing a total of 7, [3 marks]

b) find the probability of throwing any total except 7. [1 mark]

Section Seven — Statistics and Probability

Expected Frequency

You can use probabilities to work out how often you'd expect something to happen.

Use Probability to Find an "Expected Frequency"

1) Once you know the probability of something, you can predict how many times it will happen in a certain number of trials. *A 'trial' could be any activity — e.g. rolling a dice.*

2) For example, you can predict the number of sixes you could expect if you rolled a fair dice 20 times. This prediction is called the expected frequency.

> **Expected frequency = probability × number of trials**

EXAMPLE: The probability of someone catching a frisbee thrown to them is 0.92. Estimate the number of times you would expect them to catch a frisbee in 150 attempts.

Expected number of catches = probability of a catch × number of trials
= 0.92 × 150
= 138

This is an estimate. They might not catch the frisbee exactly 138 times, but the number of catches shouldn't be too different from this.

You Might Have to Find a Probability First

EXAMPLES:

1. A person spins the fair spinner on the right 200 times. How many times would you expect it to land on 5?

   1. First calculate the probability of the spinner landing on 5.

   $$P(\text{lands on 5}) = \frac{\text{ways to land on 5}}{\text{number of possible outcomes}} = \frac{1}{8}$$

   2. Then estimate the number of 5's they'll get in 200 spins.

   Expected number of 5's = P(lands on 5) × number of trials
   $$= \frac{1}{8} \times 200 = 25$$

2. I buy 400 large tins of chocolates. Each tin contains 100 chocolates altogether, and 80 of these are milk chocolate. If I select one chocolate at random from each tin, how many milk chocolates would I expect to get?

   1. First calculate the probability of picking a milk chocolate from one tin.

   $$P(\text{milk chocolate from 1 tin}) = \frac{\text{number of ways to get a milk chocolate}}{\text{total number of chocolates in each tin}}$$
   $$= \frac{80}{100} = \frac{4}{5}$$

   2. Then estimate the number of milk chocolates if I pick one chocolate from each of the 400 tins.

   Expected milk chocolates = P(milk chocolate from 1 tin) × number of tins
   $$= \frac{4}{5} \times 400 = 320$$

I predict this page could earn you 3 marks in your exam...

This is why statistics is so cool — you can use it to predict the future.

Q1 A game involves throwing a fair standard dice once. The player wins if they score either a 5 or a 6. If one person plays the game 180 times, estimate the number of times they will win. [3 marks]

Probability Experiments

The formula on page 111 only works when the outcomes are equally likely. If they're <u>not equally likely</u>, you can use the results from experiments to <u>estimate</u> the probability of each outcome.

Do the Experiment *Again* and *Again*...

You need to do an experiment <u>over and over again</u> and count how many times each outcome happens (its <u>frequency</u>). Then you can calculate the <u>relative frequency</u> using this formula:

$$\text{Relative frequency} = \frac{\text{Frequency}}{\text{Number of times you tried the experiment}}$$

An experiment could just mean rolling a dice.

You can use the <u>relative frequency</u> of a result as an <u>estimate</u> of its <u>probability</u>.

EXAMPLE: The spinner on the right was spun 100 times and the results recorded. Estimate the probability of getting each of the scores.

Score	1	2	3	4	5	6
Frequency	3	14	41	20	18	4

<u>Divide</u> each of the frequencies by 100 to find the <u>relative frequencies</u>.

Score	1	2	3	4	5	6
Relative Frequency	$\frac{3}{100}$ = 0.03	$\frac{14}{100}$ = 0.14	$\frac{41}{100}$ = 0.41	$\frac{20}{100}$ = 0.2	$\frac{18}{100}$ = 0.18	$\frac{4}{100}$ = 0.04

The <u>MORE TIMES</u> you do the experiment, the <u>MORE ACCURATE</u> your estimate of the probability should be.

E.g. if you spun the above spinner <u>1000 times</u>, you'd get a <u>better</u> estimate of the probability for each score.

Fair or Biased?

'<u>Fair</u>' means all the outcomes are <u>equally likely</u>. If something is unfair, it's called <u>biased</u>.

1) If the dice/spinner/coin/etc. is <u>fair</u>, then the relative frequencies of the results should <u>roughly match</u> the probabilities you'd get using the formula on p111.
2) If the relative frequencies are <u>far away</u> from those probabilities, you can say it's probably <u>biased</u>.

EXAMPLE: Do the above results suggest that the spinner is biased?

Yes, because the relative frequency of 3 is much higher than you'd expect, while the relative frequencies of 1 and 6 are much lower.

For a <u>fair</u> 6-sided spinner, you'd expect all the relative frequencies to be about 1 ÷ 6 = 0.17(ish).

This topic is tough — make sure to revise it relatively frequently...

Remember that relative frequency can only be used to <u>estimate</u> the probability of a result. You can increase the <u>accuracy</u> of your estimate by increasing the number of times you do the experiment.

Q1 This table shows how many times Jenny and Sandro got a free biscuit on their visits to a coffee shop.

	Jenny	Sandro
Visits to coffee shop	20	150
Got a free biscuit	13	117

a) All customers have the same chance of getting a free biscuit.
Based on Jenny's results, estimate this probability. [2 marks]

b) Whose results will give a better estimate of the probability? Explain your answer. [1 mark]

Section Seven — Statistics and Probability

Revision Questions for Section Seven

Here's the inevitable list of straight-down-the-middle questions to test how much you know.
- Have a go at each question... but only tick it off when you can get it right without cheating.
- And when you think you could handle pretty much any statistics question, tick off the whole topic.

Collecting Data and Finding Averages (p95-99)

1) What is a sample and why does it need to be representative?
2) Is 'eye colour' qualitative or quantitative data?
3) Complete this frequency table for the data below.
    Cat, Cat, Dog, Dog, Dog, Rabbit, Fish, Cat, Rabbit, Rabbit, Dog, Dog, Cat, Cat, Dog, Rabbit, Cat, Fish, Cat, Cat

Pet	Tally	Frequency

4) Find the mode, median, mean and range of this data: 2, 8, 11, 15, 22, 24, 27, 30, 31, 31, 41

Frequency Tables, Graphs and Charts (p100-108)

5) From the frequency table, calculate the mean number of pieces of homework some Year 11 students were given on a particular day.

Number of pieces	0	1	2	3	4
Frequency	3	10	17	14	6

6) 100 people were asked whether they like tea or coffee. Half the people said they like coffee, 34 people said they like tea, 20 people said they like both.
   a) Show this information on a Venn diagram.
   b) What fraction of the 100 people like tea or coffee?
7) How do you find frequencies from a pictogram?
8) The table on the right shows how some students rated a film. Draw a suitable diagram to show:

Film rating	Terrible	Bad	OK	Good	Amazing
Students	40	30	40	45	25

   a) the number of students giving each rating,   b) the proportion of students giving each rating.
9) a) Draw a line graph to show the time series data in this table.
   b) Describe the repeating pattern in the data.

Quarter	1	2	3	4	1	2	3	4
Sales (1000's)	1	1.5	1.7	3	0.7	0.9	1.2	2.2

10) Sketch scatter graphs to show:
    a) weak positive correlation,   b) strong negative correlation,   c) no correlation
11) For this grouped frequency table showing the lengths of some pet alligators:
    a) find the modal class,
    b) find the class containing the median,
    c) estimate the mean.

Length (y, in m)	Frequency
$1.4 \leq y < 1.5$	4
$1.5 \leq y < 1.6$	8
$1.6 \leq y < 1.7$	5
$1.7 \leq y < 1.8$	2

Interpreting and Comparing Data Sets (p109-110)

12) Explain the effect that outliers can have on the mean and range of data.
13) These pie charts show the results of a survey on the colour of people's cars. Compare the popularity of each colour of car amongst men and women.

Probability (p111-114)

14) I pick a random number between 1 and 50. Find the probability that my number is a multiple of 6.
15) The probability of a spinner landing on red is 0.3. What is the probability that it doesn't land on red?
16) I flip a fair coin 3 times.   a) Using H for heads and T for tails, list all the possible outcomes.
                                  b) What is the probability of getting exactly one head?
17) What are the formulas for: a) relative frequency?   b) expected frequency?
18) 160 people took a 2-part test. 105 people passed the first part and of these, 60 people passed the second part. 25 people didn't pass either test.
    a) Show this information on a frequency tree.   b) Find the relative frequency of each outcome.
    c) If 300 more people do the test, estimate how many of them would pass both parts.
19) The table shows the probabilities of a biased dice landing on each number. The dice is thrown 30 times. How many times would it be expected to land on 4?

Number	1	2	3	4	5	6
Probability	0.2	0.15	0.1	0.3	0.15	0.1

Section Seven — Statistics and Probability

Answers

> Get the full versions of these answers online
> Step-by-step worked solutions to these questions, with a full mark scheme, are included as a printable PDF with your free Online Edition — you'll find more info about how to get hold of this at the front of this book.

Section One — Number

Page 2 — Place Value and Ordering Numbers

Q1 a) One million, two hundred and thirty-four thousand, five hundred and thirty-one.
b) Twenty-three thousand, four hundred and fifty-six.
c) Three thousand, four hundred and two.
d) Two hundred and three thousand, four hundred and twelve.
Q2 56 421
Q3 9, 23, 87, 345, 493, 1029, 3004
Q4 0.008, 0.09, 0.1, 0.2, 0.307, 0.37

Page 3 — BODMAS and Wordy Questions

Remember — Brackets, Other, Division, Multiplication, Addition, Subtraction.
Q1 a) 11 b) 37 c) 3

Page 4 — Adding and Subtracting

Q1 a) Oisin is now 171 cm tall.
b) He needs to grow another 19 cm.
Q2 1.72 litres

Page 5 — Multiplying and Dividing by 10, 100, etc.

Q1 a) 1230
Move the decimal point two places to the right.
b) 0.00308 c) 12

Page 6 — Multiplying and Dividing Whole Numbers

Q1 a) 336 b) 616 c) 1664
Q2 a) 12 b) 13 c) 21
Q3 He will have 10 cm of wood left.

Page 7 — Multiplying and Dividing with Decimals

Q1 a) 179.2 b) 6.12 c) 11.847
Q2 She spends £17.78 on biscuits.
Q3 Each nephew receives £7.46.
Q4 a) 56 b) 705 c) 0.925

Page 8 — Negative Numbers

Q1 a) $-6\,°C$ b) $-5\,°C$

Page 9 — Multiples and Factors

Q1 a) 15, 30 and 45
b) 10, 20 and 30
Q2 a) 1, 2, 5 and 10
b) 1, 2, 3 and 6

Page 10 — LCM and HCF

Q1 LCM = 84
Q2 HCF = 12

Page 11 — Prime Numbers

Q1 61, 53 and 47

Page 12 — Prime Factors

Q1 a) $5^2 \times 11$ b) $2^2 \times 5^2$ c) $2^2 \times 7 \times 13$
A correct method here is either using a factor tree or just repeatedly dividing the factors until you get primes.
Q2 $2 \times 3^2 \times 5^2$, so Niall went wrong by not dividing '9' into its prime factors.
Q3 $2^2 \times 5 \times 7^2 \times 11$

Page 13 — Rounding

Q1 a) 21.4 (1 d.p.)
b) 21.44 (2 d.p.)
c) 21 (nearest whole number)
Q2 a) 4970 (nearest ten)
b) 5000 (nearest hundred)
The '6' in the original number means '9' is rounded up, and the next 'hundred' is 5000.
c) 5000 (nearest thousand)
Q3 a) 0.85 (2 d.p.)
b) 5.91 (2 d.p.)
c) 88.40 (2 d.p.)

Page 14 — Rounding

Q1 a) 10 (1 s.f.) b) 200 (1 s.f.)
c) 0.3 (1 s.f.) d) 0.09 (1 s.f.)
Q2 a) 77 (2 s.f.) b) 76.8 (3 s.f.)
c) 76.84 (4 s.f.)

Page 15 — Estimating

Q1 a) 20 b) 400
Q2 £40
Q3 a) $\sqrt{60} \approx 7.7$ (allow 7.6-7.8)
b) $\sqrt{39} \approx 6.2$ (allow 6.2-6.3)

Page 16 — Powers

Q1 a) 9 b) 49
c) 8 d) 125
Q2 a) 1 000 000 000 b) 10^5
Q3 1, 64 and 729.

Page 17 — Powers

Q1 a) 238.328 b) 14 641
c) 64.36343
Q2 a) 4^5 b) 7^3 c) q^8
Q3 a) 15 625 b) 59 049 c) 1
Q4 36

Page 18 — Roots

Q1 a) 14 b) 21 c) 3
Q2 1.2 cm
Q3 17.12422442

Page 19 — Different Number Systems

Q1 a) 7 b) 34 c) 108
Q2 a) 10110 b) 101000 c) 111111

Page 20 — Revision Questions for Section One

Q1 Twenty-one million, three hundred and six thousand, five hundred and fifteen.
Q2 2.09, 2.2, 3.51, 3.8, 3.91, 4.7
Q3 0.1
Divide the smallest number possible by the biggest number possible.
Q4 £38
Q5 a) 913 b) 629 c) 129.9
Q6 a) £120 b) 2300 c) 8800
Q7 a) 1377 b) 26 c) 62.7
d) 0.35
Q8 a) -16 b) 7 c) 20
Q9 Multiples of a number are its times table.
a) 10, 20, 30, 40, 50, 60
b) 4, 8, 12, 16, 20, 24
Q10 1, 2, 3, 4, 6 and 12
Q11 a) 14 b) 40
Q12 41, 43, 47, 53, 59
Q13 a) $2 \times 3 \times 5 \times 7$ b) $2^2 \times 3^2 \times 5 \times 7$
Q14 a) 17.7 (1 d.p.) b) 6700 (2 s.f.)
c) 0.06 (1 s.f.)
Q15 a) 891 000 (nearest thousand)
b) 4 000 000 (nearest million)
Q16 a) 100 b) 1400
Q17 a) $\sqrt{20} \approx 4.5$ b) $\sqrt{90} \approx 9.5$
c) $\sqrt{172} \approx 13.1$
Q18 a) 49 b) 1 c) 27
d) 169 e) 216
Q19 a) 3^2 b) 5^3 c) 12^2
Q20 a) 1000 b) 10 000 000 c) 10^5
Q21 a) 4^4 b) 3^{10} c) 9^3
Q22 7^5
Q23 a) 11 b) 4 c) 56
Q24 a) 4.8 b) 8 c) 11
Q25 The decimal system
Q26 a) 1100 b) 11001 c) 1011101
Q27 a) 15 b) 21 c) 91

Section Two — Fractions, Ratios and Percentages

Page 21 — Fractions

Q1 a) $\frac{2}{5}$ b) $\frac{8}{9}$ c) $\frac{3}{7}$
Q2 a) $\frac{13}{5}$ b) $2\frac{2}{7}$
Q3 $\frac{7}{8}, \frac{5}{6}, \frac{7}{9}$

Page 22 — Fractions

Q1 a) $\frac{43}{27}$ or $1\frac{16}{27}$ b) $\frac{9}{10}$
Q2 6

Page 23 — Fractions

Q1 a) $\frac{17}{18}$ b) $-\frac{43}{12} = -3\frac{7}{12}$

Answers

c) $\frac{55}{48}$ or $1\frac{7}{48}$ d) $\frac{15}{28}$

Page 24 — Fractions, Decimals and Percentages

Q1 a) 57%   b) $\frac{6}{25}$ c) 90%

Q2 $\frac{555}{1000} = \frac{111}{200}$

Page 25 — Fractions and Recurring Decimals

Q1
$$6 \overline{)1.1^{0}0^{4}0^{4}0^{4}0}$$
$1 \div 6 = 0.1666...$ so $\frac{1}{6} = 0.1\dot{6}$

Page 26 — Ratios

Q1 a) 5 : 7   b) 10 : 3   c) 1 : 6
Q2 a) $\frac{3}{2}$ b) $\frac{1}{2}$

Page 27 — Ratios

Q1 a) $\frac{2}{13}$ b) 33 litres
Q2 36 years old

Page 28 — Direct Proportion Problems

Q1 a) 80p   b) 32
Q2 £67.50

Page 29 — Direct Proportion Problems

Q1 The 770 g bottle.
Q2 $750

Page 30 — Percentages

Q1 a) 108   b) 196.95
Q2 62%

Page 31 — Percentages

Q1 £3400
Q2 £129.80

Page 32 — Percentages

Q1 4.9% (1 d.p.)

Page 33 — Repeated Percentage Change

Q1 £3446.05

Page 34 — Revision Questions for Section Two

Q1 a) $1\frac{7}{8}$ b) $2\frac{2}{5}$ c) $2\frac{4}{5}$
Q2 Amy
Q3 a) 320   b) £60
Q4 a) $\frac{25}{16}$ or $1\frac{9}{16}$ b) $\frac{44}{15}$ or $2\frac{14}{15}$
c) $\frac{23}{8}$ or $2\frac{7}{8}$ d) $\frac{11}{21}$
Q5 a) i) $\frac{4}{100} = \frac{1}{25}$ ii) 4%
b) i) $\frac{65}{100} = \frac{13}{20}$ ii) 0.65

Q6 a) A recurring decimals is a decimal with a pattern of numbers which repeats forever.
b) $0.\dot{2}$
Q7 a) 9 : 11   b) 7 : 2
Q8 $\frac{7}{9}$
Q9 80 blue scarves
Q10 a) $\frac{5}{25}$ or $\frac{1}{5}$ b) 384
Q11 960 flowers
Q12 51 ml olive oil, 1020 g tomatoes
25.5 g garlic powder, 204 g onions
Q13 The 500 ml tin
Q14 £89.66
Q15 a) 420   b) 1080   c) 112.5
Q16 20.24 m
Q17 a) 19   b) 114
c) 21.05% (2 d.p.)
Q18 14 chicken pies
Q19 35% decrease
Q20 £106.48

Section Three — Algebra

Page 35 — Algebra — Simplifying

Q1 a) $6a$ b) $7b$
Q2 $3x + 8y$

Page 36 — Algebra — Simplifying

Q1 a) e^5 b) $18fg$
Q2 a) h^9 b) s^3

Page 37 — Algebra — Multiplying Out Brackets

Q1 $-18x + 12$
Q2 $3x^2 - 15x$
Q3 $2y + 19$

Page 38 — Algebra — Taking Out Common Factors

Q1 a) $7(3x - 2y)$ b) $8(3x + 7y)$
Q2 a) $a(2 + a)$ b) $2r(2r - 11s)$

Page 39 — Solving Equations

Q1 a) $x = 6$ b) $x = 14$
c) $x = 3$ d) $x = 15$

Page 40 — Solving Equations

Q1 $x = 5$
Q2 $y = 7$

Page 41 — Expressions, Formulas and Functions

Q1 $v = 29$
Q2 $x = 11$

Page 42 — Formulas and Equations from Words

Q1 Noah = 13 tickets, Hellä = 26 tickets, Joe = 34 tickets
Q2 3, 15 and 30

Page 43 — Trial and Improvement

Q1 $x = 3.6$ to 1 d.p.
Q2 $x = 5.5$ to 1 d.p.

Page 44 — Inequalities

Q1 $n = -1, 0, 1, 2, 3, 4$
Q2 a) $x < 6$ b) $x \geq 3$

Page 45 — Rearranging Formulas

Q1 $v = 3(u + 2)$ or $v = 3u + 6$
Q2 $d = \frac{c}{6} + 2$ or $d = \frac{c + 12}{6}$

Page 46 — Sequences

Q1 Rule: multiply the previous term by 2
Next two terms: 24, 48
Rule: add 3, add 6, add 9...
Next two terms: 21, 33

Page 47 — Sequences

Q1 $7n - 5$
Q2 a) 28   b) $6n - 2$

Page 48 — Revision Questions for Section Three

Q1 a) $3e$ b) $12f$
Q2 a) $7x - y$ b) $3a + 9$
Q3 a) m^3 b) $7pq$ c) $18xy$
Q4 a) g^{11} b) c^3
Q5 a) $6x + 18$ b) $-9x + 12$ c) $5x - x^2$
Q6 $6x$
Q7 Putting in brackets (the opposite of multiplying out brackets).
Q8 a) $8(x + 3)$ b) $9x(2x + 3)$
c) $2x(2y - 5)$
Q9 a) $x = 7$ b) $x = 16$ c) $x = 3$
Q10 a) $x = 9$ b) $x = 2$ c) $x = 3$
Q11 a) $x = 3$ b) $x = 4$ c) $x = 1$
Q12 $Q = 8$
Q13 14
Q14 37 marbles
Q15 $6x$ cm
Q16 A way of finding an approximate solution to an equation by trying different values in the equation.
Q17 $x = 4.1$ to 1 d.p.
Q18 a) x is greater than minus seven
b) x is less than or equal to six
Q19 $k = 1, 2, 3, 4, 5, 6, 7$
Q20 a) $x < 10$ b) $x \leq 7$
Q21 $v = \frac{W - 5}{4}$
Q22 $x = 3y - 12$ or $x = 3(y - 4)$
Q23 a) 31, rule is add 7
b) 256, rule is multiply by 4
c) 19, rule is add the two previous terms
Q24 a) 3, 8, 13, 18
b) 503
Q25 $7n - 1$

Answers

Section Four — Graphs

Page 49 — Coordinates

Q1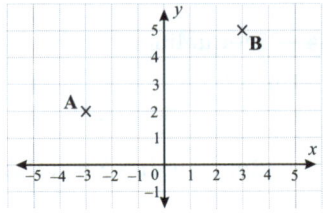

Q2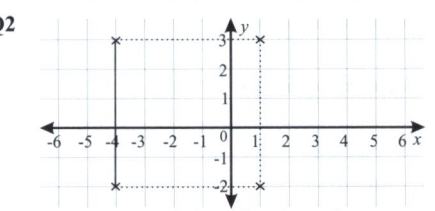

The square's third and fourth vertices are at (1, 3) and (1, –2).

Page 50 — Line Segments

Q1 a) (7, 5)
b) 7.21 (to 2 d.p.)

Page 51 — Straight-Line Graphs

Q1 a), b) and c)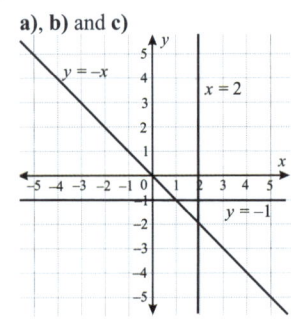

Page 52 — Drawing Straight-Line Graphs

Q1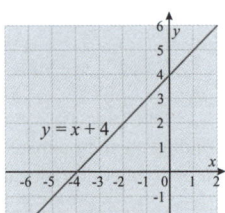

Q2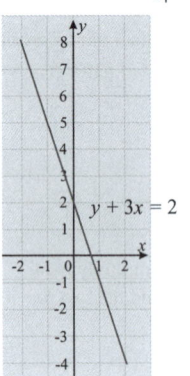

Page 53 — Straight-Line Graphs — Gradients

Q1 –5

Page 54 — Real-Life Graphs

Q1 a) 100 g
b) 50 g

Page 55 — Conversion Graphs

Q1 9600 km (allow 9400 km to 9800 km)

Page 56 — Distance-Time Graphs

Q1 a) 15 minutes
b) 12 km/h

Page 57 — Solving Equations Using Graphs

Q1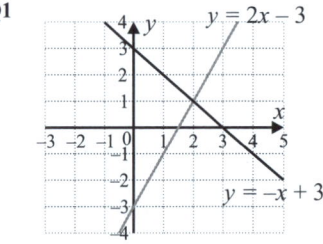

$x = 2$, $y = 1$

Page 58 — Quadratic Graphs

Q1 a)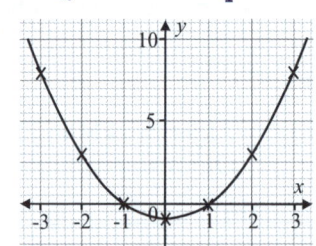

b) $x = -2.4$ (allow between –2.6 and –2.2) and $x = 2.4$ (allow between 2.2 and 2.6)

Page 59 — Revision Questions for Section Four

Q1 A(5, –3), B(4, 0), C(0, 3), D(–4, 5), E(–2, –3)
Q2 Midpoint = (2, 1.5)
Q3 9.43 (to 2 d.p.)
Q4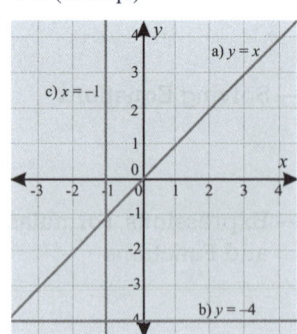

Q5 $x + y = 4$

Q6 E.g.

x	–2	0	2
y	6	–2	–10

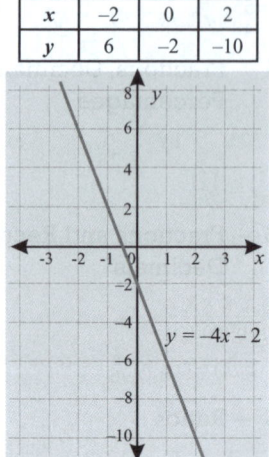

Q7 a) 2
b) –6
Q8 1
Q9 a) £10
b) 20 minutes
c) £20
d) 26 minutes
e) 67p — allow between 65p and 69p
Q10 Draw a line from a value on one axis. When you hit the line on the graph, change direction and go straight to the other axis. The values on each axis will be equivalent.
Q11 The object has stopped.
Q12 a) Beth drove faster on her way home.
b) 15 minutes
Q13 $x = -2$, $y = 0$
Q14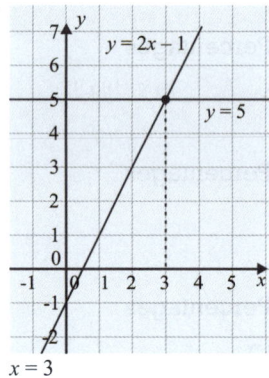

$x = 3$

Q15 They are both "bucket shaped" graphs. $y = x^2 - 8$ is like a "u" whereas $y = -x^2 + 2$ is like an "n" (or an upturned bucket).

Q16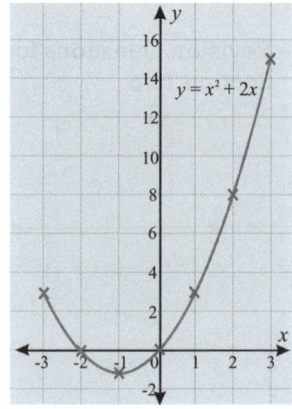

$x = -2.7$ (allow between –2.6 and –2.9) and $x = 0.7$ (allow between 0.6 and 0.9).

Answers

Section Five — Measures and Angles

Page 60 — Metric Units
Q1 a) 9300 g
b) 28.4 cm

Page 61 — Imperial Units
Q1 a) 384 inches
b) 9.6 m

Page 62 — Area and Volume Conversion
Q1 6 000 000 m²
Q2 40 000 mm³

Page 63 — Reading Scales
Q1 3.2 °C
Q2 8.5 m

Page 64 — Time Intervals
Q1 a) 2880 minutes
b) 4 minutes 25 seconds
Q2 £187.20 in a week

Page 65 — Compound Units
Q1 a) 3.5 hours
b) 50 mpg

Page 66 — Compound Units
Q1 15 g
Q2 3.45 kg/m³

Page 67 — Angle Basics
Q1 Acute

Page 68 — Five Angle Rules
Q1 $x = 108°$

Page 69 — Parallel Lines
Q1 $x = 68°$

Page 70 — Geometry Problems
Q1 $x = 123°$

Page 71 — Angles in Shapes
Q1 144°
Q2 Pentagon

Page 72 — Bearings
Q1 298° (allow 297°-299°)
Q2 030°

Page 73 — Maps
Q1 6 miles
Q2 4.5 cm

Page 74 — Maps and Scale Drawings
Q1 1 cm represents 200 m, so the woodland should be 1.25 cm by 1.5 cm, e.g.

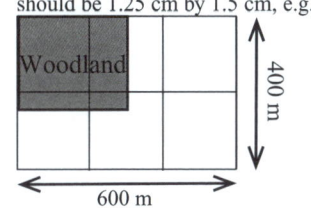

Q2

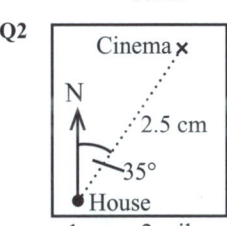

Page 75 — Pythagoras' Theorem
Q1 10.3 m (1 d.p.)
Q2 3.8 m (1 d.p.)

Page 76 — Revision Questions for Section Five
Q1 a) 380 mm
b) 5600 cm³
c) 0.731 kg
Q2 a) 48 inches
b) 3 stone
c) 16 pints
d) 240 cm
e) 2.29 litres (2 d.p.)
f) 16 km
Q3 a) 12 000 000 cm³
b) 12.8 cm²
c) 2750 mm³
Q4 To work out what a small gap represents, divide the size of the large gaps between numbers by the number of small gaps between numbers.
Q5 0.8 litres
Q6 Between 5.5 tonnes and 6.5 tonnes.
You could also have written:
5.5 tonnes ≤ elephant's weight < 6.5 tonnes.
Q7 a) 1440 minutes
b) 336 hours
c) 4 hours
Q8 9.48 pm
Q9 D / (S × T) triangle
Q10 40 mpg
Q11 2400 kg/m³
Q12 18 km/h
Q13 An obtuse angle
Q14 720°
Q15 a) 154°
b) 112°
c) 58°
Q16 40°
Q17 1080°
Q18 295°
Q19 26 km
Q20

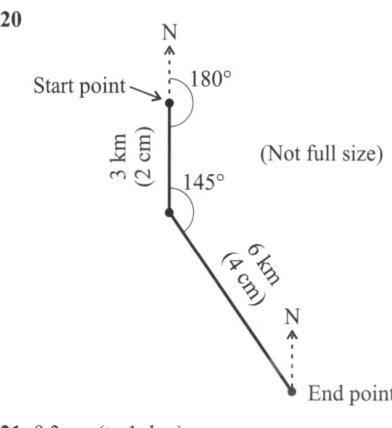

Q21 9.2 cm (to 1 d.p.)
Q22 14.5 cm (to 1 d.p.)

Section Six — Shapes and Area

Page 77 — Properties of 2D Shapes
Q1 a) E.g.
b) E.g.

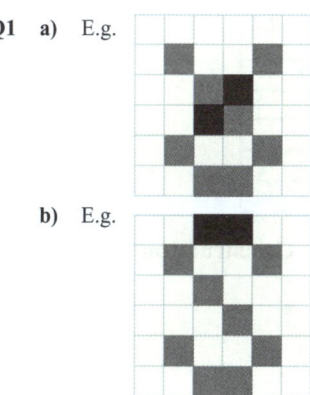

Page 78 — Properties of 2D Shapes
Q1 Rhombus
Rotational symmetry of order 2

Page 79 — Perimeter and Area
Q1 $x = 10$

Page 80 — Perimeter and Area
Q1 75 cm²

Page 81 — Circles
Q1 10 603 cm² (nearest cm²)

Page 82 — 3D Shapes
Q1 a) Cuboid
b) (i) 6 (ii) 12 (iii) 8

Page 83 — Cubes and Cuboids
Q1 288 cm³

Answers

Q2 E.g.
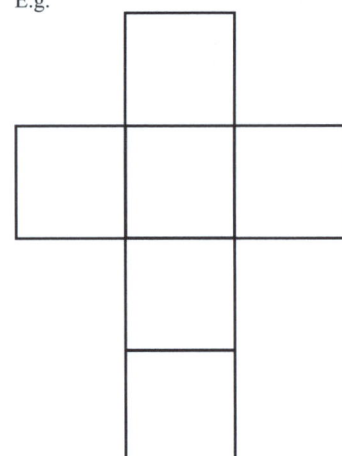

Page 84 — Prisms
Q1 360 cm³

Page 85 — Plans and Elevations
Q1 a) 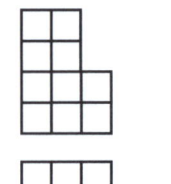 b)
c)

Page 86 — Construction
Q1 E.g.
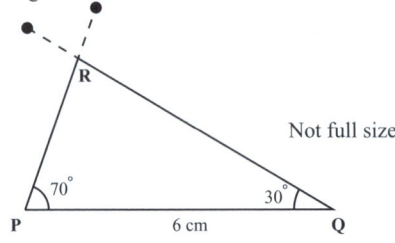
Not full size

Page 87 — Construction
Q1 Not full size
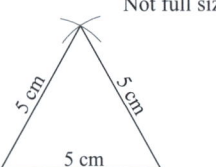

Page 89 — Loci and Construction
Q1 Visitors can go anywhere in the shaded area.
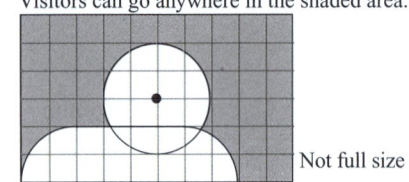
Not full size

Page 90 — Translation
Q1 (−1, −1)

Page 91 — Reflection
Q1
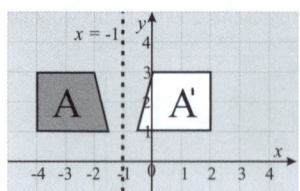

Page 92 — Rotation
Q1

Page 93 — Enlargement
Q1
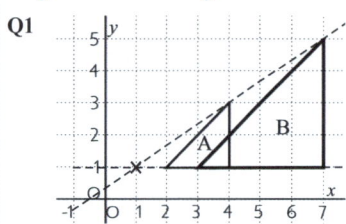
An enlargement of scale factor 2, with centre of enlargement (1, 1).

Page 94 — Revision Questions for Section Six

Q1 H: 2 lines of symmetry, rotational symmetry order 2
Z: 0 lines of symmetry, rotational symmetry order 2
T: 1 line of symmetry, rotational symmetry order 1
N: 0 lines of symmetry, rotational symmetry order 2
E: 1 line of symmetry, rotational symmetry order 1
×: 4 lines of symmetry, rotational symmetry order 4
S: 0 lines of symmetry, rotational symmetry order 2

Q2 E.g. 2 angles the same, 2 sides the same, 1 line of symmetry, no rotational symmetry.

Q3 2 pairs of equal sides, rotational symmetry order 2.

Q4 36 cm²

Q5 Area = ½(a + b) × h

Q6 32 cm

Q7 E.g.
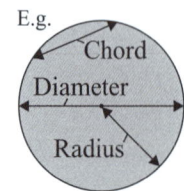

Q8 Area = 153.94 cm² (2 d.p.)
Circumference = 43.98 cm (2 d.p.)

Q9 a) faces = 5, edges = 8, vertices = 5
b) faces = 2, edges = 1, vertices = 1
c) faces = 5, edges = 9, vertices = 6

Q10 150 cm²

Q11 352 cm³

Q12 Volume = $\pi r^2 h$

Q13 360 cm³

Q14 Front: Side: Plan:

Q15 (Not full size)
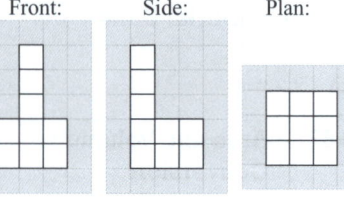

Q16

Q17 A circle

Q18
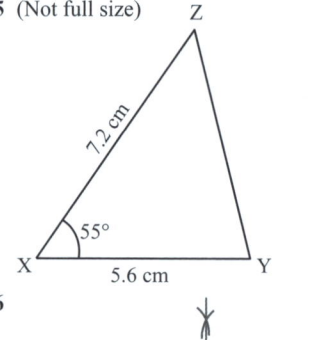
(Not full size)

Q19
(Not full size)

Q20 a) A translation of 2 units left and 4 units down.
b) A translation by vector $\begin{pmatrix} -2 \\ -4 \end{pmatrix}$

Q21 Shapes A and B are congruent.
Shapes B and C are congruent.

Q22 A reflection in the y-axis (x = 0).

Q23 a) Length and angle
b) Length and angle
c) Length and angle
d) Angle

Answers

Q24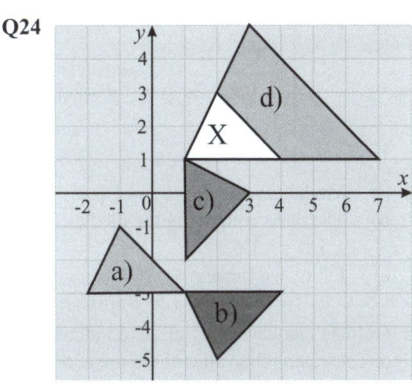

Q25 72 cm²

Section Seven — Statistics and Probability

Page 95 — Planning an Investigation

Q1 a) E.g. 'Children solve the logic puzzle faster than adults.'
b) Think about the different stages of the handling data cycle.
Collecting data:
E.g. collect primary data by doing an experiment. This data should be reliable as the researcher can measure and record the times fairly and accurately.
Processing and presenting data:
E.g. put the data into grouped frequency tables, with one for children and one for adults. Then averages, such as the mean, can be found and diagrams, such as histograms, can be drawn.
Interpreting results:
E.g. Compare the mean times for children and adults. This shows whether the children were generally faster or slower at solving the puzzle than the adults.

There are loads of things that could be included in an investigation plan — they depend on the hypothesis you've chosen.

Page 96 — Sampling and Bias

Q1 E.g. No, Tina can't use her results to draw conclusions about the whole population. The sample is biased because it excludes people who never use the train and most of the people included are likely to use the train regularly. The sample is also too small to represent the whole population.

Page 97 — Collecting Data

Q1 1st question:
Question should include a time frame, e.g. "How much do you spend on food each week?"
Include at least 3 non-overlapping response boxes, covering all possible answers, e.g. 'less than £20', '£20 to £40', 'over £40' etc.

2nd question:
Include at least 3 non-overlapping response boxes, covering all possible answers, e.g. '0-1', '2-3', etc.

3rd question:
Make the question fair, e.g. "Which do you prefer, potatoes or cabbage?"
Response boxes should cover all answers, e.g. 'Potatoes', 'Cabbage', or 'Don't know'.

4th question:
Limit the number of possible answers, e.g. "Choose your favourite food from the following options." Include at least 3 non-overlapping response boxes.

Page 98 — Collecting Data

Q1 Discrete data
E.g.

Cinema visits	Tally	Frequency
0-9		
10-19		
20-29		
30-39		
40-49		
50 or over		

Page 99 — Mean, Median, Mode and Range

Q1 Mean = 11.2, median = 12, mode = 12, range = 9

Q2 The mean of all 9 heights will be lower than 1.6 m, because the new height is lower than 1.6 m.

Page 100 — Frequency Tables — Finding Averages

Q1 a) Median = 2 **b)** Mean = 1.66

Page 101 — Two-Way Tables

Q1

	Boy	Girl	Total
Pass	13	11	24
Fail	3	4	7
Total	16	15	31

Q2 a) 15 newts
b) 14 newts
c) 38 newts

Page 102 — Venn Diagrams

Q1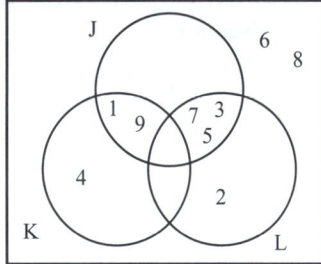

Your diagram might look a bit different — you'll get the marks as long as the data points are in the correct group. Make sure each circle is labelled with the right letter.

Page 103 — Pictograms and Bar Charts

Q1 a) 15
b)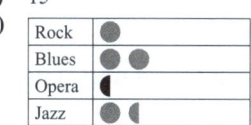

Page 104 — Pie Charts

Q1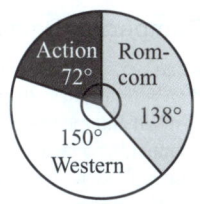

Page 105 — Other Charts and Graphs

Q1 a) Z = 55
b) Diamond-shaped

Page 106 — Other Charts and Graphs

Q1 a)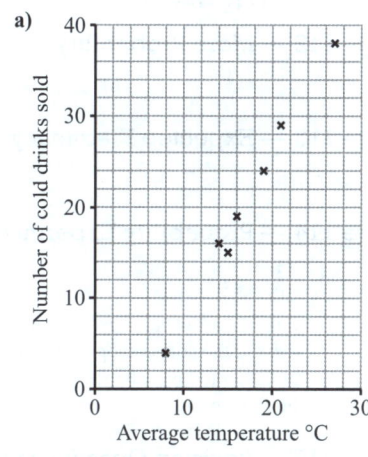

b) The data shows that as the average temperature increases, so does the number of cold drinks sold.

Page 107 — Scatter Diagrams

Q1 a) There is a strong negative correlation. The longer the run, the slower Sam's speed.
b)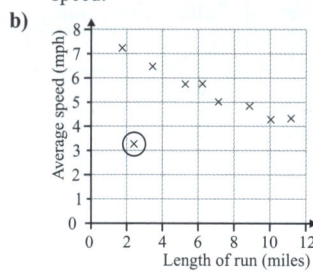
c) Approximately 5 mph (±0.5 mph)
d) The estimate should be reliable because **[either]** 8 miles is within the range of the known data **[or]** the graph shows strong correlation.

Answers

Page 108 — Grouped Frequency Tables

Q1 a) $17.5 \leq l < 18.5$
b) 17.4 cm (3 s.f.)

Page 109 — Interpreting Data

Q1 a) 3
b) Median = 2.5 pairs.
Range = 5 pairs

Page 110 — Comparing Data Sets

Q1 Hannah: median = 5, mean = 5, range = 10.
Joseph: median = 18, mean = 20, range = 19.
E.g. Joseph's mean and median are much higher than Hannah's, so on average Joseph went to a lot more matches per year. Joseph's data has a bigger range, so the number of matches he attended varied more.

Page 111 — Probability Basics

Q1 a) $P(4) = \frac{3}{10}$ (= 0.3 = 30%)
b) $P(\text{even}) = \frac{3}{5}$ (= 0.6 = 60%)

Q2 E.g.

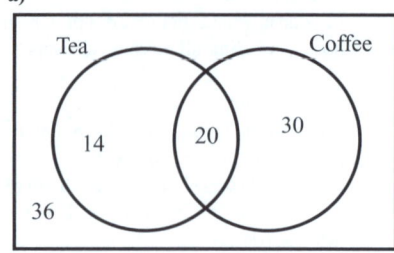

Page 112 — More Probability

Q1 a) $\frac{6}{36} = \frac{1}{6}$ **b)** $\frac{5}{6}$

Page 113 — Expected Frequency

Q1 60 times

Page 114 — Probability Experiments

Q1 a) $\frac{13}{20} = 0.65$
b) Sandro's results are based on more visits to the coffee shop, so his results are likely to give a better estimate of the probability.

Page 115 — Revision Questions for Section Seven

Q1 A sample is part of a population. Samples need to be representative so that conclusions drawn from sample data can be applied to the whole population.

Q2 Qualitative data

Q3

Pet	Tally	Frequency
Cat	||||| |||	8
Dog	|||||		6
Rabbit	||||	4
Fish	||	2

Q4 Mode = 31, median = 24, mean = 22, range = 39

Q5 Mean = 2.2.

Q6 a)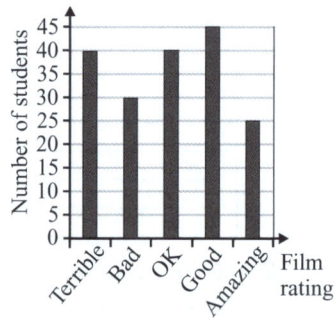

b) P(like tea or coffee) = $\frac{16}{25}$

Q7 Count the number of symbols, then use the key to work out what frequency they represent.

Q8 a) E.g. draw a bar chart.

A pictogram would also be a suitable diagram.

b)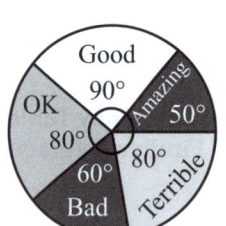

Q9 a)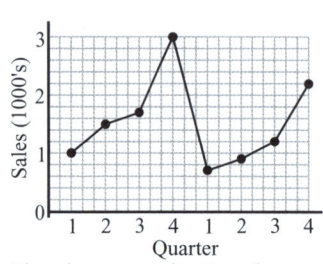

b) There is a seasonal pattern that repeats itself every 4 points. Sales are lowest in the first quarter and highest in the fourth quarter.

Q10 a) e.g.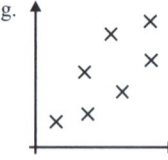

b) e.g.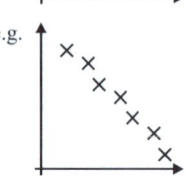

c) e.g.

Q11 a) Modal class is: $1.5 \leq y < 1.6$.
b) The class containing the median is: $1.5 \leq y < 1.6$
c) Estimated mean = 1.5763...
= 1.58 m (to 2 d.p.)

Q12 Outliers can have a big effect on increasing or decreasing the value of the mean or range, so that they don't represent the rest of the data set very well.

Q13 Black cars were only owned by men and silver cars were only owned by women. So black cars were more popular amongst men and silver cars were more popular amongst women.
There were similar proportions of men and women owning blue and green cars. So blue and green cars were equally popular amongst men and women.
The proportion of men owning red cars was nearly double the proportion of women owning red cards. So red cars were almost twice as popular amongst men as women.

Q14 P(number is a multiple of 6) = $\frac{4}{25}$ = 0.16 = 16%

Q15 P(not red) = 0.7

Q16 a) HHH, HHT, HTH, THH, TTH, THT, HTT, TTT
b) P(one head) = $\frac{3}{8}$ = 0.375 = 37.5%

Q17 a) See page 114
b) See page 113

Q18 a)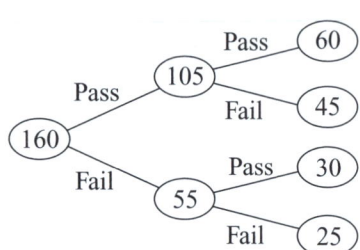

b) Relative frequency of:
pass, pass = $\frac{60}{160} = \frac{3}{8}$ or 0.375
pass, fail = $\frac{45}{160} = \frac{9}{32}$ or 0.28125
fail, pass = $\frac{30}{160} = \frac{3}{16}$ or 0.1875
fail, fail = $\frac{25}{160} = \frac{5}{32}$ or 0.15625

c) 112.5 = 113 (to the nearest whole number)

Q19 Expected frequency = 9 times

Index

2D shapes 77, 78
3D shapes 82-85

A

adding 4
  negative numbers 8
AER (annual equivalent rate) 32
algebra 35-47
  factorising 38
  inequalities 44
  rearranging formulas 45
  simplifying 35
  solving equations 39, 40
angles 67-71
  acute 67
  allied 69
  alternate 69
  angle rules 68, 70
  corresponding 69
  exterior 71
  interior 71
  obtuse 67
  reflex 67
  vertically opposite 69
APR (annual percentage rate) 32
areas 62, 79, 80, 83, 93
  circles 81
  kites 80
  parallelograms 80
  quadrilaterals 80
  rectangles 79
  rhombuses 80
  semicircles 81
  trapeziums 80
  triangles 79
averages 99, 100, 108-110

B

bar charts 103
bearings 72, 74
best buy questions 29
bias 96, 114
binary numbers 19
BODMAS 3
brackets 3, 37

C

centre of enlargement 93
centre of rotation 92
chords 81
circles 81
circumferences 81
classes 98, 108
collecting data 98
collecting like terms 35
common denominators 21
common differences 47

common factors 9
common multiples 9
comparing data sets 110
compasses 87-89
compound interest 33
compound units 65, 66
cones 82
congruent shapes 90
constructions 86-89
continuous data 97
conversion graphs 55
converting
  decimals 24
  fractions 24
  map distances 73
  percentages 24
  units 60-62, 64
coordinates 49
correlation 107
cube numbers 16
cube roots 18
cubes 83
cuboids 83
cylinders 82, 84

D

data 97, 98
decimal places 13
decimals 7, 13, 24, 25
denominators 21
density 66
diameter 81
direct proportion 28, 29
discrete data 97
distance-time graphs 56
dividing 5-7, 23
  by 10, 100, etc. 5
  fractions 23
  negative numbers 8
  whole numbers 6
  with decimals 7

E

edges 82
enlargements 93
equations 39-43, 58
equilateral triangles 78
estimating 15, 60
expected frequency 113
expressions 35, 36, 41
exterior angles 71

F

faces 82
factor trees 12
factorising 38
factors 9, 10

fair 111
Fibonacci sequence 46
flow charts 105
formula triangles 65, 66
formulas 41, 42, 45
fractions 21-25
  adding and subtracting 22
  cancelling down 21
  common denominators 21
  improper 21
  mixed numbers 21
  multiplying and dividing 23
frequency 100, 103, 108
frequency tables 100, 108
frequency trees 105
front elevations 85
functions 41

G

geometry problems 70
gradients 53, 54, 56
graphs 49-58
grouped frequency tables 108

H

heptagons 77
hexagons 77
highest common factor (HCF) 10
Hugh Jackman 56
hypotheses 95

I

imperial units 61
improper fractions 21
inequalities 44
interest 32
interior angles 71
investigations 95
isometric paper 85
isosceles triangles 78

K

kites 78, 80

L

line graphs 51-53, 106
line segments 50
line symmetry 77, 78
lines of best fit 107
loci 88, 89
lowest common multiple (LCM) 10

Index

M

maps 73, 74
  map scales 73
mean 99, 100, 108-110
measurements 63
median 99, 100, 108, 110
metric units 60
mid-interval values 108
midpoint of a line segment 50
mirror lines 77, 91
misleading diagrams 109
mixed numbers 21
modal class 108
mode 99, 100
multiples 9, 10
multiplying 5-8, 17, 18, 36, 37
  brackets 37
  by 10, 100, etc. 5
  fractions 23
  negative numbers 8
  powers 17, 36
  roots 18
  whole numbers 6
  with decimals 7

N

negative numbers 8
nonagons 77
north lines 72
nth terms 46, 47
number lines 8, 44
numerators 21

O

octagons 77
ordering numbers 2
outcomes 111, 112
outliers 107, 109

P

parallel lines 69, 70
parallelograms 78, 80
pentagons 77
percentage change 32
percentages 24, 30-33
perimeters 79-81, 93
pi (π) 81
pictograms 103
pie charts 104
place value 2
plans 85
plotting graphs 52
polygons 68, 71, 77
populations 96
power rules 17, 36
powers 16, 17
prime factors 12
prime numbers 11, 12
prisms 84
probability 111-114
projections 85
proportional division 27
protractors 67, 86
pyramids 82
Pythagoras' theorem 50, 75

Q

quadrants 49
quadratic equations 58
quadratic graphs 58
quadrilaterals 78-80, 86
qualitative data 97
quantitative data 97
questionnaires 97

R

radius 81
range 99, 100, 108-110
ratios 26
real-life graphs 54, 55
rearranging formulas 45
rectangles 79
recurring decimals 25
reflections 91
regular polygons 71, 77
relative frequency 114
rhombuses 78, 80
right-angled triangles 75, 78
right angles 67, 87
roots 18
rotational symmetry 77, 78
rotations 92
rounding 13, 14
  decimal places 13
  measurements 63
  significant figures 14
  whole numbers 13

S

sample space diagrams 112
sampling 96
scale drawings 74
scale factors 93
scalene triangles 78
scales 63
scatter diagrams 106, 107
seasonality 106
sequences 46, 47
short division 6
side elevations 85
significant figures 14
simple interest 31
simple random sampling 96
simplifying expressions 35, 36
simplifying ratios 26
simultaneous equations 57
solids 82-84
solving equations 39, 40
  using graphs 57
speed 60, 61
spheres 82
square numbers 16
square roots 18
  estimating 15
squares 78
stem and leaf diagrams 105
straight line graphs 51-55
subtracting 4
surface area 83
symmetry 77, 78

T

terminating decimals 25
three-letter angle notation 67
time 64
time series 106
timetables 64
transformations 90-93
translations 90
trapeziums 78, 80
trends 106
trial and improvement 43
triangle construction 86, 87
triangles 75, 78, 79
two-way tables 101

U

unit conversions 60-62, 64
units 60, 61

V

vectors 90
Venn diagrams 102
vertices 82
volumes 62, 83, 84

W

wordy questions 3

X

x-coordinates 49

Y

y-coordinates 49